ALSO BY ROBERT H. PATTON

The Pattons: A Personal History of an American Family

Up, Down & Sideways

Life Between Wars

*Patriot Pirates: The Privateer War for Freedom and Fortune
in the American Revolution*

Hell Before Breakfast

Hell Before Breakfast

America's First War Correspondents Making History and
Headlines, from the Battlefields of the Civil War to
the Far Reaches of the Ottoman Empire

Robert H. Patton

Pantheon Books, New York

Library of Congress Cataloging-in-Publication Data
Patton, Robert H. (Robert Holbrook), [date]
Hell before breakfast : America's first war correspondents making history and headlines, from the battlefields of the Civil War to the far reaches of the Ottoman Empire / Robert H. Patton.
pages   cm
Includes bibliographical references and index.
ISBN 978-0-307-37721-0 (hardcover). ISBN 978-0-307-90890-2 (eBook)
1. War correspondents—United States—History—19th century.
2. War—Press coverage—History—19th century.   I. Title.
PN4823.P38 2014   070.4'33309730922—dc23   2013036725

www.pantheonbooks.com

Jacket images: (top) Fort Sumter, April 12–13, 1861. Wood engraving from a contemporary American newspaper. The Granger Collection, N.Y.; (bottom) Virginia newspaper vendor, 1863, by Alexander Gardner. Courtesy of the Library of Congress, Washington, D.C.
Jacket design by Pablo Delcán
Book design by Iris Weinstein

Printed in the United States of America
First Edition
2 4 6 8 9 7 5 3 1

for Vicki, of course

and for Tom, Chris, Rob, & James—
adventurers all

There are heroisms even in the profession of journalism of which the newspaper reader in the morning over his coffee and rolls never thinks. But they are real, and without them there might sometimes be nothing for the man with his coffee and rolls to read.

GEORGE W. SMALLEY, *Anglo-American Memories* (1911)

Contents

Illustrations

Illustrations

Characters & Affiliations

The New York Herald

James Gordon Bennett—founder, publisher, editor in chief
James Gordon Bennett, Jr.—publisher, editor in chief
Henry Villard—correspondent
Henry M. Stanley—correspondent
J. A. MacGahan—correspondent
Francis D. Millet—correspondent, illustrator
John Russell Young—correspondent, foreign affairs editor
Stephen Fiske—theater critic
Edward T. Flynn—editor
Stephen Bonsal—correspondent

The New York Tribune

Horace Greeley—founder, publisher, editor in chief
Charles A. Dana—managing editor
John Russell Young—managing editor
Whitelaw Reid—managing editor
George W. Smalley—correspondent, London bureau chief
Holt White—correspondent
M. Méjanel—correspondent
Samuel L. Clemens—contributor

The New York Times

Henry J. Raymond—founder, publisher, editor in chief

Daily News (London)

Charles Dickens—founder, editor
John R. Robinson—manager
Archibald Forbes—correspondent
J. A. MacGahan—correspondent

The Times (London)

William Howard Russell—correspondent

The Graphic (London)

Frederic Villiers—illustrator

Introduction

Sometime between the American Civil War and the Spanish-American War, it became understood by many young men that being a war correspondent was the greatest job in the world. One reason was foreshadowed in a *Punch* cartoon published in London in 1854, after news arrived from the Crimean War that a brigade of British cavalry had been wiped out in a desperate assault against impossible odds. The cartoon depicts a family reacting to the report, the mother and daughters weeping, the enraged father holding a newspaper in one hand and swinging a fireplace poker in the other. Meanwhile, a young boy peers over his dad's shoulder at the dire headline. He looks thrilled.

We can't blame the correspondent who broke the news for the boy's inappropriate joy. William Howard Russell of *The Times* of London wrote his dispatch in a state of grief after helplessly watching the slaughter from a nearby hilltop. But neither his appalled description of Russian cannons shredding his countrymen nor his candor about the bungled order that launched the attack dispels the wonder of the scene. Thanks to Russell's account, the Charge of the Light Brigade has endured in poems, books, and movies as a stirring piece of history. The last thing he wanted was to make it seem romantic. Some people just saw it that way.

Russell was the first newsman to be designated a "war correspondent" by his editors. He thought the title absurd. "The miserable parent of a luckless tribe," he described himself late in his career. But those who followed in his professional footsteps generally took a brighter view. First came the Civil War's "Bohemian Brigade," rude foot soldiers in a war of newspaper circulation whose victories hinged on headlines more loud than accurate. Thirty years later the jingoistic "Yellow Kids" swarmed the Cuban battleground of the Spanish-American War. Among them were Stephen Crane, Frederic Remington, and Richard

Harding Davis, rising young journalists seeking the excitement and manly credentials that came with covering America's "splendid little war."

The period between the two saw the heyday of late-nineteenth-century progress and adventurism. America was emerging in power while the monarchies of Europe jockeyed for dominance through a succession of brief and bloody imperial wars. The correspondents who covered those wars aren't much remembered today and don't have a handy group nickname. But thanks to advances in the electric telegraph and the transatlantic cable, their work was highlighted in daily newspapers that proliferated as never before on both sides of the Atlantic, driving public opinion and fueling political changes that wouldn't resolve until World War I. The first-person narratives, with the correspondents at center stage, projected images of daring that would resonate in some of the turn of the century's most dynamic figures. Rudyard Kipling, Winston Churchill, and Theodore Roosevelt were adolescents and teenagers during this golden age of war correspondence. Which is to say, they were like that kid enchanted by the Light Brigade's sacrifice, of the perfect age and frame of mind to turn a news account of faraway horror into a glimpse of grand adventure.

The correspondents featured in this book were vulnerable to that same allure. One of them, a Scotsman named Archibald Forbes, left the military for journalism specifically because Britain in peacetime couldn't provide the excitement he'd found in Russell's story of the Light Brigade. "Cavalry regiments do not hurl themselves in wild career against hostile ranks with great frequency," he lamented. Fulfillment came with his first assignment to cover a foreign conflict. "The moon had dropped into my arms! Here I hoped to hear the trumpet sound 'charge' and see the war horse pawing in the valley." At the end of a career in which his work became a popular staple in British and American newspapers, Forbes questioned that original dream. He'd seen awful things, lost his health, buried his friends. "But the recompense!" he wrote: "To have lived at the very heart of everything that was most sensational in those sensational days." In other words, no regrets.

The clash of empires and the rise of communication technology that enabled the world to read all about it—sensational days indeed. But this book favors the personal over the epic. Its characters illuminate the stage rather than the other way around. I'd never heard of most of them before happening on their stories a few years ago, yet once introduced, I determined to write about them even before I had any idea of their larger significance. Now I know they *had* larger significance, though I'm not sure it would have mattered. It's men and women who lived at the heart of extraordinary times that are my true subject. Lived then, and I hope do so again in these pages.

Hell Before Breakfast

Prologue

In March 1889 telegrams went out from Paris summoning five correspondents of *The New York Herald* from their postings in Berlin, Vienna, Rome, St. Petersburg, and Constantinople. They were to report not to the *Herald*'s international office near the Louvre museum but to 120 Avenue des Champs-Élysées, one of the best addresses on the most glamorous street in the world. It was the home of the newspaper's owner, publisher, and editor in chief, James Gordon Bennett, Jr., who'd moved there from New York after fighting a scandalous duel twelve years earlier. "I love America," he'd said at the time. "It's Americans I dislike."

Bennett normally had little contact with his reporters. He hadn't noticed when one recently went missing in eastern Persia; the man found his way out of the desert only after a pilgrim caravan traveling to Mecca took his pleas for the babblings of a holy dervish and gave him a lift on the back of a camel. And Bennett had been merely amused by a State Department warning about a dangerous battle zone: "I'm surprised you do not know that I never withdraw my men when under fire."

He'd never been in battle himself. His naval stint in the Civil War had been little more than a vacation, patrolling Long Island Sound in his father's yacht. Not that his reputation for daring was undeserved. He played polo, raced ocean schooners and four-in-hand buggies, drank and whored with posh abandon, and partied brazenly at every Gilded Age hot spot despite any number of rivals who would gladly have seen him shot dead with champagne flute in hand, a prospect to which he sometimes made the concession of wearing a chain mail vest under his tweeds and tuxedos in hopes it would stop a bullet.

Gathered in Bennett's drawing room, the correspondents knew the occasion was serious when the man himself, and not some *Herald* staffer, entered to greet them. A kindly smile showed behind the waxed handlebars of his Wyatt Earp mustache. Most people called him "Commodore," a title drawn from his past regime at the helm of the New York Yacht Club. To the reporters he was "Tiger Jim." It fit their sense of the brute power needed to run the world's most profitable newspaper. Finding him now the picture of graciousness was unsettling to say the least.

"You men have done wonders," he began, "but the conclusion has been forced on me that people don't care for a foreign service of the high order that you have maintained." Though *The New York Herald* was thriving, its international editions were losing hundreds of thousands of dollars a year. Bennett adored his Paris *Herald,* an irreverent four-page mirror in which wealthy American expatriates could watch themselves at play. But the stodgier London *Herald,* like the British themselves, enjoyed little warmth in the publisher's heart; he was shutting it down in the first of many cost-cutting steps. "I hope you recognize how I must bow to the inevitable," he explained. "How we *all* must bow to it." He shook the reporters' hands goodbye. Only when they were outside on the street did the realization hit. Recalled the youngest of them, Stephen Bonsal, "We had all been fired."

Another thought immediately followed: "Who cares?" Bonsal was twenty-three, in Paris, with a thousand-franc note in his pocket. A roaring night ensued, ending at Café Américain with a girl on each arm and a silky chanteuse named Mademoiselle Francine singing directly, or so it felt, to him. Some veteran reporters discussed serious matters at a nearby table. "There were clouds over the Balkans," Bonsal overheard. But it was nothing new—"there were always clouds over the Balkans."

Stumbling back to his hotel around three the next morning, he found a note folded under a brass candlestick on the table outside his door. The stationery was robin's-egg blue and addressed in dark blue pencil as thick as crayon. Recognizing the handwriting, he opened the note nervously and read: "Please call on me at seven o'clock tomorrow. Bennett."

Bonsal had first seen that distinctive script in New York two years earlier. Just out of college, and having lost the last of his money at the racetrack, he'd set his sights on becoming a foreign correspondent, "where, I well knew, the goddess of chance also ruled." In pursuing that goal, the *Herald* was the best place to be. It had dominated American journalism since before the Civil War, and over the past two decades its global scope and intrepid reporters had made it required reading on both sides of the Atlantic.

Educated in Europe, Bonsal was good at languages and submitted interviews of visiting diplomats that the *Herald* accepted "on space" before hiring him full-time. Frustrated that most of his stories still weren't getting into print, he did a piece "full of gore" about a waterfront gang fight that to his surprise was published the next day. A week later it appeared on the newsroom bulletin board with a fat blue scrawl across it: "Good." One of the city editors, voice low as if afraid to anger an unseen god, regarded Bonsal with awe. Bennett was in town on a rare visit back to America, and "now he knows your name."

This latest communiqué contained a vexing ambiguity: "Seven o'clock tomorrow. Did he mean a.m. or p.m.?" Thinking it better to suffer a tongue-lashing for rousing his boss from a hangover or a showgirl's arms than to stand him up, Bonsal spent the few hours till morning at a Turkish bath. Approaching Bennett's home on the Champs-Élysées, he was eyed by a Frenchman scrubbing the marble steps. "You should know," the man warned, "that Monsieur Gordon-Bennett does not receive at these hours." Bonsal pivoted in retreat.

A voice growled behind him: "I suppose you thought, as everyone does, that you'd find me boiling drunk at seven in the morning."

It was the Commodore, tall, lean, and looking as sleek in his three-piece suit as a pasha in a silk caftan. He offered Bonsal a cigarette from a silver case and invited him inside for a breakfast, his usual, of fried mutton and plover's eggs. Terriers yipped at Bennett's feet; he instructed a servant in livery brocade to refill their bowls with Vichy water. Then he got to the point. "Have you made plans since our talk yesterday?" he asked.

Bonsal said he hadn't.

"Good. Because there's a promising rumpus going on in Macedonia." It was a curious description for the rumored unrest of mountain villagers under the distant rule of Turkey's Ottoman Empire. Accounts of murder and reprisal, of mutilated bodies strung from trees, were trickling out of the region, accounts that might be exaggerations but possibly were not; such things weren't uncommon there. "I want you to leave tonight on the Orient Express," Bennett said, "and take charge of the Balkans. My cashier will arrange what money you need."

"Take charge?"

"You have complete liberty of movement between Vienna and the Bosporus—that is your beat." Bennett's tone was crisp. "If and when hell breaks loose somewhere, I expect you to be on the spot." There was one more thing. Bonsal must communicate exclusively with Bennett and not with the *Herald*'s New York headquarters: "Envelop your mission in mystery. Only turn up when the fireworks begin."

The young man realized that his quick rehiring was to taunt the paper's newsroom professionals. Bennett liked watching them scramble to send a reporter to some distant erupting conflict that he'd seen coming for months. Belittling executives was sport for him. He'd summon them from America to Europe (a two-week trip by steamship), glance up in irritation when they entered his office, and order them home. And he once asked his managing editor in New York to name his three best aides, whereupon Bennett ordered them fired. "No one is indispensable," he said.

Within a week Bonsal had settled at a hotel in Sofia, Bulgaria, and set out on a pilgrimage to honor a personal hero. He traced the journey taken thirteen years earlier by an Ohio-born correspondent named J. A. MacGahan to a remote village sixty miles south of the capital. He took along MacGahan's journal to serve as a guidebook of sorts. With its haunting opening line, "Since my letter of yesterday I have supped full of horrors," its publication in August 1876 had shocked the world and led directly to a war that killed a quarter-million people in nine months.

The village, called Batak, smelled differently to Bonsal as he approached its outskirts than it had to MacGahan, the air fresh instead of foul, crisp instead of acrid with the odor of burned wood and fetid water. As word spread of Bonsal's arrival, people rushed out with wreaths of wildflowers honoring the American who'd preceded him there. "It was pleasant to learn," he wrote, "that in this forgotten hamlet the man who had reported their sufferings was still remembered."

James Gordon Bennett, Jr., 1890, publisher of *The New York Herald.* When the young correspondent Stephen Bonsal first went abroad to report directly to Bennett in Paris in 1886, his managing editor gave him congratulations—and a warning: "Remember. Once over there, I can do nothing for you."

Knowing what he'd come to see, a girl took his hand and led Bonsal to a six-foot pyramid of human skulls stacked in a clearing. She indicated one skull split through the cranium—her grandfather, she told Bonsal's guide. Villagers pointed out similar shrines elsewhere. "Some skulls had been perforated by bullets," he noted, "others slashed by swords. Each had preserved its identity, as it were." People's regard of the relics was so familiar as to feel almost casual, as if the event they commemorated had been in the natural course of things; "those who accompanied us told us the name of this and that victim. Many placed flowers in the gaping clefts."

Bonsal had expected this trip to fulfill his homage to MacGahan. But when told that the leader of the Turkish militia that had rampaged through here thirteen years earlier was living in the hills nearby, he decided to do as MacGahan would have done and seek the man out in order to confront him for his deeds. Achmed Agha was known locally as "Lord of the Mountains," also "Great Assassin" in recognition of the four hundred Bulgarian villagers whose throats he claimed personally to have cut. World opinion condemned him, but peace terms of the war he'd helped cause let him retire with impunity in the land he'd soaked with blood. Bonsal had a mind to rectify this, to "visit Agha in his mountain aerie and see how it had fared with the man who in that day was viewed as the outstanding mass murderer of modern times."

A meeting was arranged through tribal middlemen protective of their chieftain. Bonsal and his guide found the old warlord, white-haired and toothless, sitting on a tree stump in a forest glade smoking a rolled cigarette. Flanked by bodyguards armed with scimitars and rifles, Agha greeted Bonsal by touching his chest and forehead in gesture of humble welcome. The guide spoke in Turkish with him, then turned to Bonsal and said, "I have introduced you as the envoy from America."

"Self-appointed, yes."

"But Lord Agha has never heard of America. France and Germany, yes, but never America."

Bonsal attempted a description of his homeland. The guide translated Agha's indifferent reply: "It may be so. Allah is great and the world is big. But I can't know all the lands of black infidelity."

"Tell me," the reporter said with a rising voice, "about when under the Turkish Crescent you drew your sword on your Bulgar brothers."

"Brothers?" The old man spat. "*Dog*-brothers. Our sovereign sent word they were waylaying our soldiers and directed us to go to their villages and quiet them."

"Ten thousand men, women, and children."

"Yes." It was blunt. "The men were soldiers, the children were growing, and the women were the mothers of future soldiers. We killed them all." Agha shrugged. "What happened could not have happened had not the One God approved."

Taking a breath, Bonsal asked if it was true that he'd promised to spare the villagers if they yielded and had massacred them after they did. The guide refused to translate the question. "These things happen in war."

"Ask him!"

"There is in battle much confusion. And Agha is a very old man. He has doubtless forgotten much."

That was the end of it. A congenial meal followed ("coffee, cakes"), and it was time to go. Bonsal mounted his horse and started down the wooded valley. Passing Agha's stone house, he saw him lying outside on a fur-covered divan. "Two little boys with fly-swatters crouched beside him and bodyguards knelt nearby," he later recalled. "The Great Assassin was sleeping the sleep of the just."

Bonsal was beginning a long career in journalism that would inure him to scenes of misery yet leave him haunted by small bitter images—the staring eyes of a frozen corpse behind which he took shelter from a blizzard in 1915; the upturned face of a French supply officer mashed flat as paper by a truck; a dying Russian prince murmuring to his wife, whom the prince didn't know was already dead, to please watch over their children, also already dead. Achmed Agha napping peacefully was one of those indelible images. Like the others, it posed a dispassionate lesson that evidently was the only one the goddess of chance cared to teach. Fifty years later Bonsal would sum it up with weary resignation:

"Man is an incomprehensible animal."

1

Nobody's Child

1854–1866

An eminent journalist has expressed the opinion that no training is possible or useful for the beginner. I should reverse that, and say that there is no training, no acquisition, no form of knowledge or experience, which is not useful to both the beginner in journalism and to the lifelong practitioner.

GEORGE W. SMALLEY, "NOTES ON JOURNALISM" (1898)

William Howard Russell would call 1854 "the year of grace" when reflecting on his career-making assignment as a war correspondent for the London *Times*. His qualifications had been limited to booze, billiards, and cards, he said. Moreover, he had an aversion to blood that had forced him to quit medical school in his early twenties. He worried that sights on a battlefield might cause him, as anatomy lectures had, spontaneously to pass out.

What the "big, bluff, genial Irishman" did bring to the job was an ability to get along with all types of people. And he was instinctive, a trait evident from his first assignment in 1841. Hired as a stringer to cover elections in Dublin, he arrived late to a political debate whose skid into violence had turned it into a riot of thrown chairs and Gaelic curses. On a hunch, he took off for the local infirmary—the perfect place, it turned out, to interview the campaign's bruised and beaten partisans recovering from fights outside the polling stations. The story won him a transfer to London and a position with *The Times*, a conservative bastion so politically powerful it was nicknamed "The Thunderer." He got married, started a family, and was a jovial fixture in the Garrick Club's trendy circle of actors, writers, and idle gentlemen. The novelist William Thackeray got such a kick out of him, he offered Russell "a guinea a day" to stand in as a regular party guest. But everything changed in February 1854, when he went to cover British military operations in Crimea. "You will be back by Easter," his editor said. "And you will have a pleasant trip."

The Crimean peninsula, dangling off southern Ukraine into the Black Sea, had been the launch point for Russia's recent surprise attack on the Turkish naval port of Sinop. Ostensibly a crusade to save millions of Christians from Muslim rule, Western observers believed its true objective was Constantinople (Istanbul today), capital of the Ottoman Empire. From that gateway between Central Asia and Europe, Russian forces could pour across the Bosporus Strait and drive westward into Bulgaria, making Russia far and away the region's dominant power.

The Turks were in a fight for their lives. The French and British joined them by choice. In Paris, Louis-Napoleon's Second Empire was a shaky imitation of the First Empire forged by his uncle, the conqueror Napoleon Bonaparte; he welcomed the chance to dazzle his people with a Crimean triumph and cement his title as Napoleon III. That equation was reversed in Britain. Having avoided war ever since winning at Waterloo forty years earlier, the government had no wish to take on the Russians. The people howled for a fight, however, so a month after enjoying brandy and cigars at a farewell banquet hosted by another Garrick member, Charles Dickens, Russell found himself "nobody's child" on a foreign shore scrounging for a bedroll and horse—a confirmation of Rudyard Kipling's later contention that "an infinite adaptability to all circumstances" is a war correspondent's most valuable asset.

Russell's letters to *The Times,* which took three weeks to reach London by mail, contained unfiltered descriptions of British soldiers camped amid animal carcasses and raw sewage without proper shelter, food, clothing, or medicine. The high command, expecting home newspapers to cleanse the details and support the cause, complained that these accounts encouraged the enemy. Russell argued that in strategic terms his news was out of date by the time it appeared. The generals harrumphed that he knew nothing about war. Russell agreed, "but I suspect there are a great many here with no more knowledge than myself," he said. Eventually the fun-loving Irishman was moved to activism. "Are there no devoted women among us," he pleaded in *The Times* that fall, "able and willing to go forth and minister to the sick and suffering soldiers?" A month later Florence Nightingale arrived with thirty-four volunteer nurses to begin treating eighteen thousand stricken soldiers. Cholera was rampant. For each man killed in the fighting that winter, eight would die of the devastating bacterial diarrhea that could dehydrate the body within hours.

The visceral intensity of Russell's letters was unprecedented. A Turkish field hospital held "nightmares for a lifetime." Wounded were carried in by their comrades "with the greatest tenderness" only to waste away unattended on lice-ridden mats. A Russian facility overrun by British troops shocked Victorian sensibilities with its "maggots . . . festering corpses . . . jagged splinters sticking through raw flesh . . . features distended . . . eyes protruding . . . blood which oozed and trickled upon the floor, mingling with the droppings of corruption." Yet as hideous as the scenes were, he found them fascinating. Sometimes it took the agonized gazes of dying men ("oh! such looks!") to shame him out of his voyeurism. Terrible things can be interesting.

Russell offered a technical as well as a psychological model for future war correspondents. It came in his report from the town of Balaclava on October 25, 1854. Relative to the Crimean War's two-year total of 75,000 killed in action and at least 200,000 dead of disease, the incident was statistically trivial. But like a modern, minor news event that is magnified by virtue of being accidentally captured on film, the tragic finale to the morning's fighting was viewed by Russell from a rise overlooking the now fabled "valley of death," a mile-and-a-quarter-long gorge down which a brigade of lightly armed British cavalrymen charged at midday under heavy fire and staggered back "in miserable remnants" twenty-five minutes later. Within hours he was in his tent composing on a wooden plank across his knees: "I shall proceed to describe, to the best of my power, what occurred under my own eyes."

The dispatch set a standard of style and pacing. Halfway through, its tense changes from past to present, accelerating the narrative as wider events of the battle narrow down to the critical moment, "the

William Howard Russell, 1854,
was content to cover Parliament
for *The Times* and never could
have imagined his future renown
as a trailblazing war reporter. His
nonchalant manner led authorities
to underestimate his candor
in reporting the British army's
neglectful care of its soldiers.

melancholy catastrophe," when the British commander in chief, Fitz-
Roy Somerset, Lord Raglan, gives his vague instruction that the Light
Brigade advance "nearer the enemy." The riders head out with resignation. As they kick into a gallop and surge down the valley, cannons
erupt at the opposite end and blow "instant gaps" through their ranks.
Each man's upheld saber transcribes a glimmering halo over his head.
The climax occurs not with their retreat ("demigods could not have
done what they had failed to do") but when horsemen from each army
clash in front of the Russian artillery. Russell's stomach drops when
the guns blast grapeshot at point-blank range, "mingling friend and
foe in one common ruin." The carnage comes clear as the smoke dis-
perses. Mangled bodies litter the ground. Survivors look around in
shock before reining their horses away.

The story appeared in London on November 13 and caused a
national uproar. Britain's poet laureate, Alfred Tennyson, stoked more
outrage by publishing "The Charge of the Light Brigade" a month
after he read the *Times* account. Russell's piece opens with a rhetorical
question asking if astonishing valor can give consolation for point-
less slaughter. Tennyson, with his famed incantation of the soldiers'
doomed devotion to duty, "Theirs not to make reply, / Theirs not

to reason why, / Theirs but to do and die," replies with an emphatic no. Russell ends with a terse tabulation no less haunting: "Went into action: 607. Returned from action: 198. Loss: 409."

Forty-four years later young Winston Churchill would participate in a similarly reckless cavalry charge at Omdurman, in today's Sudan. The national myth of the Light Brigade came to Churchill's mind as he approached the battlefield. "Of course there would be a charge," he exulted. "In those days British cavalry had been taught little else. Talk of fun!" Recounting the event, he used Russell's style of switching to the present tense as the Sudanese warriors come into view: "They are advancing, and they are advancing fast. They think they are going to win." But they didn't win—trusting in faith to carry them through British machine gun fire, almost ten thousand were killed in a matter of hours. "This kind of war was full of fascinating thrills," Churchill wrote. "Nobody expected to be killed. This was only a sporting element in a splendid game."

In the fallout from Russell's Balaclava dispatch, the British prime minister and his cabinet were voted from office for mismanaging the war. Lord Raglan remained in command until his sudden death the next summer. "Not a very great general," Florence Nightingale said, "but a very good man." His illness hadn't seemed serious. It was said the war—and Russell—had broken his heart.

The thirty-six-year-old correspondent returned home in 1856 an international celebrity, credited with stirring the conscience of his nation and leading the military to improve the care of its soldiers. The drama of his reporting made for an amusing double take when readers discovered that, far from some glamorous dynamo, he was, in his own words, "bald as a round shot and gray as a badger." Meanwhile, the Treaty of Paris that ended the Crimean War left the Ottoman Empire intact and its frictions with Russia still smoldering. It was only a matter of time before they would burst into flame.

Two years later—on September 1, 1858—a pair of former warships, the American *Niagara* and the British *Gorgon,* came to shore in New York harbor and docked before the sandstone reception rotunda of Castle

Garden, on Manhattan's southern tip. Their hybrid design of sail and paddlewheel, wind and steam, captured the industrial transformation that the day's events would celebrate. The transatlantic telegraph cable connecting Europe to North America, a once unthinkable technological feat, had been laid across the ocean floor four weeks earlier. Cyrus W. Field, the visionary who'd conceived and driven the five-year project, was a New Yorker. Today the city would honor him with a parade.

Field, thirty-eight, disembarked from the *Niagara* and took in the sight of carriages, flags, and an excited crowd lining his route up Broadway. Tall and thin, he was one of those earnest types who exude confidence in the face of challenge and fidgety nervousness when at loose ends. As the mayor's welcoming party came down the pier, Field beckoned seamen and engineers from the two vessels to join him in the festivities. He wasn't one for the spotlight.

He'd already received thanks from the British and American governments for reducing communication time between their nations from a two-week voyage to a two-minute transmission. And last month newspapers everywhere had gone into rapture after he'd successfully spliced his cable to shore points in Newfoundland and Ireland and passed an electric current through it. "The Atlantic is dried up!" raved the London *Times*. *The New York Herald* likened him to "the Angel in the Book of Revelation, with one foot on sea and one foot on land." The outpouring unsettled Field. "Gas and grandiloquence," he said.

The original proposal in 1854, from a Canadian engineer named Frederick Gisborne, had asked Field to fund an underwater cable from mainland Canada to Newfoundland, first landfall for passenger ships crossing the North Atlantic. To wire foreign news inland from there rather than wait until a ship reached Boston or New York would save two days' time, Gisborne explained—an advantage governments, businesses, and newspapers would eagerly pay for. Field was lukewarm. But one evening soon afterward, he was idly spinning the globe in his library when a notion struck. Forget merely crossing the two-hundred-mile Gulf of St. Lawrence. He would stretch a cable more than two thousand miles across the Atlantic.

Retired with self-made wealth from a paper supply business, he'd had no difficulty finding backers for the venture. Many were here today, industrialists and Wall Street traders keenly aware that an international cable monopoly could reap unlimited fees. They flocked around him with backslaps and bravos after the parade ran its course from the Battery to the Crystal Palace exhibition hall, near Fortieth Street. In his subsequent remarks, he thanked them for supporting him through the early setbacks of two cable expeditions that had failed. His optimism at the time had concealed "a load in my heart almost too heavy to bear," he admitted. But everything was fine now, a pronouncement he underscored by reading aloud a telegram he'd been handed on the pier earlier today. It was a note of congratulations from some British investors—wired from London *this morning*. The crowd erupted in cheers. No one knew that Field's gratified smile was in utter, desperate relief.

His cable's first transmission after linkup the previous month had been an exchange of greetings between President James Buchanan and Queen Victoria. It took sixteen hours to transmit. Clearly there was a fault somewhere along the cable, a crack in its insulation through which electricity was bleeding into the frigid saltwater, like a punctured vein that won't clot. As accolades poured in, Field had ordered his technicians to keep the problem quiet while they tried to fix it. Transcripts of their test messages had sickened him with their futility:

"Repeat please."

"How do you receive?"

"Send slower."

"Please say if you can read this."

"How are signals?"

"Do you receive?"

"Please send something."

Thankfully, transmissions had recently improved. The reason wasn't a miracle. The cable lay almost three miles deep in some places; water pressure likely had compressed and sealed the crack. The miracle was that Field, consumed with dread, should have received at this fraught moment an overseas telegram confirming that his achievement was genuine, his tributes deserved. When the mayor presented him with a gold case engraved with the seal of New York, Field accepted it proudly: "For your kindness expressed in too flattering terms, I offer my heartfelt thanks."

His next day included a visit to Mathew Brady's photo gallery at Broadway and Tenth Street. It was an essential stop for American celebrities wishing to fix their images in the grave and striking black-white spectrum of Brady's "wet plate" ambrotypes. The "Imperial" was the photographer's top offering; larger than the murky pocket daguerreotypes available everywhere for a few dollars each, they ran as high as seven hundred dollars and made Brady, whose photographs of the Civil War would later gain him still wider fame, the era's most exclusive portraitist. "His gallery is filled with an unequaled collection of the lions of the town," said *The New York Herald*. "To see the elephant one must go elsewhere."

Field posed with one hand on a globe—the resulting image shows him with a preoccupied expression, as though not quite trusting yesterday's good fortune. At a banquet in his honor that evening, he was called from the table to take another telegram from abroad. Its message cut off abruptly. He knew what it meant. The cable was dead.

He was denounced on two continents. People suggested he'd staged the hoax to pump the stock of his Atlantic Telegraph Company. "How many shares did Mr. Field sell during the month of August?" a London paper demanded. The company's stock plummeted. For the next several years, he struggled to repay his partners. But quitting was never an option.

After the Civil War began in 1861, he focused his fund-raising in Britain, where he slowly patched together another consortium. In the meantime improvements were made in the cable's weight and flexibility. A remaining challenge was to find a ship large enough to hold the twenty-six hundred miles of cable sufficient to cross the Atlantic in one span. In the past, two vessels had carried the great spools; they'd spliced their cables together at midocean and set off for opposite shores. In 1864 a candidate, the *Great Eastern,* was proposed. The biggest ship in the world, it was three city blocks long, with six masts, five coal funnels, and room for six thousand passengers. Billed as the world's greatest luxury liner, it was too large for most harbors and too

Completing the transatlantic cable in 1858 had America bursting with pride in citizens who'd fathered the effort—Benjamin Franklin for his work with electricity, Samuel Morse for inventing the telegraph technology, William Hudson for skippering the cable ship, and Cyrus W. Field for bankrolling and overseeing the project. The celebration commemorated by this period drawing, however, proved premature.

heavy to run at speed, a colossal boondoggle now for sale at a bargain. There was a problem, however—a significant one in the superstitious world of seafaring. The ship was apparently cursed.

Twenty workers had died in shipyard accidents while building it. The *Great Eastern*'s architect, Isambard K. Brunel, who'd designed Britain's Great Western Railway system and London's Paddington Station, had suffered a stroke the day before its maiden voyage, living just long enough to learn that during the voyage an explosion had ripped apart its saloon and killed five people. And all this was before the ship's owners went bankrupt. Did Field really want any part of such an obvious agent of doom?

Pondering the question, he considered his life experience. Before the age of thirty, he'd twice clawed back from financial ruin. The blows that had staggered him—a partner's thievery, a stock market crash—had come out of the blue when all signs indicated prosperous times ahead. His first cable attempts had likewise begun amid omens of good weather and infallible machinery and been wrecked by storms and breakdown. Maybe it was time to change the pattern and stake his future on this unloved iron hulk. A colleague suggested that the *Great Eastern* was made for the transatlantic cable. But the better interpretation is that it was made for Cyrus Field.

Transatlantic telegraph fees were anyone's guess as long as Field's project remained unfinished. No doubt they'd be stiff, judging from what domestic companies charged. America's telegraph network had consolidated from many regional operators down to two main players in the decade before the Civil War, a period when lines expanded from two thousand to thirty thousand miles of cable. Western Union controlled the upper Midwest and the Mississippi valley, American Telegraph the eastern seaboard from Canada to New Orleans. It cost up to a dollar (about thirty dollars today) to transmit a ten-word telegram, and much more to send long messages. To share expenses, five New York City newspapers—including its top three, the *Herald, The New York Tribune,* and *The New York Times*—had formed an alliance, the Associated Press, to wire government items from around the country to New York. Though this made it all but impossible for them to score national scoops on one another, once the cable transcripts were in hand, their race to sell papers resumed.

The Civil War would disrupt the AP's effectiveness. What a paper spent to hire its own reporters and to get their stories from the field to the newsroom—by mail, rail, horse, boat, or telegraph—became the key factor in its obtaining the "beat," the exclusive battle dispatch that could be issued in an extra edition and hawked on the street at great profit. But until the war started and made newsgathering a contest of every man for himself, rivalry among the New York papers turned primarily on local coverage of scandal and crime and on editorial attitude expressed through political argument, moral posturing, and personal insult. All three were abundant on Monday, April 15, 1861, when protesters—inflamed as much by their newspapers as by events of the previous weekend—swarmed around a large granite building at the corner of Fulton and Nassau Streets. "The New York Herald" was carved into the edifice above its front steps, the letters smeared with the pulp of fruits and vegetables hurled at the place in fury.

Many in the crowd waved copies of the Sunday *Herald*. Headlined "Dissolution of the Union Consummated," it confirmed the surrender of U.S. troops at Fort Sumter after four days of artillery bombardment from Confederate shore batteries in Charleston, South Carolina. The *Herald*, whose one-penny first issue in 1835 had vowed always to "exhilarate the breakfast table," enjoyed the largest daily circulation of any newspaper in the world. Each morning's sheets were churned out overnight by steam presses and distributed through the city by horse-cart, around the nation by rail, and, where it surpassed the London *Times* in popularity, to Europe by ship. Sunday's issue had doubled its usual run, with more than 135,000 copies sold. It featured a blistering editorial by the paper's sixty-three-year-old founder, James Gordon Bennett, calling the Sumter attack not a Southern outrage but a triumph for fanatics of the Northern abolitionist movement. They cared more for "the nigger" than for America, Bennett wrote, and welcomed the destruction of the Union if it meant the end of slavery. He urged readers to accept Southern secession and to resist the "oceans of blood" that civil war would unleash. He punctuated his piece with a printed graphic of a Confederate flag, a ballsy flourish that even he should have known was going too far.

Others in the Fulton Street mob brandished *The New York Times*. It contained an editorial blasting Bennett's secessionist sympathy and urging him to make a public speech against retaliating for the Sumter attack: "He will receive such a greeting as will discourage his oratory if not his treason." The paper reported President Abraham Lincoln's call for 75,000 volunteer soldiers. The result was a citywide outpouring of patriotic fervor that had coalesced into this mass march on the *Herald*.

Despite its hostile rumblings, the crowd demanded only that Bennett affirm his loyalty by flying an American flag. But there wasn't one anywhere in the building, a lapse that seemed to verify allegations in the

Herald's other bare-toothed rival, *The New York Tribune,* that Bennett had stocked up on Confederate flags to broadcast his Rebel solidarity. An office boy was hustled out a back door to buy an American flag down the street. When at last Bennett stepped outside, he was draped in its furls, his buzzard features and unruly gray hair made even more vivid by the red-white-and-blue toga he wore. Satisfied, the protesters dispersed as the old man benignly waved. Once inside, he snarled an order for guns and ammo to be stored in his office lest the rabble rise again.

A pragmatist above all, Bennett published another editorial the next day renouncing his prosecession position and pledging to support Lincoln's efforts to restore the Union by force. *Times* owner Henry J. Raymond mocked these "damnable contortions," while his counterpart at the *Tribune,* Horace Greeley, called them "the most sudden and total change of opinion on record." Their papers enjoyed nowhere near the *Herald*'s daily readership. In the past, Raymond the political moderate and Greeley the radical progressive had made do with consolations of integrity over the easy slop of gossip and vice that made the *Herald* so infernally popular. But now, with the Union imperiled and their beloved Lincoln cast as its savior, Raymond and Greeley's liberal idealism seemed due for a wide embrace.

Bennett had trashed Lincoln ("illiterate Western boor") from the moment he'd emerged as a serious presidential candidate. Of Lincoln's campaign speech at New York's Cooper Union in February 1860, the *Herald* had wedged its critique between a story about an unwed mother incinerating her baby and a rave for the Barnum Museum's addition of an ape with human features to its stable of sideshow freaks; the speech has since gone down in history as a masterpiece of reasoned argument against the spread of slavery. Bennett cited self-determination and constitutional principle when defending the South's right to its "peculiar institution," but this was mostly hot air. An up-from-the-gutter millionaire shunned by polite society, he loved annoying the highbrows.

Still, with the Sumter attack galvanizing Northern calls for war, he hastened to revamp his image. On Tuesday, April 16, he invited a young reporter named Henry Villard to dinner. Villard had emigrated from Bavaria eight years earlier, writing for German-language papers before taking freelance jobs with the *Herald*. Covering Lincoln's political rise, he'd criticized Lincoln's gawky appearance and uncertain policies but had since been impressed by his character, "so sincere, so conscientious, so honest, so simple-hearted, that one cannot help liking him." Villard almost declined Bennett's invitation out of distaste for his reactionary views. But curious to observe "this notorious character" at home, he kept his qualms to himself and rode with Bennett in his carriage up Fifth Avenue and across Central Park to his mansion in Washington Heights.

They were joined at the table by twenty-year-old James Gordon Bennett, Jr. An athletic fellow with the punky look of someone afraid of no one but his father, he'd been reared in France along with his sister, their mother having moved there after her husband was repeatedly mugged on New York streets by aggrieved targets of *Herald* exposés. His had been "a queer sort of bringing up," a friend later said. "Someone, possibly a servant, led him astray when he was very young." Summoned to New York at sixteen by his father, he'd gained a reputation as a drunk, a bully, and a cheat. The last stemmed from an escapade at Plum Gut, a channel off the east end of Long Island through which he took a shortcut to win a society boat race. The *Tribune* and *Times* had trumpeted the scandal, humiliating Bennett Senior and leading him to exile his son abroad for another four years, bringing him back just a few days earlier.

Dinner with the two of them was a strange experience. Villard's German rectitude was repelled by Bennett's cackling irreverence. And he couldn't stop looking at his host's crossed eyes, a congenital tic whose sinister aspect seemed confirmed as the evening wore on: "Intercourse with the old man quickly revealed his hard, cold, utterly selfish nature and incapacity to appreciate high and noble aims."

Bennett was candid about his purpose tonight. He wanted the reporter to convey some private messages to President Lincoln—an assurance of *Herald* support for the war against the Confederacy; a donation of Bennett's yacht to the Treasury Department's revenue service; and a request that his son be commissioned a lieutenant in command of that yacht. "The last wish I thought rather amusing," Villard

James Gordon Bennett, photographed by Mathew Brady just before the Civil War, dictated *The New York Herald*'s support of Southern slavery and its criticism of Abraham Lincoln. The publisher's rivals wondered if these editorial attacks weren't merely provocations intended to keep the newspaper notorious and profitable. Bennett's political views contrasted with his iron priorities regarding the *Herald.* "Business is business, money is money," he said.

recalled. Biting his tongue, he agreed to act as go-between, for which service he received a raise to thirty-five dollars a week.

Bennett Junior was a nautical novice. He'd sailed his father's schooner, the *Henrietta,* only under the guidance of a sailing master named Samuel Samuels, top skipper for the Red Star Line of clipper ships, based in New York and Liverpool. Having Samuels as your sailing instructor was like having Babe Ruth teach you batting—his first rule had been if the kid ever touched the wheel while Samuels was steering, he'd lock him in the hold. But Lincoln saw benefit in conciliating the publisher of the most widely read newspaper in America. He fired off a note to the Treasury secretary that within days put the young man in uniform.

Fitting out the *Henrietta* with three shiny brass cannons, Lieutenant Bennett patrolled Long Island Sound through the end of the year, not surprisingly encountering no enemy raiders in the cozy basin between New York and Connecticut. He took the vessel to join a naval blockade off South Carolina, where he passed out one night on the foredeck. The hoot of an owl roused him, and he opened his eyes to see the froth of a reef off the bow. Saved by this miracle from running aground, for the rest of his life he would religiously festoon his homes and offices with images of owls as talismans to ward off misfortune. Rumor had it that one of his girlfriends had them tattooed on her knees.

Young Bennett's naval career came to an abrupt end in early 1862. Proving "a trifle presumptuous" toward his superiors, he was removed from command and assigned to a frigate. He finagled a discharge instead, unwilling to accept standard navy grub after the sumptuous fare his personal chef had served aboard the *Henrietta*.

His father installed him at the *Herald*. At the next desk sat Edward T. Flynn, the office boy sent to buy an American flag during the Fulton Street riot the previous spring. Flynn was to school the boss's son in *Herald* operations, but the instruction was flipped when the pupil became the teacher. One early lesson took place during a long lunch at Delmonico's near Union Square, a popular watering hole for businessmen looking to break up the day with mint juleps or champagne cocktails. A tipsy Bennett Junior careened to the bar and demanded to know what was delaying his drink. A voice drawled behind him, "You'da thought he ordered a case." Bennett whirled and threw a punch. The other man, pint-size compared to the lanky newspaper heir, dodged the blow easily and knocked him cold with a single left hook.

The next day Flynn had one job: "Find out who it was." The man turned out to be a professional bare-knuckle boxer named Billy Edwards, which in Bennett Junior's mind transformed the event from a shameful thrashing to a dazzling coup. Edwards was a rising contender few men dared provoke. A meeting was arranged, and soon the prizefighter and the millionaire's son were a regular pair at the best night spots in New York.

Another evening at Delmonico's ended with young Bennett leaping up at the clang of a fire alarm and dashing to the site of a neighborhood fire, where he proceeded to tell the firemen how best to fight the flames. To shut him up, they turned their hoses on him, blasting him headlong across the sidewalk. Flynn got the usual bleary question the next day, "What did I do last night?" and a subsequent instruction to buy rubber coats for the entire city fire department. "Send the bill to me. I was never so wet in my life," Bennett said. It became a pattern—by day Flynn served as a *Herald* copy editor, by night a sober sidekick to clean up the messes and pay the bills resulting from his young charge's merriment.

Meanwhile, James Gordon Bennett the elder had backslid on his promise to support Abraham Lincoln. The *Herald* resumed mocking his "village idiot" sense of humor and the sentimental "niggerism" of his concern for Southern slaves. The president took it in stride— better to suffer a few personal barbs than an editorial assault on his policies and, always vulnerable to second-guessing, his management of the war. He adopted a habit of answering Bennett's venom with sugar, sending him amiable notes and mild corrections of the *Herald*'s wild assertions. This forbearance mystified the White House staff, but Lincoln stayed fixed on the larger mission of saving the Union. "It is important to humor the *Herald*," he said.

On the same night that Henry Villard was squirming through dinner with the Bennetts, the most famous newspaper correspondent in

James Gordon Bennett, Jr., 1861. An uneventful stint as a U.S. Navy lieutenant allowed the *Herald* heir to claim lifelong credibility as a Civil War veteran with every right to put his correspondents in harm's way. Opinion about Bennett Junior ranged from barbarian to visionary; no one called him boring.

the world was bucking a nervous tide of African Americans hurrying down Meeting Street near his hotel in Charleston, South Carolina. The eight-thirty curfew bell had tolled. The slaves had half an hour to wrap up their duties and return to quarters. Any found on the streets after nine without a special pass would be arrested and punished.

The Confederate stars and bars flew over Fort Sumter at the mouth of Charleston harbor. Since leaving Baltimore four days earlier to begin a tour of the South for the London *Times,* William Howard Russell had found the region's war fever overwhelming: "I felt like a man in full possession of his senses coming in late to a wine party." Sumter's surrender had Rebel soldiers strutting around with cocky menace that Russell found laughable. He'd visited the fort earlier that day. The damage from the vaunted cannonade was "trifling," he sniffed.

He had the experience to back up his opinion. Two years after the Crimean War ended, he'd been plucked from comfortable London life and sent to India, arriving in January 1858. The native Bengal army had turned on its British colonial masters after long-festering discord was tipped into violence by new government-issue bullet cartridges greased with pork and cow fat, substances taboo to the Bengal army's 90,000 Muslims and Hindus. Rumors (false, but it didn't matter) of the army's impending forced conversion to Christianity had sparked a mass mutiny whose death toll quickly ran into the tens of thousands.

Most victims died in massacres and summary executions. One of the worst incidents occurred as a force of British redcoats closed on the Bengal-held town of Cawnpore. Panicked rebels hacked to death two hundred captive women and children and threw their bodies down a well. Russell, indulging his fascination for places "where great crimes have been perpetrated," toured the building where the killing occurred, its floor caked with drying blood. Workers who exhumed the bodies could barely express their trauma. "A sickening anguish," one said. "There is no object in saying more."

British troops answered the Cawnpore atrocity with firing squads and mass hangings; they strapped Bengal mutineers across cannon barrels and blew their midsections into the sky. "A glorious sight," said a British officer of a pile of two thousand dead natives. Russell denounced the actions as excessive and racist: "I believe we permit things to be done in India which we would not permit to be done in Europe." This scolding irked a British public steeped in hellish accounts of the Bengal army's barbarity, most of them unsubstantiated. One example described Anglo-Saxon babies "put alive into boxes and set fire to. Others were spitted on bayonets and twisted round in the air, and to make the tortures more exquisite all this was done in the presence of the mothers, who were compelled to look on in a state of nudity."

Posed against such lurid images, Russell's call for moderation made no dent in a government crackdown whose pitilessness was exemplified by the policy of making captured mutineers, as a curse on their souls prior to hanging, lick the bloody floor mats taken from the building where those British civilians had been killed. He railed against heretical tortures of "sewing Muslims in pigskins, smearing them with pork fat before execution, burning their bodies, and forcing Hindus to defile themselves." *Times* readers were unsympathetic, however, and greeted Russell with derision when he returned from India after order was restored.

His assignment to cover North-South unrest in America offered a happy escape. Welcomed at the White House, he appreciated the president if not the first lady: "The impression of homeliness produced by Mrs. Lincoln is not diminished by closer acquaintance." In New York he interviewed the prosecession owner of the *Herald,* James Gordon Bennett. "His game," Russell wrote, "is to abuse every respectable man in the country in order to take his revenge on them for his social exclusion." He found Bennett's counterpart at the *Tribune,* Horace Greeley, only a slight improvement. The fifty-year-old reformer oozed with the self-righteousness of the New England Puritan, who, having "hunted down all his Indians, burned all his witches, invented abolitionism as the sole resource left to him for the gratification of his favorite passion."

Greeley predicted that Russell would be repelled by the South's "slave pens" once he saw them, and indeed the sight of an African sold at auction appalled him. Russell called slavery "a cancer" but acknowledged other reactions within him that revealed a reporter's detachment and a candidly human inappropriateness. Slavery's "whippings and brandings, scars and cuts," didn't stop him from wondering "whether it might not be nice to own a man as one might possess a horse—to hold him subject to my will and pleasure, to hold his fate in my hands."

Russell detested the presumption of Southern planters that Britain's dependence on imported cotton would force it to back the Confederacy. His editors disagreed. Their support of the Confederacy for reasons of trade over morality left Russell doubly isolated. Southerners resented his disparagement of their cause, while Northerners felt the same about *The Times*. His celebrity favor evaporated as a result, and in July, with opposing armies gathering near Manassas, Virginia, thirty miles west of Washington, commanders rebuffed him. He'd encountered the same attitude from the British military in 1854. Now in America on the eve of the Civil War's first major battle, he must again, he wrote, "take the field without tent or servant, canteen or food—a waif to fortune."

Problems in finding a mount brought him late to the fighting near Bull Run creek on July 21. He missed the Union assault that buckled the Confederate line and sent journalists dashing to the nearest telegraph station with excited reports that soon were splashed across the country: "Brilliant Union Victory!" But the Rebels didn't break. General Thomas J. Jackson rallied them and thereby gained his nickname, "Stonewall." Russell's tardiness put him in perfect position to detect that the tide had turned. While reporters at the front grappled with gunfire, dust clouds, and hysterical rumors of advance and retreat, he saw a stream of blue-clad soldiers stagger out of the chaos lamenting, "We're whipped." Offended by their hangdog collapse and forlorn parade of hospital wagons packed with unwounded men, he urged them to summon their pride and resume the attack, "but I might as well have talked to the stones."

By the time his London dispatch was reprinted in America a month later, the fact of Bull Run as a Northern disaster had been absorbed. Russell's analysis pulled off the singular trick of equally insulting each army—the Union for yielding to panic, the Confederate for calling it a great victory. He made matters worse by chiding America's traditional condescension toward the British monarchy. "The stones of their brand new republic are tumbling about their ears," he clucked. "It will be amusing to observe the change in tone."

American papers excoriated "the snob correspondent from the London *Times*." His candor about missing Bull Run's combat brought him ridicule. He was likened to an old woman flouncing about red-faced, fat, and miles from the fighting. And it was claimed he'd been drunk, having admitted riding out that day well supplied with brandy from whose flask, to Russell's chagrin, a parched trooper had taken "a startling pull which left but little between the bottom and utter vacuity."

He took the jibes with humor at first, telling friends that he was "the best abused man in America." But when some Yankee reporters started hinting at his cowardice, he lashed out at their self-proclaimed coolness under fire and their florid descriptions of rivers of blood and gore. "I failed to discover any traces of close encounter or very severe fighting," he sniffed. After all, he'd been to Crimea where many thousands had died; the death toll at Bull Run was barely eight hundred.

He received death threats. Then word came down from the White House that his press privileges were revoked. "My unpopularity is certainly spreading upwards and downwards," he observed, "and all because I could not turn the battle of Bull Run into a Federal victory." He sailed for home the next spring. In its send-off, *The New York Times* acknowledged that his dispatches had included some brilliant passages. Bennett of the *Herald* was unmoved: "He hates our country; let him leave it."

Russell was glad to go. A storm rocked his ship on its first night at sea but didn't alter its heading, "thank Heaven, towards Europe." He took with him a lasting view that American journalism was "degraded and odious." He also brought along a new nickname, "Bull Run Russell," that would dog him all his life.

The Times forgave his shabby exit and awarded him an annual pension of three hundred pounds. He was far from finished as a correspondent. Ahead lay the Austro-Prussian War of 1866, the Franco-Prussian War of 1870–71, and the Russo-Turkish War of 1877–78, a trio of bloodbaths that would be as alluring to American newsmen as the Civil War had been to Russell. They would bring an aggressiveness suited to the tastes of their readers, leaving the languid, diligent

Russell yet again dismayed as to what exactly was happening to the profession he'd pioneered.

Henry Villard was one of the Bull Run reporters who caught Russell's ire for bragging that "bullet, ball, and grapeshot never had much terror for me." Once the battle's morning euphoria gave way to sober truth, Villard wired a corrected dispatch to the *Herald.* James Gordon Bennett ran it in a special edition, but people dismissed it as a gimmick hatched to pump sales. When Villard followed with a full account of the Union fiasco, Bennett, fearing he would again be mobbed by Lincoln partisans, deleted all mention of the army's failings before printing it.

Bull Run's most comprehensive early report appeared in *The Philadelphia Press.* Its author, John Russell Young, had, like Russell, enjoyed the peculiar advantage of covering the fight from the rear, having overslept that morning. In collecting accounts from soldiers, Young noted that they weren't the only ones fleeing: "A number of distinguished representatives of the New York press took this occasion to leave the scene of danger."

His piece begins straightforwardly: "There is no use concealing that the army of the Union has been completely routed." Proceeding in a tone of calm critique ("The causes of defeat appear to be these"), it ends with a vision of the sun rising "in bloody splendor" over the four-mile train of bone-weary troops trudging back to the capital. Born in Ireland, Young had supported himself from childhood and joined the *Press* at age fifteen. Now a newsroom veteran of twenty, he knew how to end with a flourish: "Amid a shower of falling rain, we saw our dear old flag, God bless it, still streaming to the breeze—emblem of a glorious past; harbinger of a more glorious future; and, although covered today in temporary disaster, soon to float again over a Rebellion crushed, a Constitution defended, a Union restored, and the majesty of a mighty and invincible Republic."

Thus was introduced to American readers a "humdrum laborer" (his words) whose lifelong career in journalism would generate a trove of writings, mostly forgotten today, bringing an almost religious equa-

John Russell Young was twenty-five when he became *The New York Tribune*'s managing editor in 1866. Remembering his early triumph in covering the Battle of Bull Run as a field correspondent in 1861, he hoped someday to visit war zones in Europe where he might experience the thrill of "a hairbreadth escape."

nimity to the era's full range of newsworthy subjects, from a political scandal to a theater performance, a pretty painting to a wartime atrocity. The poet Walt Whitman called Young "a lovable cuss." Lifelong friends, the two first met in Washington soon after Bull Run. Whitman had published his collection *Leaves of Grass* to little notice six years earlier and now was an aide in the army hospital. "You ran into him in out of the way places," Young wrote, "riding in horse cars talking to the driver, giving pennies to ragged groups of Negro children, sailing down Pennsylvania Avenue in frowsy raiment and that wonderful hat with packages under his arms for the hospital." The earthiness of Whitman's poetry was "among my earliest indiscretions," he said. "He was a gentleman of the pavement, a shaggy, lounging wayfarer." Whitman put his regard for his friend more plainly: "He's a man with real guts to him."

In contrast to the firestorm caused by the foreigner Russell, Young's Bull Run story was received as a patriot's earnest admonishment. Soon the "slight and boyish" Philadelphian was recalled from the field and made editor of the *Press*. Three years later Horace Greeley would bring him to New York to run the *Tribune*. His youth wouldn't sit well with old-timers at the paper. Editors were supposed to be grizzled

and coarse. Young resembled a mild-mannered owl. But there was grit
behind the sweetness. "As lovely as a woman," a colleague said of him,
"but when challenged no man in his profession struck with greater
power."

Young later described his editorial philosophy this way: "There is
nothing in this world entirely right or entirely wrong." His approach
to dire events and controversial people was fair-minded and humane
as a result. Consider his "pen pictures" of New York's newspaper kingpins, Greeley of the *Tribune,* Raymond of the *Times,* Bennett of the
Herald—together they embodied American journalism in all its arche-
typal styles, Young wrote. Greeley was "the advocate—strident, implacable, resolved that mankind should not go to perdition." Raymond
was detached and ironic, taking in life's panorama "like the lounger
at the club window, thinking only of its movement and color." And
Bennett was the steely capitalist whose dominance resembled "a vast,
sinister shape which had come out of the infinite to overspread and
darken the heavens." Young's own style is illustrated by the annual
entry on June 21 in the diary he kept all his life. It's the day his mother
died and left him an orphan at age eleven. Each year he wrote the same
reflection—that she'd showed him "beauty of being." It was something he thought worth commemorating again and again.

After Young's *Press* account fully aired the Bull Run debacle, Greeley
was savaged in *The New York Times* and the *Herald.* His *Tribune* had
led the howls of "Forward to Richmond!" that had pushed Lincoln to
strike south before the army was ready. This war cry had been driven
by the paper's managing editor, Charles A. Dana, "brilliant, capable,
irresponsible—not above setting things on fire for the fun of watching them burn," in Young's description. Dana's hawkishness would
eventually find him a welcome perch as Lincoln's assistant secretary
of war, but it got him fired from the *Tribune* after Bull Run. Greeley
felt responsible for not restraining him in the run-up to the battle and
wrote an apology to Lincoln of such abject defeatism ("the Union is
irrevocably gone") that people wondered if he'd gone mad—and in
a way he had, for the disaster gave him "brain fever" from which he
emerged in the fall of 1861 to find his reputation in tatters and the *Tribune's* circulation in freefall. The chastened publisher imposed a new

editorial policy of printing facts not comment. The paper continued to struggle, however, disheartening its staff despite a staunch facade of elevated purpose, a fact Bennett gleefully publicized when he printed an internal Greeley memo complaining, "The *Herald* is constantly ahead of us."

More than five hundred reporters would cover the Civil War. The *Herald* employed the most by far, as Bennett poured half a million dollars into the project. He ridiculed the *Tribune's* scanty coverage next to "our heavy battalions." A competitor characterized the *Herald* ethos as perfectly reflecting its irascible owner: "The whole world was to him a reporter's district, and all human mutations plain matters of news. Battles and sieges were simply occurrences for its columns. Good men, brave men, bad men, died to give it obituaries."

The paper extended its dominance after Lincoln's hard-nosed secretary of war, Edwin M. Stanton, imposed press censorship in early 1862. Beyond the vexation of seeing troop movements publicized, officials had had to cope with reporters racing to print eye-popping news whether warranted or not. When mere "unorthodox remarks" were overheard at headquarters, for example, the next day's headline screamed, "GEN. WILLIAM T. SHERMAN INSANE!" Sherman came to hate reporters as a result, going so far as to applaud their death in battle: "That's good news! We'll have dispatches now from hell before breakfast."

Secretary Stanton placed all telegraph lines under government control and began building thousands of miles of military cable. He forbade the transmission of anything but "past facts" cleansed of all reference to the disposition of troops. The clampdown drew protests from most every paper except the *Herald*. Bennett was backing Lincoln more than ever these days, pleased that the president had rebuffed abolitionist pressure to widen the war's aim from restoring the Union to also freeing the slaves. Lincoln opposed slavery, of course—"I cannot remember when I did not so think and feel." But winning the war was his top priority, and that was hard enough without adding the controversy of emancipation. "If I could save the Union without freeing any slave I would do it," he wrote Greeley in August 1862, "and if I could save it by freeing all the slaves I would do it; and if I could save it by freeing some and leaving others alone I would also do that." For this reluctant pragmatism, Bennett praised him as "the only man of moral and political stamina in the country."

But two events a month later would rattle the *Herald* owner and slow his paper's momentum. First was the Battle of Antietam, fought at Sharpsburg, Maryland, on September 17. The second event came five days later, when Lincoln announced the profound change in policy he'd been secretly planning for months—to declare every slave free as of January 1, 1863. "God Bless Abraham Lincoln!" Greeley cheered. "Unnecessary, unwise, ill-timed, impracticable," grumbled Bennett, "and full of mischief."

The *Herald* had immediately hailed Antietam as a backbreaking blow to the Confederacy and a credit to the generalship of George B. McClellan, a favorite of Bennett's due to their shared proslavery views. The hasty announcement had helped encourage Lincoln's belief that the time was right to add the moral dimension of emancipation to his war aims. In truth, the battle was far from decisive. McClellan and one of his corps commanders, Ambrose E. Burnside, failed to crush the Rebels at ripe moments during the battle and afterward, when General Robert E. Lee dragged his battered army south. McClellan was fired as a result. Burnside, as genial as he was untalented, was appointed his successor, a Lincoln decision of tragic consequence on account of the prodigious loss of life that Union troops would suffer under his poor leadership.

The Battle of Antietam put Dunker Church, Bloody Lane, and the Cornfield into Civil War lore as hallowed killing grounds. The *Herald,* in its rush to print good news, got it wrong. It took a rookie reporter named George W. Smalley to expose Antietam's strategic inconclusiveness and terrible human cost. The Civil War's most famous battlefield "beat" was reprinted in papers across the country. And Horace Greeley, Smalley's *Tribune* employer and Bennett's favorite whipping boy, had the satisfaction of running it first.

Smalley, twenty-nine, was a sturdy, square-jawed athlete who'd captained Yale's rowing team in 1852. While studying law in Boston before

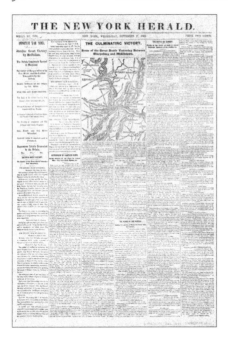

"The Culminating Victory" was the *Herald* headline after the first day's fighting at Antietam on September 17, 1862. In getting the story wrong, the *Herald* gave its struggling rival, *The New York Tribune,* a chance to score the Civil War's most famous "beat" with a dramatic report of the battle's horrific casualties and strategic stalemate.

the war, he'd been outraged to see an escaped slave seized under the Fugitive Slave Act and returned in chains to Virginia: "In broad daylight a citizen of Massachusetts was carried down State Street by Boston troops and sent back into slavery!" Joining the abolitionist cause, he was welcomed as "a natural soldier" and made a bodyguard for its fiery spokesman, Wendell Phillips. He fell in love with Phillips's adopted daughter, Phoebe, but with no money to marry, he sought an interview with the owner of America's leading antislavery organ, *The New York Tribune.* Greeley distrusted college-educated journalists but made an exception this time. Smalley expected to start in the newsroom. Instead he was told to pack for the war's front line. No problem, he said—"the adventure is entirely to my taste."

At Antietam he was attached to the army of Joseph "Fighting Joe" Hooker. The general ran a headquarters described as a combination of bar and brothel, yet Smalley admired his leadership. "I say this the more unreservedly," the straitlaced New Englander wrote, "because I have no personal relation whatever with him, never saw him till the day before the fight, and don't like his politics or his opinions in general." Smalley wore "a sort of uniform" to blend in with Hooker's staff, with the result that "nobody took the trouble to ask who I was or why I was there." This facilitated an exchange with the general early on the battle's first day. Patrolling the skirmish line on horseback while barking orders "in language of extreme plainness," Hooker was a prime target for Rebel marksmen; many of his staff were shot while riding alongside him. Shorthanded as a result, the general had no time to question Smalley's affiliation when he turned to him with urgent orders for one of his commanders.

Summarily drafted as a courier, Smalley crossed the battlefield as gunfire cracked around him. "Corpses are strewn so thickly," he observed, "that you cannot guide your horse's steps too carefully." The flanks of his horse, grazed by Minié balls, were slick with blood when he galloped up to the commander and recited Hooker's order to renew the attack: "It is time to end this business."

The man waved him off. "It must come to me from a staff officer."

"Then I'll report to General Hooker that you decline to obey."

"Oh, for God's sake don't do that! The Rebels are too many for us, but I'd rather face them than him."

Smalley rode back with his report. Before sending him on another mission, Hooker said with a scowl, "Don't let the next man talk so much."

Hooker later said he'd never seen "more tranquil fortitude and unshaken valor than was exhibited by that young man." Nor was Smalley above throwing his bravery in the faces of his peers. "Is that all you have done?" he challenged a fellow reporter as they wrote their stories that night. "Haven't you been in battle under fire?" The man took offense and threw a punch. Afterward he whined to his editor that Smalley was bossy and patronizing: "He gave me to understand by the tone of his voice that he considered me a coward."

Smalley's prose was as forthright as his character. "Fierce and desperate battle between 200,000 men has raged since daylight," his Antietam dispatch begins, "yet night closes in on an uncertain field." The first day leaves the Union at a slight advantage, as "everything is favorable for a renewal of the fight in the morning." But matters change the next afternoon, when McClellan's field commanders implore him to call up a reserve of 15,000 fresh troops, and Smalley realizes that "the moment has come when everything may turn on one order given or withheld, when the history of the battle is only to be written in thoughts and purposes and words of the general." Time seems to stop while McClellan ponders. At length he sighs and says there's nothing more he can do. "Men had died by hundreds and were yet to die," Smalley later would say, "because he could not make up his mind."

By the time Lincoln's Emancipation Proclamation was formally issued four months after Antietam, James Gordon Bennett had put his disappointment behind him. Though still dismissing any assertions of equality between blacks and whites, he supported, in his way, African Americans joining the Union Army: "They are just as good for killing as anyone else." Even his bigotry yielded in matters where deeper dislikes were aroused, as when Lincoln's otherwise annoying racial crusade at least offered an upside of disarming Horace Greeley and the abolitionist kooks: "There being no slavery, there can be no antislavery. This knocks the foundations from under this association of pestilent agitators and crazy fanatics."

Lincoln's call for military conscription in July 1863 brought a similar mix of high pronouncement and low vendetta. Bennett supported the measure as the quickest way to replenish the army and bring the war to conclusion. But public resistance was violent, and a citywide eruption of antidraft riots targeted New York's black citizens as the handiest scapegoat for the war's soaring bloodshed. The *Herald* sold in record numbers as it luridly described the white thuggery that left hundreds of innocents dead in the streets. When protesters threatened to smash the offices of the *Tribune* and the *Times* for helping expand the war from punishing Southern secessionists to freeing African slaves, Bennett smiled to see Greeley and Raymond scrambling for their lives. They blasted him for inciting the mob with his racist rhetoric. How hypocritical, he snorted, to denounce the rioters as Irish scum when most of the police protecting the city were Irish: "Apparently Greeley and Raymond hate the white race as much as they adore the black."

His editorials during the 1864 presidential campaign were no less opportunistic. They swung between routine jabs at Lincoln ("incompetent driveller") to grudging respect for "Honest Old Abe." Even faint praise helped in Lincoln's tight New York race against George McClellan, Bennett's former favorite, whose failings the publisher now conceded. The *Herald*'s choice for president was the stellar commander Ulysses S. Grant, "who knows how to tan leather, politicians, and the hides of rebels." Since Grant had already announced that he wouldn't quit the battlefield for the campaign trail, Bennett knew the endorsement was as good as supporting Lincoln's reelection. He signaled his price for this tacit boost through White House go-betweens, as Lincoln explained to an Illinois friend, Leonard Swett: "Bennett has made a great deal of money, some say not very properly. Now he wants me to make him respectable."

There it was. Despite having worn his social exclusion as a badge of pride for decades, Bennett craved acceptance. He was one of the richest, most ornery men in America, yet in negotiating a swap for his campaign neutrality, he wondered plaintively, "Will I be a welcome visitor at the White House if I support Mr. Lincoln?"

Lincoln's secretary, John Hay, was aghast. "What a horrible question for a man to be able to ask," he thought. Yet while he almost pitied Bennett, Jay counseled the president not to receive him in public: "He is too pitchy to touch."

In consolation, Lincoln opted for a different payoff three months after the election, nominating the *Herald*'s reviled owner to be America's ambassador to France.

The sixteen days Bennett took to reply were as much to savor the offer as to ponder it. "Accept my sincere thanks for that honor," he finally wrote. "I am sorry to say that at my age I am afraid of assuming the labors and responsibilities of such an important position." But his warm sign-off to Lincoln, "with sentiments of the highest respect," marked a turning point between them. To the amazement of many, Bennett became one of the president's heartiest supporters, acknowledging in an editorial, "He has proved himself, in his quiet way, the keenest of politicians." Just weeks after Lincoln's second-term inauguration, Bennett was already proposing that he run again in four years.

And on April 4, 1865, he gave his highest praise, calling the president's speechwriting so brilliant that whenever his political career ended, there'd be a job as a war correspondent waiting for him at the *Herald*. "Should he accept," Bennett said, "he can have one hundred dollars a week, his rations, and a fresh horse every six months."

Lincoln was assassinated ten days later. Bennett wrote several editorials praising the "morally magnificent" leader. It would require the broader perspective of history, he said, "to comprehend the genius of a character so externally uncouth, so pathetically simple, so unfathomably penetrating, so irresolute and yet so irresistible, so bizarre, grotesque, droll, wise, and perfectly beneficent as the great original thinker and statesman for whose death the whole land, even in the midst of victories unparalleled, is today draped in mourning."

More distraught over Lincoln's death than anyone could have predicted, Bennett, seventy now, at once cut back on his involvement in *Herald* operations. He came to the office rarely. With "entire confidence" he placed his twenty-four-year-old son in charge, ignoring his editors' warnings that Bennett Junior was, to put it delicately, "not very steady." They were privately furious that the drunken brat would be their superior ("he is more changeable than his father, his judgment more defective"), but the old man was firm. "No other person has my confidence but my son," he insisted. "What is said to him will be the same as if said to me."

America's most powerful publisher was content to putter about his mansion in carpet slippers tending his pet canaries, named after local politicians and vanquished business rivals. As word spread of his abdication, a poem about him circulated among newspapers around the country. It begins, "Should history condescend to pen it, / What would its verdict be on Bennett?" The anonymous author goes on to answer the question:

> *He was the scandal of his age,*
> *A coward, liar, pimp, and sneak.*
> *Though his age preserves him from our blows,*
> *We despise him as he goes.*

Daniel Chester French completed his sculpture for the Lincoln Memorial in 1919. Five years earlier he'd created a small monument that stands near the White House (see page 294). It commemorates two of French's friends, an army major and a famous painter. The latter, Frank Millet, supported his art career by covering the war between Russia and Turkey in 1877–78 for *The New York Herald,* becoming for a time the most influential war reporter in the world.

Bennett was past caring what people said about him. As often happens to lifelong battlers once they quit the arena, old age, it was said, came on him "overnight."

Henry Villard had a difficult war. Starting with the *Herald*'s sanitization of his Bull Run dispatch, he'd been unable to pull off a breakthrough "beat." It wasn't for lack of trying. Joining the *Tribune* in order to find more like-minded editors, he filed a stirring account of the slaughter at Shiloh in 1862 only to have it lost in transit to New York; and his sharp critique of Burnside's disastrous leadership at Fredericksburg later the same year was considered too demoralizing to publish. But more than professional setbacks discouraged him. At Shiloh he'd surveyed the carnage with a calm eye. "I lingered to see the effect of sudden violent death on features and limbs," he wrote. "It surprised me that the faces of the victims bore a peaceful, contented expression." A few months later the sight of wild dogs scavenging the unburied dead brought revulsion that all but incapacitated him: "Decomposition had swelled the bodies into awful monstrosities. The nasty beasts were hard at work disemboweling them and gnawing into the skulls for their brains. Such is war!"

Seeds of pacifism were planted in him along with a thirst for recognition that made him eager to find another line of work. In 1873 an introduction to some German-American railroad men led him to invest money inherited from his father. Eight years later Villard gained control of the Northern Pacific Railway. Some of his new fortune went for an early stake in Thomas Edison's company, the future General Electric. Some went to purchase New York's *Evening Post* and its weekly offshoot, *The Nation,* publications reflecting his antiwar views. Villard was a capitalist titan when he died in 1900. His wartime journalism was deemed the least of his accomplishments. One of his last comments on the subject suggests he shared the opinion: "If I were a commanding general, I would not tolerate any of the tribe within my army lines."

George Smalley, by contrast, was a newsman to the core. His Antietam report had won him a promotion to the *Tribune's* New York headquarters, where he spent the duration of the war. The starch in his personality limited his office popularity, however, so when Greeley went looking for fresh talent to revive the paper, the publisher brought in the youngster from Philadelphia, John Russell Young.

Young managed the newsroom with a subtle hand. In July 1866 he ambled by Smalley's desk with a month-old London newspaper under his arm. It was almost a pity, he said idly, how the end of the Civil War had put a stop to battle news: "With no more fighting, there is no occasion for war correspondence." Unfolding the paper and perusing it as if for the first time, he remarked that maybe he'd spoken too soon. Austria had declared war on Prussia, the former a vast and wobbly conglomerate of Germans, Slavs, Hungarians, Romanians, and northern Italians, the latter a compact, muscular kingdom in central Europe.

Like most Americans at the time, Smalley knew little about foreign affairs. "We were still in that state of patriotic isolation," he recalled, "when events in Europe seemed to us like events in an ancient world." Austria and Prussia might as well have been Sparta and Athens for their relevance to daily life in light of the Civil War, the Lincoln assassination, and the turmoil of Reconstruction. But Young suspected that soon would change. "A journalist of genius," Smalley later wrote, "Mr. Young was not satisfied with the existing supply of European news. He wanted better news and more correspondence."

Smalley was married now to Wendell Phillips's daughter, and they had two young children. His career was the higher priority, however, and after Young proposed that he become the *Tribune's* European "special," the reporter was at sea two days later. Though it would have far-reaching implications, the task at hand was nothing new: "I went to Europe to see the Austro-Prussian War."

His ship was the Cunard liner *China*, carrying almost a thousand passengers. Its two-hundred-dollar first-class ticket bought a berth in the main cabin, all meals for the two-week voyage, steward fees, and access to cash saloons on the upper deck; for half that price, you could bunk with seven hundred others down in the forward hull, enjoying mess hall food and limited use of latrines and outside walkways. Smalley liked to think of himself as a man of the people, a disciple of Greeley's social progressivism. But he was damned if he would travel in steerage.

Midway across the North Atlantic, the *China* encountered a singular sight. On the horizon was the unmistakable silhouette—five smokestacks, two fifty-foot paddlewheels—of the massive vessel *Great Eastern*. Owned by Cyrus Field's new company, Anglo-American Telegraph, it steamed slowly west while feeding thousands of miles of one-inch cable over its stern down into the depths. To maintain flexibility, the cable was coiled in the hold in huge saltwater tanks whose weight was said to be enough "to sink the Spanish Armada." A recent technical advance enabled a continuous electric current to run between Ireland and an on-board station as the cable unspooled; the line's integrity was monitored through news announcements received daily from Europe. One item reported that armies from Prussia and Austria were massing near the town of Königgrätz on the Elbe River, a hundred miles east of Prague.

The *Great Eastern* had almost succeeded in connecting the cable last summer, coming within two hundred miles of Newfoundland before the line was accidentally severed. Confidence was so high on this trip that Field, who on previous voyages had paced the deck at night and slept by day to conceal his nervousness from the crew, gazed out the windows of the *Great Eastern*'s saloon with expectant calm. On July 26, 1866, land was spotted. The next day the cable was joined to the Newfoundland telegraph and the North American network beyond. Field wired a message to the New York newspapers: "All well. Thank God, the cable is laid and is in perfect working order."

The New York Times declared that European dispatches sent by ship would henceforth be "little more than wastepaper" by the time they arrived. The London *Times,* forgetting that its star correspondent, William Howard Russell, exemplified the traditions of in-depth, unhurried reporting, proclaimed the lightning speed of the international telegraph "a glory to our age." In its excitement, *The Times* pushed another bit of news to the back page: "Treaty of peace signed between Prussia and Austria."

The war Smalley had hoped to cover had ended while he was still at sea. At a stroke, the unsung Prussian Army had smashed the Austrians at Königgrätz and supplied the conflict's alternative name in history, the Seven Weeks' War. Learning of the decisive battle on disembarking in Liverpool, he was upset to have wasted his time. "It would have made a difference to us in America," he lamented, "if the war news of June could have reached us by cable." But then he remembered Young's wider directive to gather foreign news wherever it happened. Smalley would go to Berlin to see the victorious army return to its capital. These Prussians evidently were on the rise in Europe. There might be a story there.

For Cyrus Field and his company, Anglo-American Telegraph, acclaim and money poured in. It was the dawn of America's Gilded Age, a period of postwar economic expansion when flaunting wealth would be as respected as making it. This national transformation would see urban populations boom, literacy rates double, and daily newspapers more than triple in number across the country. City editions would expand from single to multiple folded sheets with upward of a dozen pages, and advertising revenue would soar from personal classifieds, department stores, and patent medicines. Anglo-American was deluged with clients willing to pay any price for fast international communication. With his profits, Field bought mansions in America and Europe and one of the largest emeralds in the world, which he wore as an everyday tiepin.

He came to grief, however. His daughter was hospitalized with mental illness. And his two sons, given total access to his seemingly limitless bank account, would meet misfortune as entrepreneurs in the late 1880s. Needing emergency funds to pay off their debts, Field sought the aid of his next-door neighbor, the railroad magnate Jay Gould. Knowing Field was desperate, Gould lived up to his reputation as a robber baron and drove terms for the bailout that eviscerated Field's fortune.

The greater agony to Field was that one of his sons, Edward, was willfully hateful in embezzling the family's few remaining assets. Edward continued to lie and write bad checks until by 1891 there was truly nothing left. Field was seventy-two and frail. To see Edward arrested and then learn he'd suddenly died in custody would seem an almost biblical blow for a father to endure. But it was a blessing to Field, for an autopsy found massive lesions on his son's brain probably caused by injury years before. So Edward wasn't a crook who'd despised his father. He'd simply been unwell.

Field died a year later. His gravestone inscription commemorates his perseverance and energy in creating the transatlantic telegraph, of which by then there were several lines owned by several companies— but his had been the first. Of the many newspapers around the country that eulogized him, one of them used the occasion to criticize Jay Gould. Most papers feared offending the powerful financier lest he retaliate without mercy. But this one let fly with both barrels, calling Gould a foul skunk whose wealth had been built "from the bankruptcies of scores of honest men." The editorial ran in *The New York Herald* and was penned by its owner and editor in chief, James Gordon Bennett. The son.

2

American Methods
1865–1870

I could not help feeling that from the pluck and enthusiasm that had brought them over the sea the world might one day reap real victories.

MONCURE D. CONWAY, "THE INTERNATIONAL BOAT-RACE" (1869)

In the summer of 1865 James Gordon Bennett the elder decided to use the *Herald*'s wartime profits to build a magnificent new headquarters. When a lot at the corner of Broadway and Vesey Street became available, his determination to buy it was too strong for the seller not to exploit. And it wasn't just any seller. The lot was the site of Phineas T. Barnum's American Museum of "curiosities and monstrosities such as the eye of man never before gazed upon." Its recent destruction by fire had left the impresario broke but not broken, and Bennett's eagerness gave Barnum a plum opportunity to play out his credo, "There's a sucker born every minute."

The two men had tangled before. In 1850 Barnum had made a fortune with an opera tour of the "Swedish Nightingale," Jenny Lind, despite Bennett denouncing its high ticket prices for such "claptrap" talent. When Barnum later had one of his several brushes with bankruptcy, Bennett pronounced it fair justice for the huckster foisting on the public a carnival sham of "Fiji mermaids, woolly horses, Negroes turning white, and impostures of all kinds." But now the tables turned. Barnum hoodwinked his old nemesis with an inflated property appraisal that would have been justifiable, he joked privately, if the land were paved in gold.

When Bennett discovered the ruse and demanded his money back,

Barnum laughed, "I don't make child's bargains." At once all mention of his new production at Broadway's Winter Garden theater was dropped from the *Herald*. He stormed into the newsroom and pounded the desk of the managing editor, Frederic Hudson, shouting, "My advertisement is gone! Is there a screw loose?"

"You must ask the Emperor," Hudson said.

Barnum looked around furiously. Outside a corner office an imperious young man conferred with some *Herald* underlings. "Him?"

Hudson rolled his eyes at the notion of wild Jimmy Bennett actually replacing his father. "Not yet."

The land dispute sparked a two-year freeze in which the *Herald* refused Barnum's business and panned every one of his shows. The feud ended only after work was completed on the marble temple that became the *Herald*'s new home. In addition to a gaudy array of Corinthian columns, it had massive doors of black walnut constructed without locks or bolts. People speculated that this was done on the order of Bennett Junior to symbolize that work inside never stopped.

With his father increasingly removed from *Herald* operations, the young man behaved as acting chief with the same impudence that he brought to New York's stodgy social clubs when senior members eyed him warily. In the clubs he'd put on shows of drunken riot to confirm their worst suspicions. In the newsroom he might call together the staff to lay down his latest whimsy. "I want you fellows to remember," he announced, "that I am the only one to be pleased. If I want the *Herald* turned upside down, it must be turned upside down." Lest any of the veterans think he was kidding, he popped that illusion fast. "I can hire all the brains I want for twenty-five dollars a week."

Free to tap into the paper's huge profits, he indulged every whim. He frequented horse tracks, gambling parlors, and a top-shelf brothel run by a madam named Josie Woods; so classy was her establishment, the doorman's uniform featured silver buttons in pornographic mold. When dining out, he might yank the tablecloths from under the place settings of adjacent parties and make amends by paying their bill. Informed at a restaurant door that the kitchen had closed for the night, he'd buy the joint on the spot in order to dine at leisure. Six thousand dollars (more than a hundred grand today) was a reasonable bet on a gentlemen's footrace after lunch at a Fifth Avenue hotel. And thanks to him, "Bennetting" was the sport of charging one's Thoroughbred through pods of schoolgirls outside their academies and scattering them like bowling pins.

Such heedless flash was almost a social requirement among the gilded stars of New York's postwar boom. It enhanced young Bennett's standing among the elite who'd spurned his father for years. His role model and main cohort was the stock market speculator Leonard Jerome, a generation older in years but a virtual teenager in his pursuit of maximum fun. Said a friend of the high-living financier, "One rode better, sailed better, banqueted better when Mr. Jerome was of the company." Carousing with Jerome at the height of the financier's "merry despotism," Bennett learned that the nightly company of theater starlets never got boring, that nothing beat the style of "a howling swell" in spats and a boutonniere, and that peeling down Broadway in a runabout buggy drew cheers as well as gasps. He took Jerome's equestrian kick a step further by dropping the traditional top hat and waistcoat and racing at night along the country roads north of Manhattan wearing nothing at all. He'd lash the horses and rattle the reins like a nudist Ben-Hur in quest of some elusive sensation he could articulate only one way: "I want to be able to breathe."

Then there came a boozy night at the Union Club on Fifth Avenue in October 1866. Some gentlemen mariners ("It depends what you mean by *gentlemen*," Leonard Jerome liked to say) were debating centerboard- versus keel-design sailboats. Arguing for the former was George Osgood, grandson of the shipping magnate Cornelius Vanderbilt and board member of the New York Yacht Club, who'd just taken possession of his new schooner, the *Fleetwing*. On the other side, swearing that his shallow-draft, centerboard *Vesta* was the fastest ship in the world, was Pierre Lorillard, tobacco baron and builder of the original Breakers estate in Newport, the Rhode Island resort for which his company's most popular cigarette is named. With no skin in the game, Leonard Jerome's brother, Lawrence, challenged, "Put it to the test. Race them across the Atlantic." It was agreed. For a prize of $30,000 (about half a million dollars today), the *Fleetwing* and the *Vesta* would compete—and as soon as possible, to avoid the North Atlantic's winter storms.

Young Bennett, who'd been listening nearby, approached the table. He wanted in on the bet—but with stakes raised to thirty grand each, winner take all. Osgood asked if he intended to enter the *Henrietta,* which Osgood had beaten in a race the previous summer. Absolutely, Bennett said. The prospect of easy pickings convinced the two older yachtsmen to include him. Bennett had one stipulation: he wanted the race run two months from now, in December. Too dangerous, they said. He insisted: "Only then can we count on wind enough for all." Osgood and Lorillard looked at each other. They wouldn't be going themselves; hired captains would face the dangers. The match would test the schooners—each more than a hundred feet long with upward of two dozen crewmen—not their owners' seamanship. Fresh drinks were ordered all around. The ocean race was on.

Bennett was hell-bent on manning the wheel but took the precaution of bringing along his old sailing teacher, Samuel Samuels, whose Atlantic crossings for the Red Star Line were so fast it was said he knew a "secret ocean path between New York and Liverpool." Two of Bennett's friends would also go—Stephen Fiske, the *Herald*'s theater critic (he'd got the job after accusing his predecessor of filing reviews without seeing the plays); and Charles Longfellow, son of the Boston poet Henry Wadsworth Longfellow. "Charley" was a world-class sailor who'd followed his near-fatal wounding in the Civil War with a life devoted to sport and definitely not to poetry, to which he felt such an aversion that he admitted to reading his father's verse only "from a sense of filial duty."

Bennett sequestered his pals aboard the *Henrietta* the night before the race lest they lose nerve and jump ship. "The season selected is the most inclement of the year," warned *The New York Times*. "The excursion is likely to be anything but a pleasure trip." Spectator boats full of "fair ones and their gentlemen friends" dotted New York Bay before the start on December 11; these moneyed contests were like professional sporting events today, with fans watching and wagering with partisan fever. The three great schooners "throbbed on the swell" until, as if choreographed, they tacked simultaneously toward the starting line, their bowsprits crossing in unison as the gun sounded at one p.m.

Still in sight of one another that evening, by the end of the next day sixty miles separated first from third. The *Fleetwing,* the leader, tacked north, looking to draw level with Britain's Isle of Wight and ride the west winds straight to the finish. The *Vesta* took a more southerly course, while the *Henrietta,* on Samuels's counsel, opted for "the steamship route," heading directly northeast from New York to England. Five days out a winter gale struck. Six crewmen on the *Fleetwing* were swept overboard by "a specially malignant billow," the ship's log recorded. Two clung to a line and were saved; four were lost. The *Fleetwing* searched for four hours before pushing on. "We are sure that the agony of the strongest swimmer must have been brief," the London *Telegraph* later said. "To be washed into a frantic sea in the darkness, and, as their vessel vanished in the storm, to struggle with the waves and feel the chill of death knowing there is no manner of hope, is to meet a bitter end."

Each vessel hove-to during the gale, lowering its sails till the gusts and rollers abated. But the *Henrietta* was fortunate. The storm had come out of the southwest, driving the vessel along her course; without a stitch of canvas aloft, she made more than a hundred miles a day, pushed by the wind and waves. That the *Fleetwing* and the *Vesta* caught no such break and still closed on the finish line within hours of the *Henrietta* eight days later confirms the general belief that Bennett's schooner was the slowest. But he'd known that already and had sought the December start in order that wintry conditions would make the race a test, he said, "of endurance rather than speed."

Nothing was heard of the contestants for thirteen days. Breathless American press coverage preceding the race was matched with dire speculation in Europe. No paper saw its circulation spike as much as the *Herald,* whose publisher's son had been the only one of the race's three principals "who goes in his own boat." The profit windfall didn't escape Bennett Senior. He'd condemned the race as extravagant nonsense, but when results arrived by telegraph he emerged from retirement to run a proud headline: "HENRIETTA THE WINNER OF THE OCEAN RACE." Nor could the old provocateur resist adding, "A Challenge Is Hurled to the Old World."

The *Herald* chronicled the parades and banquets thrown in honor of the *Henrietta's* crew. Knowing his son's habits, the publisher inserted a warning into an otherwise rapt editorial: "We hope the young gentlemen concerned have borne and will throughout bear themselves in a manner worthy of all praise." Bennett Junior stayed on his best behavior—he gave the entire winning purse to his shipmates—clearly signaling a personal change. "When he returned to New York he began to devote himself to business," Stephen Fiske wrote. This wasn't well received in the *Herald* newsroom. No one believed the young man was anything but "a creature of unrestrained desires," as one employee put it. "If impulse called, he obeyed, and no rule existed but to be broken."

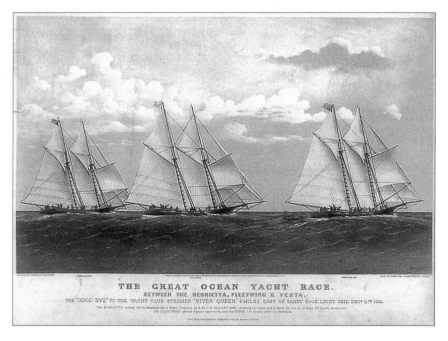

The start date of the Great Ocean Race in December 1866 was chosen deliberately by James Gordon Bennett, Jr. Winter crossings of the North Atlantic were arduous and deadly, but he knew it was the only way his schooner *Henrietta* could beat the faster *Fleetwing* and *Vesta*. Taking the helm in the perilous race solidified his legend as a daredevil and sent the *Herald's* circulation to new heights.

Bennett Senior had been a beast to work for—but now that his son was angling to replace him, staffers spoke nostalgically of the old man's "kindly heart" rather than his lightning temper and incendiary politics. One can imagine their reaction when on April 27, 1867, top billing on the *Herald* masthead, "James Gordon Bennett, Proprietor," suddenly featured "James Gordon Bennett, Jr., Manager" underneath. Two months later the founder's name vanished entirely, and "James Gordon Bennett, Jr., Editor-in-Chief and Publisher," stood alone.

But not for long. Within hours, Bennett Senior stormed into the *Herald* building and ripped into his son at full volume before the whole newsroom. It was the old man's last hurrah. "Though the announcement disappeared," Fiske wrote, "the fact remained." The prince was now the emperor.

Charles Dickens had nothing good to say about the effect of the telegraph on the quality of news reporting. It was December 1867. John Russell Young, twenty-seven, was hosting a *Tribune* banquet in honor of the English novelist, who was visiting America to deliver a series of public readings. Dickens, a red flower decorating his black velvet lapel, was at the height of his fame after publishing *Little Dorrit, A Tale of Two Cities,* and *Great Expectations* in recent succession. "In soul I long had worshipped Dickens," Young later wrote. It made him reluctant to dispute the author's poor opinion of the telegraph and the editorial constraints it imposed. "Tolls are dear and condensation is the rule," he said to Dickens affably. "There go the adjectives."

"Yes. The adjectives and adverbs and all the horticulture of newspaper genius."

Young thrilled to so connect with his idol: "This royal visitor from the land of romance—why, the very gods were dowering me with Olympian splendor!"

He'd organized the night's affair and arranged the seating in hopes of exactly such an exchange. Dickens was one of the cofounders of London's liberal *Daily News,* and Young nudged the conversation to the respective qualities of British and American journalism. Dickens was curt: "Your newspapers are properties. Ours are institutions."

The comment took Young aback. "But of course all editors are beholden to their business departments."

"Not ours. This will come to you in time, as many other things will come. There can be no true journalism where editorial prerogatives are impaired."

Young appreciated the sentiment but not its tone. As their conversation continued, his annoyance grew. "Instead of being spoken to man-to-man, I began to feel as if I were being soothed." Dickens's condescension was unmistakable. "Somehow, I did not like him. Here he was, but where were the illusions? The gods wore wooden shoes after all."

After dinner they strolled through a light snowfall to Dickens's hotel near Gramercy Park. They began discussing *A Tale of Two Cities* and its depiction of Paris during the French Revolution as crazed with lurid bloodlust. Young ventured that this was surely a dramatic exaggeration. It was an opinion Dickens didn't appreciate: "Have you been to France?"

Young had married a Philadelphia girl, Rose Fitzpatrick, two years earlier and had a baby son and a New York apartment to go along with his dream job at the *Tribune*. Visiting France was not a priority.

"Should you ever go," Dickens continued, "you will comprehend what I was trying to say."

They walked on. Young turned the topic to American literature and his personal favorites, Edgar Allan Poe and Walt Whitman.

The Englishman replied, "Yes, yes, quite so—*but*," and then delivered deft dissections that thoroughly cut down those writers.

Young had had enough. Returning to the sore spot of *A Tale of Two Cities,* he said that frankly he'd found it a letdown after the teeming satire of *David Copperfield*. This stopped the dialogue cold. Dickens eyed him through the veil of snowflakes. *A Tale of Two Cities* and its vision of France in revolt represented some of his best work, he growled—and until Young saw more of the world, he'd best not criticize. Listening with a fixed smile, Young found himself recalling a colleague's muttered dig at Dickens's crowd-pleasing brilliance: "Shakespeare, with some threads of the Negro minstrel running through him." He rather agreed with that now, for the author did seem kind of a windbag.

Charles Dickens was "a small and slender figure, rather fancifully dressed," in Mark Twain's description of one of Dickens's readings in America in 1867. *Tribune* editor John Russell Young was in awe of Dickens until his illusions deflated on meeting the great author in person.

Contrary to Dickens's skepticism, Young's experience with the transatlantic telegraph had been positive. The reporter he'd sent to Europe the year before, George Smalley, had prudently sent long stories by mail and wired urgent news in concise summary. His first cable to America, published in the *Tribune* on August 1, 1866, had outlined the terms of the Austro-Prussian armistice. The Seven Weeks' War had killed more than 80,000 soldiers and civilians and vaulted Prussia to the top of Europe's power structure. On hearing a rumor that peace talks had hit a last-minute snag, Smalley paid five hundred dollars ("we wasted no words at that price") to wire an item hinting that hostilities might resume. When it didn't happen, Young forgave him his mistaken prediction. In this fledgling stage of rushing foreign news to American readers, the headline's "sufficiently startling" shock value was what mattered most.

In September 1866 Smalley had gone to Berlin to watch the Prussian army's triumphant return from the field. As troops streamed through the multicolumned Brandenburg Gate, he'd sensed that the thousands of spectators would have preferred to see them in torn and muddy fighting gear, though even in crisp blue tunics and red trousers, "they looked like what they had proved themselves—irresistible." Flags and decorations lined the boulevard with a constrained grandeur that he attributed to a still-emerging German identity. "It was a declaration of independence," he wrote of the Berlin parade, "and of something more."

King Wilhelm I, a doddering sixty-nine-year-old who'd ascended Prussia's throne following his brother's death six years earlier, led the procession. "But the three men behind him were the real heroes," Smalley wrote. In a wide gap between blocks of troops marching in lockstep rode Albrecht von Roon, the war minister who'd organized the military's innovative use of rail transport and the newly invented "needle gun," whose breech-load efficiency had devastated Austria's musket-carrying infantry; Helmut von Moltke, the general who'd directed the fighting; and Otto von Bismarck, the coldly calculating prime minister who'd instigated the war to advance his plan to unite Europe's many German-speaking states into one empire. Aligned shoulder to shoulder, the triumvirate barely acknowledged the rapturous crowd. Popularity meant nothing to these men, Smalley wrote. What they wanted—and now manifestly possessed—was the power to dominate Europe.

He left a letter of introduction at Bismarck's government office after the celebration. The prime minister's immediate invitation to call at his residence made him suspect that Bismarck meant to use him to spread his nationalist message to the *Tribune*'s German American readers; it was a deal the reporter was happy to strike. Ringing at the gate at ten-thirty that night, Smalley was impressed by the austerity of Bismarck's office, "the very center of the spider's web." The fifty-one-year-old prime minister greeted him briskly. Bismarck's wife entered and, after an irritated cluck about her husband's late hours, mixed him a brandy and soda. She didn't offer one to Smalley, who figured she wanted him to go. But the prime minister—trim and mustachioed, his uniform in perfect order even at this hour—pushed him into a stuffed chair. "Sit," he said in clipped English. "I want to talk to you." There was no saying no.

The *Tribune* article drawn from their subsequent three-hour interview won wide attention for its portrait of Bismarck's smoothly Machiavellian style. "A virtual introduction of the Count to the American world," Young declared when the manuscript arrived in New York. Among the nuggets Bismarck divulged was that he'd pushed his nation into war with Austria "over the heads of the Prussian parliament and people, and against the wish of the king." Subterfuge had been needed because Prussia was too soft, too sentimental about its traditional ties to German-speaking Vienna, and too full of lazy aristocrats. "There is nothing so selfish as second-class royalty," Bismarck had said.

Smalley had asked about rumors suggesting that the prime minister had secretly siphoned money from his king's private bank account to fund war preparations. The prime minister replied with a smile, "I told him as much as was necessary for the time being, till it was time to throw off the mask." Austria had learned of Prussia's mobilization even before Wilhelm did, and demanded that Prussia stand down at once. "Then I knew," Bismarck said, "the Lord had delivered her into our hands." In conveying Austria's ultimatum to the king, Bismarck had presented it as an affront less to Prussian sovereignty than to Wilhelm's masculine honor. It worked like a charm: "The king took fire at once. From that moment the difficulty was to restrain him." His manhood insulted, Wilhelm's furious call for war was everything Bismarck could have wished for. "All the rest," he told Smalley, "was in the hands of the god of battles."

The gamesmanship hadn't ended there. Jubilant in triumph seven weeks later, Wilhelm had wanted to march into Vienna at the head of his conquering army. Bismarck was sympathetic—after all, "when an enemy's capital lay at the victor's feet, why should he not enter it?" But the prime minister's long-term plan for German unification depended on the adversaries now becoming allies, a goal that humiliating the Austrians would have undermined. He'd persuaded Wilhelm to let Austria keep its dignity in defeat, and as a result, Bismarck said, "Please God we shall all be friends again. The fruits of our triumph are yet to gather."

The meaning of this last remark was unclear. But Bismarck's confidence, together with the power of his parading army ("The machine was in its best working order," Smalley wrote), were clues to Prussia's next move: targeting France's Second Empire and its unpopular ruler, Louis-Napoleon, Napoleon III. Smalley didn't grasp the implications in 1866, but in time he would understand that he'd been looking "at the beginnings of what was foreordained to happen."

Returning to London, he set about fulfilling John Russell Young's demand for foreign news, ranging from political trends and market prices to royal gossip and racing results. Young retained several other American expatriates, in addition to Smalley, to send the *Tribune* items from around the continent—a slapdash arrangement directed from New York with little coordination. Smalley, on a visit back to America in the fall of 1867, advised him to streamline the process by appointing a London-based editor to hire correspondents, delegate assignments, and edit copy before transmitting it across the Atlantic. Young loved the idea. "The proposal was far-reaching and had no precedent," Smalley recalled, "not that want of a precedent troubled him much." Young's willingness to yield some managerial control to improve the paper's operation might seem a minor thing, Smalley continued, "but in truth it was vital. Once it had been decided to establish a *Tribune* office in London, a revolution had taken place." Journalism's first international news bureau was about to be created.

Smalley didn't want the job, but Young insisted the conception was his and so should be its implementation. "Remember, I don't care about methods," he told him. "You will use your own methods. What I care about is results."

Young gave the undertaking a confident headline: "Mr. Smalley sails for Europe today to act as Foreign Commissioner for the *Tribune*." Reaction from New York's other papers was sneering. Leading the catcalls was the *Herald*'s young loudmouth, James Gordon Bennett, Jr., who, in his usual refusal to cede authority to anyone, made it clear that under no circumstances would he set up "a rival office to New York."

Smalley took a flat with his wife and family and set about creating a system whereby news gathered from around Europe would be sifted and polished at his office at 11 Pall Mall and sent to the *Tribune* in concise, cost-effective form. With tensions calm in the wake of the Seven Weeks' War, he spent time cultivating connections among the British establishment. It didn't come easily—he bore an avowed "hearty hate of all things English" stemming from his Puritan upbringing and fierce devotion to the Union. Young earlier had cautioned him that

Otto von Bismarck was contemptuous of the press and eager to exploit it. On the eve of war in 1870, the Prussian prime minister told his generals that providing journalists "very detailed accounts of our army in the field" would boost their glory—and Germany's.

his political commentary must mirror the *Tribune*'s progressivism and also Greeley's resentment of Britain for its support of the Confederacy—no problem for Smalley since he shared the same views. Sensitive to any condescension toward America that he detected in *The Times* and its liberal counterpart, *The Daily News,* he posted frequent letters to their editors protesting the snobbery. Many Britons thought him the greater offender, injecting acrimony into everything he wrote.

Personal considerations gradually turned Smalley away from his paper's liberal line. Greeley was cheap with his payroll; Smalley's effort to pad his income with essays for British journals forced him to downplay his American partisanship. But moderating his tone helped him do the *Tribune*'s work as well, for an essential tool of his newsgathering was to socialize with the upper classes. "In London," he said of his constant round of dinners and cocktail parties, "there are few better ways for the purposes of high politics." Young began featuring his commentary in a weekly column. Smalley relished the exposure and soon was calling his life abroad "paradise" and his managing editor "the Pope" for arranging it. Then in May 1869 Young was fired from the *Tribune*.

Problems between him and Greeley had been brewing for some time.

In 1867 Young had disagreed with the publisher's call for the pardon of Jefferson Davis, the former president of the Confederacy imprisoned since the end of the Civil War. The sentiment baffled those who'd looked to Greeley as one of the South's sternest critics, but Greeley insisted it was time for reconciliation. Young admired him despite the backlash it drew from *Tribune* readers, observing, "We might question its necessity, its timeliness, but it was the act of a patriot who felt that the dearest of his life were as nothing when the country could be served."

A year later Greeley criticized Young's editorials demanding the impeachment of President Andrew Johnson. Johnson's ostensible crime had been to defy restrictions against his removing cabinet officials who'd carried over from the preceding Lincoln administration even though they were politically opposed to him. But really what turned Congress (and Young) against him was his reluctance to push postwar Reconstruction measures that imposed penalties on the secessionists and promoted civil rights for freed slaves.

The *Tribune* led the way in seeking Johnson's removal from office. The daily drumbeat caused circulation to soar. "There is joy in the exchequer," Young exulted. Greeley likewise favored impeachment but disapproved of his paper's fevered tone, fearing it resembled the "crazy reprehensible French methods" of mob incitement in the French Revolution. Johnson's arrogance would cause his downfall sooner or later, he said; "let us not turn a case of desirable suicide into one of undesirable martyrdom." Young commended his boss's integrity: "He saw the material gain, the bounding circulation, but as in the case of the bailing of Jefferson Davis, it would not have weighed a feather against the higher voice of his conscience."

Greeley took steps to rein in his managing editor. Skeptical of Young's support for the presidential candidacy of Ulysses S. Grant in 1868, he said that electing the taciturn, apolitical general would constitute "a grab-bag experiment" in American governance. He undermined Young's newsroom authority by hiring a reporter named Whitelaw Reid as the *Tribune*'s "writing editor." Reid's professed "instinctive dislike of men of General Grant's caliber and character" matched Greeley's skepticism better than Young's worshipful view of the Civil War hero.

Horace Greeley, photographed here during the Civil War, directed his *New York Tribune* against slavery and in support of social reform. Beginning in 1866, the *Tribune's* aggressive use of the transatlantic cable to expand its foreign coverage vaulted it ahead of its competitor, *The New York Herald.*

Matters came to a head when Young was accused of abusing the *Tribune's* membership in the Associated Press, the consortium formed before the war to share telegraph costs. *The Sun* made the charge under the headline "Sneak News Thief" in April 1869. That paper's new owner, Charles A. Dana, formerly of the *Tribune* and Lincoln's wartime cabinet, wanted to redeem its reputation as one of the city's seamier rags and raise it to the upper ranks of New York journalism by breaking a major scandal. He claimed Young had "fleeced and bled" the AP by giving cable transcripts to a nonmember paper, *The Philadelphia Morning Post,* in which Young was an investor. "A false treachery," Young responded. Greeley published a statement exonerating him but still asked for his resignation rather than put the *Tribune's* reputation at risk.

In a remembrance of Greeley written years later, Young noted the publisher's exasperation over a world "permeated with Democrats, free traders, and idle folks given to drink." He didn't mention his dismissal from the *Tribune*—but Young's diary does. "Greeley surrendered me to a fantasy," it says.

Whitelaw Reid replaced him as the *Tribune's* managing editor. "Everybody liked him and nobody was afraid of him," said the *Her-*

ald's Stephen Fiske. Already soured on Reid for succeeding his friend, Smalley was prickly in defending his turf as London bureau chief; the fact that he and Reid had never met and could communicate only long distance didn't help matters. Far removed from the *Tribune*'s New York headquarters, Smalley continued to diverge from its politics and write more sympathetically of the Tory conservatism of his new cronies in Britain. Greeley sniffed out this rightward drift and told Reid to fire him. Reid protected Smalley out of respect for him as a reporter and editor, but Smalley, not knowing this, continued to treat him as an interloper.

In the summer following Young's ouster, Smalley threw himself into a project he hoped would confirm his status in the *Tribune* hierarchy. The first-ever race between university rowing teams from Harvard and Oxford, set for August 28, 1869, was bigger news than any war or cultural event in recent memory. Harvard's captain issued the challenge in April to his counterparts at Oxford and its perennial rival, Cambridge University. The latter begged off in concern that it couldn't field a competitive team at such short notice, an excuse mocked by Harvard's boosters. Oxford meanwhile was praised for its "manly response" in the affirmative. American journals were afterward relentless in deriding Cambridge as eternally inferior to Oxford, "the winning college, having beaten her adversary nine successive years."

Hyped as "immortal in Anglo-American annals," the race was breathlessly previewed in every aspect, from the teams' training diet to the physics of their rowing styles. Oxford deployed long pulls on the oars that maximized a blade's draw through the water but with fewer strokes per minute. Deemed obsolete by American rowers, the system had been replaced at Harvard by one using shorter, faster strokes.

One American who doubted Harvard's chances was Smalley. Having rowed for Yale before the Civil War, he appreciated Oxford's forty years of rowing experience and its competitive edge on the four-mile course on London's River Thames, where Oxford and Cambridge annually raced. This made Smalley seem a turncoat to many sports fans in the States, his pessimism attributable, they said, to a Yalie's "juvenile grudges" against his collegiate rival.

The British were less cocky only because the stakes were so high.

Losing the race would be like losing the American Revolution all over again, said *The Times,* reviving "bitter memories of the national disgrace, the surrender of Burgoyne or Cornwallis." Commentators praised Harvard for braving the challenges of competing abroad but ripped the American press for "uncalled-for remarks on the chances of fair play," namely that British bookies would plant culinary saboteurs in the kitchen at Harvard's London lodgings. Then again, the Americans' training diet would doom them whether or not it was poisoned. "How could men expect to win that had been living on mush and rice and such things?" it was asked. The Oxonians, by contrast, were loading up on beef and ale, "fare with muscle in it."

Fifteen American newspapers sent reporters to cover the event, but every advantage belonged to Smalley and the *Tribune.* He hired a British expert to provide postrace analysis and the secretary of the Harvard Boat Club to give an inside account. Since their stories would be too long to send by cable, he arranged to rush them to ships sailing for America that night. Most important, he booked Anglo-American Telegraph to wire the result to the *Tribune* immediately after the winner crossed the finish line.

A million spectators gathered in sweltering heat along the riverbank prior to the five p.m. start. Brass bands blared out "Yankee Doodle" and "God Save the Queen." Moncure D. Conway, an American chaplain serving in Britain, was gratified that people were so nervous they forgot to misbehave. "The usual amount of drunkenness was absent and no race has ever been known here for years about which there were so few bets," he wrote.

At the sound of the starting gun, Harvard jumped out to a lead. Its churning oarsmen set a course record at the one-third mark. Panic swept the home crowd. "Oxford shows a lack of spirit!" someone wailed. Conway saw an elderly English clergyman shake his head and remark calmly of the trailing boat, "That rowing is *moral.*" The point was reiterated in much of the postrace chatter, as Oxford's gradual gain on Harvard, its "almost superhuman" sprint into a neck-and-neck position at the final turn, and finally its pulling away to a length-and-a-half win, were attributed to "infallible truths" about rowing and each team's contrasting national heritage. For Oxford to have stayed patient in the face of Harvard's early surge was deemed a triumph of discipline. Conway agreed: "All this loyalty to law, this fidelity to the true thing amidst whatever misgiving, has its moral side. It represents that which is best in the English character." Harvard had rowed with a passion reflecting America's proverbial vigor. "Our boys scattered their splendid qualities as Americans are said to scatter their money," Conway wrote. "They won hearty bravos from astonished thousands, but they did not win the race."

The Times echoed this view, opining, "The victory was a victory of education, and here the advantage was all on our side." The day's top speaker gave the simplest analysis, however. Charles Dickens, toasting the teams at a banquet that evening, characterized the race as a showcase for two equally worthy opponents. No doubt Oxford was as relieved as it was proud to have won, Dickens said, and Harvard should hold its head high: "Such a defeat is a great, noble part of a manly, wholesome action, and I say that it is in the essence and lifeblood of such a defeat to become at last a sure victory."

The race's afterglow lingered for weeks. Smalley shared in none of it. His meticulous plan to be first in America with a recap had collapsed. His British expert had refused at the last minute to comment, out of fear that *Tribune* readers would think he was biased. And a snafu with Anglo-American caused dozens of American papers to receive the cabled result before the *Tribune*. Smalley's own account didn't appear until three days later. In frustration, he lashed out at Whitelaw Reid for revising its technical jargon of rowing into something barely English: "If I should ever send you another telegram, I pray you to have it published unmutilated."

Reid dismissed the matter as mere bad luck. He found Smalley's snit comical and told him to let it go. "You may laugh at me if you like," Smalley wrote back, "but the disaster was a blow to me which I have not got over. It left me unfit to do anything but sit on a beach and curse the idiot who caused it."

Determined to redeem himself, Smalley put feelers out to British newspapers about jointly sending stories in the future. He told them, "It does not matter how a piece of news is transmitted, whether by rail or by steamship or by wire. What matters is that it should get there."

He set up a meeting with John R. Robinson, the forty-one-year-old manager of London's *Daily News,* to discuss a partnership. It didn't go well, as "Mr. Robinson could see no advantage to his paper of such an agreement." Bespectacled and impeccably dressed, Robinson had a reputation for cutting wit that Smalley seems not to have appreciated. Scoffing at "American methods" of aggressive reporting, the British editor pronounced the languid, reflective letters of William Howard Russell to be the pinnacle of news correspondence.

Smalley, with his usual tactlessness, disagreed. Russell's reporting from the Crimea was a fine public service, he said, "perhaps the greatest which any journalist in the field ever performed. But it was not exactly journalism. It had little or nothing to do with speed and accuracy in the collection and transmission of news." Robinson declared the meeting over. Other editors, with equally low regard for organizations outside their convivial group at Fleet Street, were no less dismis-

The university crew race between Oxford and Harvard in August 1869, depicted here in a Currier and Ives lithograph, was an epic clash between British tradition and American vigor. The *Tribune* hoped to showcase its international news operation with up-to-the-minute coverage of the race. Ultimately it would take war between France and Prussia one year later to give the paper its moment to shine.

sive. "They sat content, true Britons that they were, in their belief in their own supremacy," Smalley wrote.

He had better luck with telegraph officials. His obsessive hunt for the culprit who'd botched his race report had turned up an office boy at Britain's cable monopoly, the British & Magnetic, where all dispatches had to be cleared before transmission overseas. The clerk had dallied in his paperwork and caused the delay of Smalley's cable. After chewing out Henry Weaver, an executive at Anglo-American, for enforcing British red-tape requirements, Smalley threatened to pull the *Tribune*'s business entirely if the policy wasn't changed. Weaver shocked him by falling for the bluff: "I will agree to your proposal on one condition— that you tell nobody you are allowed to hand your messages to us. We do not intend to alter our rule. We make an exception in your case."

"I do not suppose Mr. Weaver was aware that he was giving me a great advantage," Smalley marveled later. "Direct access to Anglo was a great security and great saving of precious time." Moreover, no one else knew of the *Tribune*'s favored position—"the fact did not become known in the world of journalism till sometime in the late autumn of 1870."

The date was significant. Though events on the continent seemed placid at the moment, a major war was coming. "The year 1870 is a year of transition if not of revolution," Smalley wrote. "I think we are entitled to remember with satisfaction that in telegraphic news enterprise it was an American journal which led the way, and that journal was the *Tribune*."

Under the burgeoning leadership of James Gordon Bennett, Jr., *The New York Herald* continued to reign as the most widely read paper in the world. Its coverage of political events was the fairest of the New York journals mostly because Bennett's convictions were as indifferent as his morals. And though at five cents a copy it was more expensive than its competitors, it sold better and carried many more advertisements. In a policy originally implemented by his father, the *Herald* accepted all types of ads, from the respectable to the dubious. The latter category included plugs for quack medicines and pages of "personals"—advertisements, say, from "chic ladies with cozy suites" and "a TRUE man seeking to care for a SWEET girl"—that moral watchdogs blasted as a brazen bazaar of vice and adultery. Bennett Senior had insisted that his paper reflect social reality. On that score the ads gave a true civic picture, making the *Herald* a commercial democracy in ways surpassing its priggish competitors and bringing in $800,000 in annual advertising revenue to boot.

Still, the wide praise given Smalley's profile of Bismarck in the fall of 1866 had emboldened Horace Greeley to proclaim his newspaper's resurgence. In foreign news especially, "We make bold to say that the *Tribune* is surpassed by no other paper of the age." Annoyed, Bennett Junior paid a whopping $7,000 to Anglo-American Telegraph to wire the complete transcript of King Wilhelm's speech detailing final peace terms between Prussia and Austria. Spending whatever was needed to maintain the *Herald*'s supremacy soon became the young publisher's first reflex—as when in 1867 he tried to poach a promising *Tribune* freelancer who'd recently made a splash at the paper.

Samuel L. Clemens had come to prominence two years earlier, after his comic tall tale, "The Celebrated Jumping Frog of Calaveras County," appeared in a New York magazine and was reprinted around the country under his pen name, Mark Twain. In the spring of 1867 the thirty-one-year-old humorist met with John Russell Young, then still editing the *Tribune,* about his upcoming five-month "pleasure pil-grimage" to Europe and the Holy Land aboard the cruise ship *Quaker City.* He'd already arranged to mail letters from the trip to San Francisco's *Alta California* newspaper and hoped to publish some in New York as well. Young contracted for six, printing them as they arrived through the summer and fall.

The letters poked fun at Clemens's fellow tourist-bumpkins and the grand decrepit cultures they encountered with guidebooks and vanities in hand. "We always took care to make it understood that we were Americans—Americans!" read one. "When we found that a good many foreigners had hardly ever heard of America, and that a good many more knew it only as a barbarous province away off somewhere that had lately been at war with somebody, we pitied the ignorance of the Old World but abated no jot of our importance."

The letters enchanted readers and in 1869 would be included in Mark Twain's best-selling first book, *The Innocents Abroad.*

Determined to grab Clemens for the *Herald,* young Bennett contacted him the day the *Quaker City* returned to New York that November, sending a messenger to intercept him outside his hotel with a fifty-dollar offer to write an essay about the excursion. Clemens shrewdly played one paper against the other, securing lucrative terms in which the *Tribune,* his primary venue, ran signed letters and the *Herald* unsigned ones—a subordinate arrangement Bennett normally would never have tolerated.

Clemens was established enough in his career to extract concessions that another writer who solicited Bennett that same month couldn't match. Welsh-born John Rowlands had come to America eight years earlier as a merchant seaman, changing his name from that of his drunkard father to Henry Morton Stanley after jumping ship in New Orleans. He'd served in and deserted from both the Confederate and the Union armies, had gone to Turkey where he'd barely dodged a murder charge, and had wound up a reporter in the American West describing "these blazing farms, these mutilated corpses, these scalped and wounded men" that marked the borderlines between white settlers and displaced Native Americans.

Twenty-six years old when he approached the *Herald* that December, Stanley hoped to obtain a freelance assignment profiling the British explorer and medical missionary David Livingstone, who'd been incommunicado in central Africa for two years. Unfortunately, just days before Stanley's appointment with Bennett, the London *Times* reported that Livingstone was alive and well near Lake Tanganyika. This forced the reporter to change his pitch at the last minute. Instead of a Livingstone story, he proposed to cover an upcoming British military expedition to squash unrest in Ethiopia.

Bennett, also twenty-six, with a tailored hauteur that the squat, swarthy Stanley found "fierce-eyed and imperious," didn't let on that boosting his paper's foreign coverage was a top priority. After suggesting that Americans didn't care about Africa, he allowed that submitting lively dispatches from Ethiopia on speculation (payable on acceptance) might earn the reporter a permanent job with the *Herald.*

Mark Twain, shown here in a painting by Frank Millet in 1875, had high ambitions both literary and financial. "Am pretty well known now," he wrote his mother after signing deals with the *Herald* and the *Tribune*. "Intend to be better known."

He then gave Stanley a letter affirming his press credentials and sent him on his way.

Stanley bribed the telegraph clerk at the North African port of Suez to place his future dispatches atop the stack of outgoing cables. But his real break came from luck rather than shrewdness. The Ethiopian story itself was a winning mixture of imperial muscle and tragic irony. After British troops crushed the uprising in April 1868, the rebel leader killed himself with a pistol given him earlier by Queen Victoria—in reward for being a faithful British subject. Accounts of the episode poured into the Suez telegraph station; a glitch in the line stalled all except Stanley's. The *Herald* got the news before its rivals, leading Bennett to gush about the "superiority in writing style" of this new reporter he'd discovered. He put Stanley on the payroll at $2,000 a year.

Stanley's first local beat was New York's police court. "It widened my knowledge," he later recalled. "The people were far more interesting than the people I met in Ethiopia." Next came an assignment to Spain to cover discord between left and right, republican and royalist, that was on the rise throughout Europe. Meanwhile, in October 1868 *The Times* updated Livingstone's whereabouts with word that the doctor, unseen by white men since 1866, was making his way from the

African interior to Zanzibar on the eastern coast. Stanley was told to meet him there. Just as quickly, however, rumors of the sighting were debunked, and Stanley's mission was scrapped.

A year later he was summoned to Paris, where Bennett had temporarily taken residence to escape the fallout from the "Black Friday" stock market crash caused by Jay Gould's attempt to corner the world's gold reserves. Bennett and Gould hated each other. Acquaintances since boyhood, their antagonism at this point was personal; later it spilled into business as Gould expanded his hunting ground from railroads and the stock market to Bennett's turf of newspapers and telegraph interests. Bennett was friends with the financier's partner in the gold scheme, James Fisk, and had obligingly published a *Herald* piece whitewashing Fisk's culpability. While lying low in Europe till the fallout passed, he saw a report in *The Times* that Arab slave traders in East Africa had encountered a white man deep in the Tanzanian jungle. It seemed a perfect story to change the subject from Bennett's tainted Wall Street associations to international derring-do. He'd cabled Stanley at once.

He was in bed in his suite at the Grand Hotel (it was three in the afternoon) when the reporter arrived. Bennett professed not to know who he was.

"My name is Stanley."

Bennett rolled out of bed, donned a silk robe, and found his way to the point. "Where do you think Livingstone is?"

Stanley said he was probably dead.

"Well, I think he is alive, and that he can be found, and I am going to send you to find him."

"Do you mean me to go to Central Africa?"

"I mean that you should go and find him wherever you may hear that he is. Of course you will act according to your own plans, and do what you think best—*but find Livingstone!*"

Bennett then gave an instruction that seemed to contradict his urgency. He told Stanley to wait an entire year—until January 1871—before starting the quest. Did this mean the enterprise was mere whimsy, just another mad impulse in a man famously prone to them? Or was it a tactical gambit drawn from past experience? Bennett's friend Stephen Fiske had no doubt: "He developed journalism by a new method, creating news instead of waiting to record it." Four years earlier Bennett had raced across the wintry Atlantic to settle a drunken bet, rocketing the *Herald*'s circulation in the process. Now he might reap another jackpot by creating a publicity campaign around the search for Livingstone.

Whatever its logic, his delay in sending Stanley into the jungle proved a brilliant move. In the interim year, nothing was heard of the doctor. Public curiosity turned morbid as a result. African cannibals surely had eaten him, and anyone crazy enough to follow his footsteps would doubtless meet the same fate—making for an entertaining tale indeed.

"Everybody is going to Europe!" Mark Twain had exclaimed when he too was fixing to join the craze with that gaggle of tourists aboard the *Quaker City*. It was true. Foreign travel boomed after the Civil War. By the end of 1868, more than two thousand Americans were arriving monthly in Britain to kick off sightseeing tours. Among them was a part-time Ohio schoolteacher whose humble background (he was born on a farm called Pigeon Roost Ridge) contrasted with his opulent Irish name, Januarius Aloysius MacGahan. Bored with a life of "mere existing," the twenty-four-year-old was bound for exotic Paris. He'd promised his widowed mother he would study languages and international law, but to friends who knew of his love for classical literature, he'd confessed another ambition: "to write a book that will bring me fame."

Called Jan for short, he dressed in a rumpled, colorful style that smacked of theatricality. He had a weak spot for women but not much for alcohol, and though comfortable in rough company, he wasn't one to cuss or boast. A boyhood friend recalled how MacGahan's "chivalric tenderness for the weak" had led him to confront bullies whenever they'd menaced his schoolmates. Instinctive rather than doctrinaire, his politics were defined by the same sense of fair play.

His first years abroad were nomadic, poor, and blissful. His letters describe wanderings between Paris and Brussels in connection with "the world of art" that involved study but little progress toward a paying profession. In Écouen, just north of Paris, he shared a flat with a Bostonian named J. Wells Champney, who, like many aspiring American painters, was taking classes with French masters. The roommates were proverbial starving artists—and loved it. "I think I was never better off in my life," MacGahan wrote, "and as to enjoyment, there are not two fellows in this round old earth that know better how to find it than we."

Without yet seeing it as a clue to a possible career, he enjoyed France's politically charged atmosphere. Emperor Louis-Napoleon, Napoleon III, was struggling to suppress republican radicals fomenting revolt against his regime. Fluent now in French, MacGahan heard talk of revolution on visits to Paris in 1869. Being "upon a volcano, each moment threatening eruption," brought anticipation rather than dread. "The air is full of rumors," he wrote his mother. "It is exactly the picture of Paris of olden times, as Hugo pictures in *Les Misérables*." He revered Victor Hugo and that novel's passionate depiction of the student uprisings in Paris in 1832, when eight hundred protesters died at makeshift barricades under banners of socialist red. MacGahan was sure the same rebel ardor "by the liberal party and especially by men of action is on the point of returning to France."

In June 1870 he visited Cologne, part of the North German Federation of thirty-nine independent states recently welded together by Prussia's Prime Minister Bismarck. His letters reveal a young man testing his powers of description. Medieval castles overlooking the Rhine River's "sheet of molten silver" were a particular fascination: "You take a book, perhaps stretch yourself on the grass in sight of a broken arch and falling tower, and you find the most exciting romance tame beside the events and creatures of your imagination." For a young man full of poetic yearning, the impression of those barren gray parapets could only be tragic, signifying "the flight of centuries since human passion held sway and human hearts have loved and sorrowed, joyed and died, where now all is ruin and desolation."

He had yet to attempt even a page of the masterpiece he hoped to produce. Its subject still eluded him; in contemplating popular tastes, he at least knew what didn't appeal: "French literature is without the

Januarius MacGahan left Ohio for artistic pursuits in Europe in 1869. Startled one afternoon in Paris by the sound of a distant cannon, he asked a passerby what it was. "Oh, a revolution probably" was the shrugged reply. A year later MacGahan jumped at the chance to cover the Franco-Prussian War for the *Herald*.

slightest particle of invention or novelty. It is always a man, married of course, who has a mistress, and a married woman who has a lover. All of which is interesting at first but old, old, *old* after being seen a few times." Clearly, whatever he wrote would have to be fresh, vivid, and big.

He spent the early fall traveling through villages along the Rhine out of touch with wider events. Returning to France, he discovered that the previous summer's political tension had erupted. He posted home a wildly excited letter whose first line would prove a declaration of much more than the news of the day. In *"Voilà la guerre!"* MacGahan had found his calling.

3

Wild Work
1870–1871

To have lived ten lives in as many short years; to have held in the hollow of the hand the exclusive power to thrill nations; to have looked into the very heart of the turning points of empires and dynasties—*what joy!*

ARCHIBALD FORBES, "HOW I BECAME A WAR CORRESPONDENT" (1885)

The Franco-Prussian War took everyone by surprise. In early July 1870, just weeks before the shooting started, a veteran diplomat told George Smalley he'd never seen Europe's political horizon "so free from clouds." But the unrest MacGahan had noticed in Paris's streets and cafés hinted at domestic pressures pushing France toward war that weren't apparent at the international level, where friction between France and Prussia had been constant since the end of the Seven Weeks' War in 1866.

At that time, France had expected its noninterference in the conflict between Prussia and Austria to warrant a gesture of gratitude from the victor, namely a gift of territory. Emperor Louis-Napoleon considered himself top dog on the continent and entitled to respectful concessions. He wanted the fortified city of Luxembourg as a strategic buffer between France and the Prussian Rhineland. But Bismarck, having consolidated his power as the "Iron Chancellor," wasn't intimidated. He and his colleagues, Roon and Moltke, had just smashed the army of the Austrian Empire and absorbed its northern provinces into a German federation ruled from Berlin. Confidence in their military, coupled with their belief that France's Second Empire was crumbling under corruption and decadence, made the idea of giving anything to Paris laughable to them.

Rebuffed, Louis-Napoleon heard his people's complaints of French weakness and tried to restrain the upstart Prussians. He warned Bismarck not to encroach on the still independent German states of Bavaria, Württemberg, and Baden, whose acquisition would have made Prussia a true colossus looming just over the border. Louis-Napoleon's headstrong wife, Empress Eugénie, voiced her nation's fear of attack from so near an enemy: "I will go to sleep French and wake up Prussian." But Bismarck was defiant, forging alliances and agreements with those states that blatantly signaled his ultimate goal of adding them to the Prussian-German conglomerate.

Angering conservatives in his country by not declaring war at once, Louis-Napoleon simultaneously angered liberals by running a regime built on graft and nepotism. He placated rural peasants and farmers with government handouts but couldn't buy off disgruntled urban laborers, intellectuals, students, and middle-class workers, many of whom called for socialist revolution and the creation of a "red republic." After a nationwide round of local elections saw most of the vote

Louis-Napoleon's wife, Empress Eugénie, was determined that their son take the French throne as Napoleon IV. But he was killed in 1879 at age twenty-three by Zulus in Africa. The Scottish correspondent Archibald Forbes was with the search party that found the prince's mutilated body. "A miserable end," he wrote, "for him who once was the Son of France."

go to opposition candidates, Louis-Napoleon, despite a fog of opiate painkillers for hemorrhoids, gout, and kidney stones, got the message that his empire was in trouble.

His remedy, as in 1853 when he'd leaped into the Crimean campaign to clinch his hold on power, was to find a convenient national enemy. The obvious choice was an easy sell to his people, for no matter what their domestic politics were, everyone hated Prussia. Bismarck was likewise itching to fight, but he wanted Louis-Napoleon to make the first move. The impression of France as aggressor would isolate it from any sympathetic assistance from other nations and let Prussia contend one on one against France's formidable army.

With the same craftiness he'd used to provoke Austria to declare war on Prussia four years earlier, Bismarck goaded Louis-Napoleon. He proposed that Prussia's King Wilhelm pronounce himself kaiser of the German fatherland, a slap at France's edict against any expansion of the North German Federation. He financed a railway linking Prussia and Italy through Switzerland, fueling French fears about a Prussian-Italian alliance. In a third provocation, he helped orchestrate Spain's offer of its throne, vacant since 1868 when Queen Isabella II had been toppled in a popular uprising, to Wilhelm's nephew, a Roman Catholic only remotely linked to the Spanish line of succession. Even Wilhelm was annoyed by this last stunt, which he knew would push France to the brink. "I owe this mess to Bismarck," he admitted. "He has cooked it up like so many others."

Louis-Napoleon's fear of being hemmed between nations whose rulers were cousins led him to take action. Through an emissary, he demanded assurance from Wilhelm, who was vacationing at a spa in the German village of Ems, that Prussia never again put forward a candidate to the Spanish crown. Wilhelm said *forever* was impossible to promise, but given that his nephew had declined the Spanish offer, it surely was no longer an issue. The matter would have died there but for Bismarck's meddling. He wrote and released for publication the "Ems Dispatch," whose twisted wording implied that Wilhelm, enraged by France's ultimatum, had expelled its ambassador and cut off communication with Paris, a breach of diplomatic decorum. In a further poke at what Bismarck called "Gallic overweening and touchiness," the chancellor timed the document to appear in newspapers on July 14, Bastille Day, France's national holiday.

Roon and Moltke were dining with Bismarck while he gleefully composed the dispatch at the table. Anticipating Louis-Napoleon's reaction, they relished the prospect of battling France. Moltke thumped his chest: "If I may but live to lead our armies in such a war, the devil may come afterward and fetch away my carcass." Roon chimed in, "God will not let us perish in disgrace!" Both men near seventy, with a lifetime's experience of war, they joined Bismarck in raising their glasses to a final dream fulfilled.

Receiving the Ems Dispatch in Paris, Louis-Napoleon took the bait and ordered his army to mobilize. Crowds thronged the streets. "On to Berlin! Down with Wilhelm! Down with Bismarck!" There was dissent in the legislature, with many liberal republicans condemning the "fabricated crisis." But the emperor's royalist supporters, led by his chief minister, Émile Ollivier, proclaimed utter faith in the cause. Ollivier went so far as to say he welcomed war "with a light heart." Opponents jeered, but the vote was taken, and 400,000 French troops lumbered eastward toward the German border.

Prussia's national ethic of military preparedness put a million men in ready reserve. French commanders expected their superior arms to compensate for their lesser numbers. They had the two best weapons in the world, the chassepot rifle and the mitrailleuse machine gun. The latter was similar to the American Gatling gun, shooting two hundred rounds a minute. The chassepot was a light infantry rifle that fired more rapidly and with three times the range as the once state-of-the-art Prussian needle gun, shooting a bullet of unmatched stopping power that left gaping wounds as it passed through flesh. Foreign observers called the chassepot "a gorgeously worked murder weapon" and, no less admiringly, the mitrailleuse a "hell machine."

To counter these technical advantages, Prussia had the experience of the Seven Weeks' War, when Moltke had developed and since refined nimble modes of rail supply and field maneuver surpassing anything the French had encountered. The Prussian army was a precision machine geared for attack. Even its artillery was mobile, and its cavalry was positively fluid in its role as a probing, harassing, encircling presence designed, in Moltke's conception, "far less to deploy in great masses than to be *everywhere* at once."

French commanders knew of these tactical refinements but assumed their better weaponry would prevail. Too, they had Louis-Napoleon's sweeping war plan to bolster their confidence. Certainly it looked good on paper, combining ground and sea forces in coordinated strikes into Prussia upward through southern Germany and downward from the North Sea. But the expertise needed to execute the plan was beyond the capability of the moribund French military. The naval deployment sputtered. The ground thrust across the Rhine and Saar Rivers in the last days of July 1870 advanced just far enough into Germany to expose its flanks to an enveloping counterattack. The two French armies conducting the offensive fell back across the rivers to fortified positions around Strasbourg and Metz, where they soon found themselves cut off from each other and from the French interior.

Over the next month came a succession of battles matching French defensiveness against Prussian aggression. Manpower ultimately trumped firepower as the Prussian infantry spent what lives were needed to press yard by yard through murderous fire from the chassepot and mitrailleuse. Agile deployment of artillery used these incremental gains to rain ever closer bombardment on French defenders, who, depleted and dispirited, were then again assailed by relentless waves of bayonet-wielding Prussian infantry—after which Prussian artillery would reposition forward to continue the inexorable compression. It was World War I trench warfare in prototype and would kill more than 200,000 combatants before the end of the year.

In America, James Gordon Bennett, Jr., his *New York Herald* still struggling in its foreign operation, reacted to the war's sudden outbreak by throwing money at two dozen mostly untried reporters to blanket the battlefront. This amused the *Tribune*'s George Smalley. To cover a war, he wrote, "one way is to send into the field everybody you can lay hands on and to take your chance of what may turn up. The other is to choose the best two men available and send one to the headquarters of each army. I preferred the latter." His editor in New York, Whitelaw

George W. Smalley was nicknamed "Bruiser" for his athletic physique and stubborn character. Having proved himself fearless under fire in the Civil War, the *Tribune*'s London bureau chief demanded nothing less from the correspondents he sent to the front in France in 1870.

Reid, remembering Smalley's work at Antietam, wanted him to be one of those men. But Smalley insisted that as bureau chief, he must stay in London, where he could be "master of the situation."

He hired a half-English, half-French freelancer named Méjanel to follow French forces and a recent Oxford graduate named Holt White to join the Prussians. One of White's first reports concerned an engagement at the border town of Spicheren on August 6. With only 50,000 troops involved and 7,000 casualties, the battle was "not an important one," Smalley wrote, "except it was the first." He'd instructed White to hand-carry accounts of major battles to London (a day's travel from the front) but to cable summaries of any skirmishes. Receiving White's recap from the telegraph station at Saarbrücken, a six-hour ride east, Smalley declared it "the first battle story of any length ever sent by wire from the continent to London."

Sticking to the facts of Prussia losing men and France losing ground, White didn't describe the shell blast that threw him into a ditch or the soldierly Scotsman with a notepad and knapsack who extended a walking stick to help him climb out of it. The stranger's name was

Archibald Forbes. A thirty-two-year-old reporter for London's *Morning Advertiser,* Forbes had come late to journalism after a disappointingly peaceful stint in the Royal Dragoons. A fictional war story he'd written had convinced the paper's editor to hire him—so detailed were its battle scenes, British veterans suspected the author was a deserter. Now here he was at the front. "As a child might sigh for the moon," Forbes wrote, "this work had been the dream of my life."

Smalley wired White's Spicheren dispatch from London to New York without delay, thanks to the arrangement he'd struck with Anglo-American after the Harvard-Oxford race. It was the first big item in the *Tribune's* wartime cable bill, which would eventually exceed $100,000. He then took the story to John Robinson at the *Daily News,* where Smalley's proposal of a newsgathering alliance had been snubbed less than a year earlier. The British editor eyed the ratty sheets with suspicion. "The battle was fought only yesterday."

Smalley nodded. "Yes."

"It could not have come by post."

"No."

"Well, how then?"

"By wire."

"A dispatch of that length! It's unheard of."

Smalley showed him the cable receipt.

"And you expect me to print this tomorrow in the *Daily News*?"

"Print it or not, as you choose. It will certainly appear in the *Tribune.*"

Smalley's coy routine didn't induce Robinson to reconsider the partnership offer, so the American got blunt. British newsgathering was stodgy and slow, and Smalley, far from some ignorant rube, had "four years' experience of our own war, when news was collected on a scale and by methods before unknown." He was prepared to spend vast quantities of *Tribune* cash to maximize use of the telegraph. The *Daily News* could have access to those cables if Robinson put his office at the *Tribune's* disposal, "conceding to us the privilege of seeing news, proofs, and everything else at all hours, whether relating to the war or otherwise."

Robinson listened "for civility's sake" before rejecting the outrageous proposal. Smalley turned to Frank Hill, an acquaintance at the *Daily News* who "knew his way to Mr. Robinson's mind much better than I did." Hill successfully pitched the plan—and ever afterward Smalley made sure to praise Hill's "singularly open mind" and to denigrate Robinson's. Nor did he back down when this version of events was questioned later: "I am aware that this may not have a friendly reception in England, but it is strictly and literally true."

Robinson published White's story the next day. But he declined to credit the *Tribune* as its source, giving *Daily News* readers, Smalley noted icily, "every opportunity to admire the enterprise of that journal." Smalley afterward wrote a piece for *Harper's* magazine asserting that the *Daily News's* war coverage owed a huge debt to him. Furious, Robinson took to calling the pushy American "a very Napoleon of journalism." Smalley didn't care. "We had ceased to be on good terms," he said of Robinson later. "I forget why."

On the same day as Spicheren, another battle occurred fifty miles east at the town of Wörth. Twice as many troops were involved with three times the casualties, most of them Prussian, thanks again to French weapons and Prussian obstinacy. But numbers prevailed, and Prussia absorbed its heavy losses en route to outflanking the French commander, Patrice de Mac-Mahon, and forcing his retreat. Receiving news of the rout as a persuasive lesson, Mac-Mahon's superior, Achille Bazaine, a political appointee possessing what Archibald Forbes called "a modest mistrust of his own intrinsic capacity," withdrew to Metz with 200,000 troops and awaited Moltke's attack.

The war's next battle took place at Mars-la-Tour ten days later. Largely an artillery duel (though the Prussian cavalry brigade that lost half its riders in one charge might have disagreed with the description), it left 16,000 casualties on each side, an acceptable toll to Prussian leaders, whose ranks swelled with reinforcements. The French marshal, Bazaine, took comfort in calling Mars-la-Tour a draw, not grasping the reality of a quarter-million enemy troops now deployed between him and Paris. On August 18 his grandly titled French Army of the Rhine met the enemy just outside Metz at Gravelotte. At a day's cost of 12,000 French and 20,000 Prussian casualties, the battle left

Bazaine stuck in Metz and Moltke with a clear road west to pursue Mac-Mahon's fleeing army.

Gravelotte was the war's first set-piece battle for the combatants, who chose their ground, arrayed their forces, and executed plans as best they could; and for the international press as well, which converged on the scene in the certainty that a great moment was at hand. Reporters were everywhere, their wish freely to roam the battlefield helped at French headquarters by administrative mayhem and at Prussian headquarters by Bismarck's love of publicity. At the top of the hierarchy sat the Crimea's old warhorse, William Howard Russell, dispatched from London in panic by his editors ("we shall be outstripped!") when *The Daily News* began featuring, thanks to its collaboration with Smalley's *Tribune,* fresh dispatches *The Times* couldn't match.

Welcomed by the Prussians, Russell traveled the war theater by coach with Wilhelm's son, Crown Prince Friedrich, who led Prussia's Third Army from the front rank with courage and also misgivings. He'd mused to Russell while surveying the battle dead at Wörth, "These are terrible and painful sights. How many such are we to have, and worse?" The crown prince hated war. "If I should reign I would never make it," he said. He proved true to his word but would reign only ninety-nine days after his father's death, dying of cancer in 1888 and making way for Wilhelm II, a militaristic bumbler who led Germany into World War I.

Russell felt self-conscious that every time he jotted something in his notebook, the soldiers around him would stop and stare. But his legend was undeniable. Forbes didn't resent it when, while cooking his lunch on the ground outside an inn one day, he glimpsed through a window Russell and Hilary Skinner, a longtime correspondent for *The Daily News,* taking tea in the dining room. "I should not have thought of accosting them," he wrote. "They were the elite of the profession. I was among the novices." As a member of the elite, Russell felt no obligation to rush his dispatches to *The Times.* He posted them via the military mail system, which could take a week to get a letter to London. Meanwhile, the *Tribune* and *Daily News* had authorized reporters to cable even long dispatches. One of them, "a quiet little man" named Joseph Hance, wired Smalley an item on Gravelotte from the

Saarbrücken station. Its substance seemed "no great achievement" to Forbes when he read it, but its publication in America two days after the battle was nothing less than astonishing.

Forbes wrote one of the best pieces on the battle. At a makeshift command center in a forest clearing, King Wilhelm sits on a ladder slung between a shattered gun carriage and a dead horse, his unease evident in his darting gaze and twitching hands at each distant shudder of cannon. Nearby, "Bismarck, with an elaborate assumption of coolness which his restlessness belied, made pretence to be reading letters." Suddenly the implacable Moltke rides up, "his face for once quivering with emotion," and announces that Prussia has won the day. The king bursts into tears. Bismarck tries to look casual, as if he'd never doubted the outcome, but Forbes sees him sigh with secret relief and crumple the letters, clearly a prop, in his fist. Unfortunately for the Scotsman, the evocative story traveled "by the slow and tortuous mail train," attracting little notice when it appeared in Britain days later.

Russell's Gravelotte dispatch in *The Times* describes Crown Prince Friedrich's usual qualms over the bloodshed: "Where is all this to end? It is quite frightful." It records the prince's pity for the king under whose banner so many thousands were dying; "my father felt it very deeply, it made him quite unwell." But Russell's observations were undercut by their slowness. His editors begged him to pick up the pace: "Who won? Get that on the wire." But set in his ways, he continued using the usual mail. And there were other reasons for his torpor. Writing about war was getting harder for him, inducing "a strange mental condition—lethargy and intense despondency." Thus he felt only foreboding when one morning before dawn he was invited to watch the day's fighting from a hill overlooking Sedan, a fortress town on the Meuse River near the borders of Luxembourg and Belgium.

Sedan's stone ramparts may have been formidable in the seventeenth century, but they were no match for modern Prussian artillery. Holed up inside were 100,000 weary troops under Patrice de Mac-Mahon. The French commander had made the mistake of trusting that his colleague, Marshal Bazaine, would break out of Metz and link up with him on the road to Paris. But Bazaine had sat tight, on the convenient rationale that "it is not the besieged army that ought to come to the relief of the free and mobile one." So Mac-Mahon's army alone carried the future of the Second Empire strategically and in the person of Louis-Napoleon. His regime crumbling, the emperor had joined Mac-Mahon at Sedan in hopes of participating in a last-ditch victory to rally his people. But if French leaders saw reason for optimism, Russell could have corrected them. From his hilltop he saw "the prodigious force which was encompassing them, whose bayonets glittered for miles, and whose columns darkened the ground, advancing, as sure as fate itself, in one great cloud of war against an almost helpless enemy."

The Prussian cannonade began at sunup. Russell had a perfect view of shells exploding amid the French ranks. He'd spent his career doing this yet now felt nauseated by the sight. "It is not a pleasant thing to be a spectator of such scenes," he confessed. "There is something cold-blooded in standing with a glass to your eye, seeing men blown to

This 1870 engraving, "The Effect of the Mitrailleuse in the Battle of Gravelotte," illustrates the French machine gun's fearsome effect. France had better weapons than Prussia in their nine-month war, but Prussia had more soldiers and an iron resolve to sacrifice them in the service of victory.

pieces or dragging their shattered bodies to places of safety, or writhing on the ground too far for help, even if you could render it."

This was a young man's game, after all.

Fought on September 1, 1870, Sedan was the first major battle of the Franco-Prussian War in which French casualties exceeded Prussian ones, and by a two-to-one margin. Artillery and the grinding attrition of a month's steady combat had negated the superior killing power of the chassepot and mitrailleuse. Twenty thousand Frenchmen were killed or wounded, and more than 80,000 surrendered, including Louis-Napoleon. Though war would continue across France for months, its outcome was decided.

Russell was still polishing his report two days later. So was *The Daily News*'s Hilary Skinner; they found themselves writing at side-by-side tables. Having known each other for years, they decided to call it a draw and ride together to London. It was all very genial until they arrived to find that *The Daily News,* thanks to Smalley and the *Tribune,* had already published a telegraphed account of the battle. He and Skinner told themselves their stories were better written—but they were old news and consequently, Russell had to admit, "had lost all their bloom."

The Battle of Sedan was fought on a Thursday. On Friday, with no escape from the encircling Prussians, Louis-Napoleon composed a note to King Wilhelm: "Since I could not die in the midst of my troops, I can only put my sword in Your Majesty's hands." A staff officer carried it across the battle line under a waved white napkin. French dead were everywhere, most of the bodies obliterated by shrapnel— "there were human hands detached from the arms and hanging up in the trees; feet and legs lying far apart from bodies to which they belonged." On Saturday morning the British press agency, Reuters, ran a brief bit on the battle. Though it gave few facts, it left Smalley fuming in his office, "wondering what I was to do and still more what the *Tribune* correspondents in the field were doing." A telegram arrived. Holt White, the young Oxford graduate, would be in London that afternoon—with news.

White hadn't slept since early on the day of battle. He'd slipped through French and Prussian checkpoints after nightfall and ridden for Brussels, hoping to get a cable out to London. Belgian border guards "made a pretence of guarding their frontier" and held him up for hours. At the Brussels telegraph station, he was told that no war-related cables were permitted due to their volatile effect on financial markets. So he hopped a train to Calais, a ferry to Dover, and a train to London. The second he staggered into his office, Smalley, never one for small talk, hit him with a question: "Is your dispatch ready?"

White shook his head. "Not a word of it written."

Smalley said take a seat and get busy.

"I cannot. I am dead tired, and have had no food since daybreak. I must eat and sleep before I write."

Only now did Smalley take in White's appearance, "a mere wreck of a correspondent, haggard, ragged, dirty." Not that it mattered. "It was no time to consider anybody's feelings. A continent was waiting for the news locked up in that man's brain." That continent was North America, and Smalley, redemption for his Harvard-Oxford fiasco finally at hand, wasn't about to relent. "It was an opportunity for the *Tribune* as seldom had come to any newspaper. It was necessary," he recalled with typical understatement, "to use a little authority." He got White some food but disallowed sleep till the piece was finished. Sitting opposite him at a table, he transcribed White's scrawl into legible form for the transmitter. By two the next morning, the six-column story was on its way to New York in time for Sunday's *Tribune*.

Sedan was one of history's most pivotal battles, crowning one empire and breaking another, and the *Tribune* captured it first. Some of the paper's rivals ran snide editorials suggesting the news was mistaken or made up. Smalley scoffed: "They were angry, naturally enough, and resorted to conjectures which might as well have been left unexpressed." It was a moment to enjoy—though not for long. One day after publishing White's big "beat," Smalley was impatient for more. "There was a lull," he lamented. "The English papers of Monday morning were a blank."

Then late that afternoon there strolled into his office Monsieur Méjanal, from whom he'd heard nothing since sending him to cover

John R. Robinson of London's *Daily News* resisted the American idea of using the telegraph to rush news of the Franco-Prussian War to British breakfast tables. When he finally relented in the fall of 1870, *The Daily News*'s circulation soared as a result. A colleague quipped to the editor, "You and Bismarck are the only persons who have gained in this war."

French operations at the start of the war. Taken into Prussian custody at Sedan, Méjanel had ambled to London after being released as a non-combatant. "He had a Gallic indifference to time," Smalley grumbled. But all was forgiven now. "An angel from heaven would have been less welcome." With calmness that the anglophile editor attributed to Méjanel's "English side—his mother was English—and that half of him was imperturbable," the reporter sat down and cranked out his report, laying down his pen at midnight: *"Enfin, j'ai vide mon sac."* It was cabled to the *Tribune* for Tuesday's edition, complementing White's dispatch and giving American readers accounts of the battle from both the French and the Prussian sides. "A unique performance," Smalley crowed.

Pleased as he was, it irked him that his groundbreaking achievement owed little to his eminent partner: "Mr. Robinson at the *Daily News* had nothing." That paper's circulation had tripled since the start of the war, leading *The Times* to scold its staff, "The *Daily News* has beaten us hollow." The boon was thanks to Smalley's reporters and the system he'd established three years earlier. Yet *The Daily News,* he complained, "never thought it worthwhile to state the truth."

In the weeks following Sedan, all Europe expected the next engagement to come at Metz. Almost 200,000 troops under Marshal Bazaine sat surrounded by less than two-thirds as many Prussians; a French breakout seemed certain. Paris was the ultimate prize, but with two million inhabitants and a garrison of 300,000 soldiers and National Guardsmen, it seemed too formidable for Prussian attack. One reporter took it on himself to make sure, and after discovering that Moltke was quietly shifting his forces from pinning down Bazaine to weaving "coil upon coil about the French capital," Archibald Forbes rushed to London with a scoop to shock the world.

No one wanted it. His editor at the *Morning Advertiser,* subscribing to conventional wisdom about Metz, declined it immediately, while *The Times* asked him to submit the piece in completed form prior to any decision. Surveying the other publishers along Fleet Street, a dejected Forbes, still scraggly and unwashed from the field, flipped coins to narrow the choices of where next to apply. After eliminating *The Daily Telegraph* and the London *Standard,* he walked to an office around the corner on Bouverie Street and asked for "a Mr. Robinson."

Though Smalley wasn't a fan, the *Daily News* manager was one of the profession's sharpest minds. He'd noticed Forbes's stories in the *Morning Advertiser.* Yet as eager as he was to find someone equal to the *Tribune* correspondents whose battle dispatches were carrying *The Daily News* these days, he kept his air of reserve. "That sounds interesting," he said of the Paris scoop pitched by the Scotsman. He offered to pay for three columns about Moltke's secret deployment.

Elated, Forbes ran to his flat and dashed off four columns, throwing in the extra for free. A positive nod from a deputy editor fueled another two columns on the spot. "I always felt that the faster I wrote, the better I wrote."

The story ran the next day. Forbes was invited to the *Daily News* office to discuss future projects. But before they sat down to talk, Robinson retracted the offer: "I don't think we'll trouble you to write those contributions." Forbes, his hopes shot down, tore into the editor in "language more vigorous than courteous" and stormed outside to the street. Someone ran up and grabbed his shoulder breathlessly. "Don't be a fool!" It was Robinson. "I was going to say that I want you to start tonight for Metz." The reporter was hired at twenty pounds a week.

Forbes would reflect on this career break years later: "It is possible

Archibald Forbes joined the London *Daily News* in 1870 and immediately drew criticism from *The New York Tribune* for receiving credit for *Tribune* dispatches. After he proved almost unbeatable in the contest of reporting the Franco-Prussian War, his success became a boon to both newspapers thanks to their wartime business partnership.

that had I declined I might have been a happier man today. I might have been a haler man than I am at forty-five, my nerve gone and my physical energy but a memory." But the lure of the work surpassed its personal cost.

He was at Metz when Bazaine's army surrendered on October 29. The marshal wasn't there—he'd smuggled his wife through the Prussian cordon two days earlier, collected his wages from the army paymaster, and skipped town under cover of darkness, leaving thousands of humiliated men and officers to stand in a gray rain and hand over their weapons without firing a shot. After writing up these events all night in his quarters, Forbes started out the next morning for the Saarbrücken telegraph station. In his exhaustion he rode at a comfortable pace. It was a mistake he wouldn't make again.

One of Smalley's freelancers, a German-American named Gustav Müller, had also witnessed the Metz surrender. He made straight for London to write it up in Smalley's office. "It was cabled forthwith to New York, and a copy handed to the *Daily News*," where Forbes's wire hadn't yet crossed Robinson's desk. So compelling was the story, the London *Times* bought reprint rights and ran it the next day, giving credit where it seemed due, to its arch competitor, *The Daily News:* "We congratulate our contemporary on the energy and enterprise of its correspondent."

Smalley was outraged. "Mr. Robinson did not think it needful to explain that it was in fact a *Tribune* dispatch," he fumed, "and that it was a *Tribune* correspondent who had wrung from *The Times* this testimony." Nor did Robinson, in the days ahead, correct the impression that the story had originated with his newspaper. Smalley tried hard to strip the laurels showered on its presumed author: "He had nothing whatever to do with this Metz dispatch." The real author was a *Tribune* reporter and not, as everyone presumed, *The Daily News*'s new hire, Archibald Forbes.

Notwithstanding this dispute, the two papers' relationship quickly transformed. To Smalley's surprise, "The *Daily News* service became efficient." The reason was Forbes—upset over getting beat on the story of the French surrender at Metz, he vowed never to come in second again. Said a colleague, "His one great aim was to get the first and best news of any fighting that might take place, and he never spared himself until it was done." He worked in the American style, in short, and as Smalley was pleased to acknowledge, "the *Tribune* in the end profited by it."

The shift came just in time, for Smalley's vaunted "specials" suddenly fell down on the job. The Metz correspondent, Gustav Müller, returned to the field with a hefty *Tribune* advance to expedite future cables and promptly disappeared. Smalley mourned his apparent death from "a bullet or a brigand's knife" until he learned that Müller had pocketed the money and skipped off to America. Adding insult to injury, Smalley wrote, "he seemed to think his conduct in no need of defense!"

Smalley had likewise sent the two reporters who'd broken the Sedan story back to work with high expectations. But Méjanel's Gallic languor finally tried his patience too much and he fired him, while White dropped out of sight until he turned up dead in a foreign field hospital, a sad end that Smalley, with his usual stringency, deemed a personal failing on the man's part. In his later memoirs, however, Smalley's verdict softened: "Holt White is entitled to be remembered as a man who at one supreme moment accomplished one of the most brilliant exploits in the history of journalism. Let us judge him by his best—and so judged, his name must take its place with those of Russell, Forbes, and MacGahan."

Januarius MacGahan was one of two dozen rookie reporters hired in haste by *The New York Herald* to cover the Franco-Prussian War. Unwilling to install a foreign bureau chief, as the *Tribune* had done, James Gordon Bennett, Jr., cabled their orders long distance. "Every man is expected to write from half to three columns a day," MacGahan told his family, "but the *Herald* does not use one-tenth of what they get."

His published submissions ran without byline, in keeping with journalism's then-common practice of attributing dispatches to "our correspondent" rather than to named individuals. MacGahan's earliest pieces are hard to identify; the quirky expressiveness that distinguishes his prose had yet to emerge. His main contribution initially was "heavy interpreting," for Bennett's clumsy centralized system often put multiple men at the same locale with none but MacGahan able to speak the local language. "How they manage to get on I do not understand," he wrote in dismay.

In January 1871 the twenty-six-year-old Ohioan was sent to the late-developing theater of fighting around Dijon, near the Swiss border, to follow General Charles Bourbaki, a former corps commander under Bazaine. Fed up with Bazaine's passive entrenchment at Metz, Bourbaki had sneaked through the Prussian lines, six weeks after Louis-Napoleon's surrender at Sedan, and tried to initiate peace talks between Bismarck and Louis-Napoleon's wife, Empress Eugénie, who'd taken refuge in Britain. Prussian forces, though bound for victory, were stretched to the breaking point. Bismarck would have welcomed French concessions of money and territory in exchange for ending hostilities. But Eugénie, still hoping her husband's Bonaparte dynasty could survive with their son on the throne, played for time by stalling in her reply. Bismarck was not pleased.

Nor did he appreciate that liberals in the French legislature, led by a fiery nationalist, Léon Gambetta, had exploited the vacuum created by Louis-Napoleon's capture at Sedan to seize control of the government. Declaring the Second Empire dead and themselves leaders of a new Third Republic, Gambetta and his supporters claimed a righteous duty to repel the German barbarians. They vowed to redeem French honor by reviving the military campaign and driving out the invaders. The killing would continue.

That autumn Prussian forces closed around Paris in a series of lop-sided engagements whose death tolls skewed ten to one against the French, thousands dying compared to Prussia's hundreds. As fighting dragged into winter, a frustrated Bismarck decreed that French citizens be made to feel the pain of war as never before; increased atrocities such as rape and civilian massacre were the result. The chancellor's demand for "no laziness in killing" vexed his generals, who argued that shelling population centers only hardened resistance and incited international outrage. Not that they were shining humanitarians. They told Bismarck to be patient, that blockading French cities would soon have people dying "like mad dogs." The promise came true in Paris certainly, where the death toll from hunger, disease, and Prussian bombardment soon exceeded 3,000 per week.

General Bourbaki reluctantly accepted Gambetta's request that he join the republican cause and lead an army against the Prussians' southern supply lines. But by now results were foregone wherever French defenders met the enemy. On January 26, after ordering the remnants of his army into a last retreat, the proud Bourbaki shot himself in the head. The bullet furrowed messily between his skull and scalp but didn't kill him, and after the war he became a politician of modest success.

His army's surrender on February 2, 1871, came on the heels of an armistice between Bismarck and Gambetta, whose hopes for a national surge of patriotic commitment had fizzled when France's rural peasants, 75 percent of the population, failed to report for combat, preferring to stay home rather than fight for a liberal republic they'd neither sought nor trusted. Annoyed by Gambetta's earlier belligerence, Bismarck made sure to humiliate as well as destroy. He staged a glittery coronation of Wilhelm as kaiser of the new German empire at the epicenter of former French glory, the palace of Versailles located ten miles west of Paris. The king, pushed around yet again by his chancellor, accepted the title and garish ceremony grudgingly. "This is the end of old Prussia," he sighed.

Under terms of the armistice, France had three weeks to form a legislative assembly and ratify formal terms of surrender. A nationwide election was held, sweeping into office an overwhelming majority of antiwar candidates with conservative, Catholic, and rural leanings. Almost two-thirds of them were outright royalists hoping to establish another monarchy, and even the Assembly's liberal minority was mostly middle-class moderates eager to settle with Prussia and begin rebuilding France's economy on traditional capitalist principles.

Paris was the angry exception to this conservative tide. Most of its citizens had leftist leanings and an unbowed will to keep fighting the Prussians, against whose siege of starvation and bombardment they'd held out with more grit, they were proud to claim, than shown anywhere else in France. Having agitated for years against the despotic Louis-Napoleon and believing his downfall their opportunity to create social reform, many Parisians felt betrayed by their more moderate countrymen.

France's swing from empire to republic and potentially back to empire was dizzying but understandable; conservatives were blamed for starting the war and liberals for prolonging and losing it. But though endorsed at the national ballot box, this royalist revival was rejected in Paris. Vowing to force reform by any means necessary—eliminating class enemies, abolishing private property, and divesting the Catholic Church of its wealth and property—the Paris radicals were a fringe group with limited nationwide influence. But inside the city they dominated.

The newly elected National Assembly chose as its president seventy-four-year-old Adolphe Thiers, a cabinet minister under Louis-Napoleon who'd opposed the emperor's rush to war and later refused to join Gambetta's short-lived Government of National Defense. Negotiating the Treaty of Frankfurt that officially ended the Franco-Prussian War, Thiers had no choice but to grant Bismarck's demand for the prosperous border region of Alsace Lorraine and a huge indemnity of five billion francs. Bismarck wanted more French territory but relented in exchange for the right to march 30,000 troops through the conquered capital, a pleasure he'd denied himself after defeating Austria in 1866 but in no way would forgo this time.

Most French citizens deemed the treaty's heavy price a necessary hurdle toward getting on with rebuilding their nation. But being forced to host a German parade down the Champs-Élysées was a bitter insult to Parisians already furious at the Assembly's royalist tilt and prostration before Bismarck; many Prussians, including Crown Prince Friedrich, likewise thought it a vulgar provocation. The spectacle took place on the first day of March in an atmosphere of clenched loathing. There were rumors that the city's National Guard, a diffuse but well-armed militia that had kept civil order during the siege, might attack the Prussian marchers, but it went off without major incident. At one point Bismarck strayed from the viewing stand near the Arc de Triomphe and found himself surrounded by glowering Frenchmen. He took out a cigar, approached the toughest-looking man there, and asked for a light. Here he was, unarmed and alone, mastermind of the war that had crushed them, and no one raised a hand against him. The humbling of France was complete.

He left for Berlin five days later, leaving behind an occupation force to block Paris's eastern approaches till the indemnity was paid. His nine-month war had killed or wounded more than 100,000 Prussians and at least twice that many French. He'd driven a superpower to its knees, saddling it with a doddering president and a crippling debt. Diplomats from other nations said his peace terms defied standards of good-faith negotiation. Bismarck scoffed. "So moderate a victor as the Christian German does not exist in the world anymore," he said.

His departure was reported by Russell of *The Times* and by Forbes, now of *The Daily News*. Traveling with the conquering army, both had been accosted by seething Parisians the moment they'd wandered away from their military protectors. "Prussian spy! Kill him!" people yelled at Russell as he clambered aboard a train out of the city. The prospect of a mugging in France compelled him speedily to London, where for once his dispatch was on time. Forbes meanwhile was seen tipping his cap to the Prussian crown prince during the parade. This offended "disturbant elements simmering in the vicinity" who'd shown little courage in battle, he wrote scornfully, "but let them only catch an unfortunate civilian and then just mark their valor." They beat him with sticks and dragged him to the banks of the Seine, a true fright given that a week earlier an alleged spy had been flung into the river, where he'd floundered under a hail of thrown stones until sinking under the water.

Forbes screamed to a National Guardsman for help, but the man only laughed. His assailants dumped him at the police station, from

This triumphal vision of the Prussian army's march through Paris in March 1871 was careful to place King Wilhelm at top center and the crown prince at his right hand. That would have been fine by Roon, Moltke, and Bismarck, who preferred not to advertise their absolute power.

which a British embassy official secured his release that evening. The Scotsman's dislike of the French ran deep after that. Paris, he swore, would endure more "wild work" before cleansing the resentments and loathing of the "stunted, thin-faced, evil-eyed, scraggy-necked, knob-jointed, white-livered horde of miscreants" that populated the city. It was something he looked forward to, clearly.

He returned to London and began putting in ten-hour workdays to finish a two-volume memoir of the war. Paris simmered in the mean-time. The Thiers government had only one active military division due to the rest having been demobilized during the armistice or not yet returned from Prussian detention. Paris's National Guard, pared to a gritty core of hard-line dissidents once its "bourgeois battalions" disbanded to resume civilian life, was suddenly the most lethal force in France after hauling two hundred cannons from around the city to its stronghold in the working-class section of Montmartre.

On March 18 Thiers sent two brigades to repossess the guns and nip this street insurrection in the bud. Launched in stealth just after midnight, the operation might have succeeded had it brought enough horses to haul away the cannons, a screw-up on par with the army's wartime performance. The delay gave time for hundreds of local resi-dents to converge on the scene, many of them women, whose socialist militancy made them seem bloody-eyed demons to the middle-class folks they denounced. By sunup, they'd driven back the government troops, who couldn't bring themselves to shoot the rioters, and seized one of the commanders, Claude Lecomte, dragging him before a self-appointed "Vigilance Committee" of rebel firebrands.

Montmartre's twenty-nine-year-old mayor, Georges Clemenceau, future prime minister of France during World War I, tried to pro-tect Lecomte but was shoved aside after another captive was brought in—an old retired general, Clément Thomas, who lived nearby and had walked over in curiosity at the commotion. A show of hands was taken, "immediate extinction" the unanimous vote.

The two were stood against a wall in the backyard garden at No. 6 Rue des Rosiers. Thomas—white beard, frock coat, an elderly pensioner out for a stroll—went first. A squad of riflemen raggedly formed up. The old general shook his fist and shouted, "Kill me! You won't prevent me from calling you cowards and assassins!" They fired two volleys, but he stayed upright through the barrage, cursing them nonstop till someone stepped up and put a round through his eye.

In the abrupt quiet that followed, Lecomte, waiting his turn a few feet away, was spun around and pushed face first against the wall. A witness was scornful: "This man, who in the morning had three times given the order to fire upon the people, wept, begged for pity, and spoke of his family." He was killed with one shot in the back of the head.

The gunmen kept firing into the bodies; an autopsy found forty holes in Thomas. Women straddled the corpses and urinated on them as a string of hardscrabble kids watched from atop the wall. Clemenceau, arriving too late with help, was shaken by the raw savagery. "All were shrieking like wild beasts," he recalled, "without realizing what they were doing."

A city election held ten days later resoundingly supported the uprising. The municipal council's first order of business was to rename itself the Paris Commune. It placed Guardsmen at the ramparts of the many forts arrayed along Paris's outskirts and blocked the streets with barricades built of sandbags, stones, and piled furniture. From his base in Versailles outside the city, President Thiers prepared to retake the now Communard-held capital by force.

In London, John Robinson's harangues couldn't get Forbes to set aside his book and go cover this major story. Finally finishing on May 19 and leaving for Paris that night, Forbes arrived in time to see Thiers's troops overrun the Commune defenses in a final week of house-to-house fighting. Atrocities were commonplace, and Forbes's descriptions caused a sensation in Britain and America. Still, his tardiness allowed other papers to gain a head start. Thanks to its no-name stringer from Pigeon Roost Ridge, one of them, an international laggard no longer, was *The New York Herald*.

4

Paris Is Burning

1871

VICTOR HUGO: *Is France such a happy country that an American should come so far to see her?*

J. A. MACGAHAN: *There may be more to see and learn in an unhappy country than in a happy one.*

BORDEAUX, MARCH 2, 1871, *The New York Herald*

Victor Hugo was in Paris burying his son the same morning that Generals Lecomte and Thomas were shot in the garden on Rue des Rosiers. The funeral procession, winding its way to Père-Lachaise cemetery through narrow streets echoing with distant gunfire, attracted from adjacent cafés a trail of artists, workers, and National Guardsmen chanting *"Vive la République!"* in honor of the sixty-eight-year-old author, whose common-man epics such as *Les Misérables* and *The Hunchback of Notre Dame* had been an inspiration to France's reform movement. At the cemetery, the crowd buoyed Hugo in his bereavement. "People threw flowers on the tomb," he wrote. "How the people love me, and how I love the people!"

Januarius MacGahan had interviewed Hugo at his home in Bordeaux two weeks earlier. His original assignment had been to profile another resident, the Third Republic's pugnacious leader, Léon Gambetta, still bitter about France's capitulation to Prussia and his subsequent ouster at the polls. "The old story," Gambetta grumbled. "Want of perseverance, want of tenacity. The French have always been so. If we don't succeed at the first trial, we are lost."

Hugo, too, was critical of his countrymen when MacGahan sought him out two days later. Said the white-bearded author, "They have been so enervated by twenty years of Empire that they are lost to all sense of honor, patriotism, or justice, and prefer selling their brothers to the Prussians to losing a cow or pig."

An ardent disciple of Hugo's work, MacGahan had been nervous at meeting the writer. "You do not know how you will be received," he fretted, "by one who judges everything by standards of his own and cares as little for the opinions of the world as for the winds that blow." Noting with approval the workmanlike furnishings of Hugo's home, his pulse jumped when the great man appeared. Hugo was "strong and robust, with dark blue eyes that look upon you like the blue sky seen from the bottom of a deep well." Since appointments with prostitutes were part of Hugo's daily regimen well into his seventies, MacGahan's impression of a "temperate life" and "vigorous constitution" was at least half right.

He asked Hugo's opinion of France's newly elected National Assembly. Despite their royalist sympathies, Hugo replied, its members would never submit to another absolute ruler like Louis-Napoleon. He was adamant on another point. Someday France and Germany would meet again in "a war that will be the most terrible ever recorded."

"What will be the result?"

France would win, Hugo said—but unlike Prussia, it would then extend a hand of friendship to the defeated. "Then will be realized the grandest dream of the nineteenth century—a United States of Europe."

He ended the interview with a request that the reporter convey his regards to America. MacGahan did him better, closing his story with two paragraphs of praise for "this statesman and philosopher, this poet and prophet" who'd courageously written against the Second Empire and its pretentious ruler, *"Napoléon le Petit,"* and had suffered scorn and exile as a result.

The prominence his Bordeaux interviews received in the *Herald* marked MacGahan's first notable impression on his editors and their hard-to-please boss. MacGahan had begun to wonder if he was cut out to write the sort of stirring dispatches that could support a career.

Victor Hugo, 1870. Though his novels were an inspiration to the French socialist movement, Hugo fled to Belgium after the Paris Commune seized control of the city in March 1871. He issued a statement calling the rebellion justified but its means criminal, a middling comment that pleased no one.

"I had supposed it took somebody like Russell of *The Times* to be a war correspondent and did not think it worthwhile for an unknown person like myself to try it."

As it turned out, his best work was closer to Russell's leisurely ruminations than to the facts-first urgency of Smalley and Forbes. The *Herald* at last had embraced the international cable technology first exploited by the *Tribune* and now regularly featured news wires from Europe. MacGahan contributed few of these items. His descriptions of life inside the embattled city came by mail to the *Herald* weeks after he'd written them. Despite the delay, James Gordon Bennett, Jr., printed them under eye-catching banners, presumably because Mac-Gahan, though nameless to readers, wrote with the natural eye of a regular fellow caught up in crazy events.

His profiles of Gambetta and Hugo ran side by side in the *Herald* on March 24, 1871, by which time MacGahan had left Bordeaux for Paris. He had a firsthand view of the Commune in the wake of the city election that brought it to power. "The mob is triumphant and virtually possess the city," he wrote with alarm. "Only wine shops are open. Drunkenness is rampant. Even women are armed." Dozens of suspected government sympathizers, ranging from priests to bankers, had been rounded up and jailed. Three were executed for their ties to the military. Many of those remaining were soon released. Though the atmosphere was far from calm, it seemed thankfully free of the manic bloodlust of the previous century's French Revolution.

Through a series of meetings at its headquarters in the Hôtel de Ville near Notre Dame cathedral, the Commune laid out its mission as civic administrator and revolutionary beacon to the world. Among the initiatives were child care for working mothers, women's rights of ownership and inheritance, education reform, and workplace safety. Moderates and hard-liners angled for position in the hierarchy. In general, the former handled communal matters of labor and finance while the latter, with palpably sinister overtones, set themselves up as judges, armed security, and political enforcers.

The result was that, despite the Prussian army blocking its eastern boundary and French government troops massing at Versailles to the west, the city of Paris functioned pretty well. The several hundred British and Americans who remained in the city were amazed at the normalcy of daily life—produce markets operated, refuse was collected, milk and coal were delivered, fishermen lined the Seine at dawn, and families strolled the boulevards at evening. World opinion nevertheless condemned the Commune. Its "principles of disorder" boiled down to more money for less work, the *Herald* pronounced from New York. "The idle and hungry will prey upon the owners of property; there will be no end of stealing," said the paper. "All people should rally round the Republic and the Assembly."

MacGahan agreed, asserting that "the watchword of the Commune is 'Death to the rich, death to the land owners, death to the priests.'" Such declarations promoted an outside perception that the Commune was both evil and petty, a "pitiful pygmy of insurrection" destined for a proper spanking. That spanking commenced on April 2, Palm Sunday. Promising the Assembly a campaign "painful, but short," President Thiers opened with an artillery barrage whose indiscriminate targeting (a girl's school was demolished the first day) was a hallmark of the siege from then on. The Commune, having come to believe it might be permitted to exist as an autonomous municipality within greater France, issued a stunned proclamation: "The royalist conspirators have attacked. Despite the moderation of our attitude, they have ATTACKED."

The city's National Guard retaliated the next day. Led by idealistic commanders with tons of confidence and little combat experience, the Guardsmen resembled "a horde of turbulent picnickers" as they rambled singing and hooting toward Versailles. Shells from government batteries fell harmlessly at a distance, and the attackers picked up the pace. Then two shells burst in their midst, wounding several men and sending two halves of an officer, split at the waist, flying through the ranks. Retreat was sounded at once.

During the previous day's action, a government military surgeon had been killed (mistakenly, the rebels said) while waving a white flag. Versailles officials used the incident as an excuse to declare war without mercy—any insurgent who fell into their hands would be shot. Commune leaders announced a reciprocal policy of killing three hostages for every executed Communard. It was unclear whether "hostages" meant captured government troops or anyone deemed a counterrevolutionary by the Commune's increasingly paranoid enforcers. The mood of the city, oppressed now inside and out, darkened. "The word *guillotine*," MacGahan reported, "is spoken in whispers."

On April 6 Thiers appointed Patrice de Mac-Mahon, recently released from Prussian internment following his defeat at Sedan, to lead the government's siege of its own capital. This time the marshal was up to the task. Over the next seven weeks, while continuing to pour cannon shells into the heart of the city, he mustered 200,000 troops to overwhelm the Communard garrison. Beginning with Fort Issy, between Versailles and Paris, Mac-Mahon methodically dislodged the rebels from their outer defenses and pushed them across the Seine to Paris's densely crowded poorer sections to the north and east, pounding them with artillery as they were squeezed into tighter and tighter confines against Prussian checkpoints at the far side of the city. Initially neutral in this affair, fear of socialist revolution next door to the German empire led Bismarck to forgo the fun of watching Frenchmen kill Frenchmen. He would support Thiers by blockading Paris and denying the Communards any escape. Plus he wanted his five billion francs.

Around the world, headlines changed from "The Red Rebellion" to "The Dying Commune" as news cables recounted the growing hysteria, defiant and desperate, of the cornered Communards. These reports in the *Herald* appeared alongside MacGahan's letters written many days earlier. It gave a divided impression, for while the *Herald* applauded the Commune's destruction, its reporter on the scene had clearly begun to have mixed feelings. After MacGahan interviewed a young Communard commander named Jules Bergeret in early May, for example, the *Herald* gave it the snide banner "Bergeret's Bosh" when running it two weeks later. But the piece itself is sympathetic. Bergeret's god is "universal harmony," his hope for immortality limited to being well remembered after his death, his goal beyond the revolution merely to return to his workshop "no richer than when I left it." His marriage views especially impressed MacGahan, who likewise considered love sacred whether avowed in church, a civil court, "or alone under the starry canopy of heaven." All in all, the reporter concluded of the reviled revolutionary, "not a bad doctrine, certainly."

A similar split arose between him and the *Herald* when he profiled Charles Delescluze, a lifelong agitator for social justice who became the Commune's war minister in the late days of the rebellion. Dispelling the man's caricatured image as a shabby old Jacobin, MacGahan's dispatch presents a dignified reformer who suffered years of persecution and slander under the empire with little lingering bitterness. When MacGahan warns Delescluze that his coverage of the Commune might not be sympathetic ("it is not for me to support either side"), the old man urges him to go anywhere and write anything. In a follow-up story, MacGahan takes a moment to address his readers: "I cannot allow this opportunity to escape without bearing testimony in favor of the manner in which I have been invariably received by the leading lights of the Commune." If the aside was meant for his editors as well, they didn't get the message, printing the story under the derisive headline "The Last Communist Dictator."

MacGahan's generous portrait of "Citizen Delescluze" is a far cry from when he initially called the Commune's leaders "men of bloodless faces, lusterless eyes, and villainous hearts." The change was inevitable given the hardship of life under siege that he shared as well as reported. This was nowhere more apparent than in his story about the May 17 explosion of a Communard weapons factory on Avenue Rapp that killed two hundred women and children working in the basement facility. Rushing to the grisly scene, he shudders at the "human pulp" hanging from the trees and buildings around the cratered, smoldering armory. Beneath a rain of government artillery that deafens and jars the rescuers, "mutilated forms were to be seen on every side groaning and writhing with agony." MacGahan puts down his notepad to help carry a stretcher. Something catches his eye: "On one body clung the scorched fragments of a hooped skirt. On the finger of one hand was a wedding ring, showing that the unfortunate woman was a wife and probably a mother, whose children had shared her fate."

In the aftermath, MacGahan stepped forward to protect some onlookers from arrest as suspected government collaborators who must have helped target the armory. Don't be foolish, he told the National Guardsmen as they corralled the terrified bystanders—the explosion was obviously an accident caused by untrained workers. His dispatch is harsh in its criticism of the Guardsmen. Carousing as if at a nightclub when the dead are laid out for families to claim, "they smoked, drank, conversed and laughed." With defenders like that, is the implication, the Commune was doomed.

Beyond his empathy for the Parisians, MacGahan's sentiments were influenced in another way that would figure throughout his career—basically, he was a sucker for colorful characters. His tendency to admire men for their panache attracted him to flamboyant figures regardless of their politics or, in some cases, their brutality. A tip from Delescluze put MacGahan on to the first such hero to star in his stories. Polish-born Jaroslav Dombrowski was a thirty-five-year-old career soldier who'd been fighting oppression ever since participating in the January 1863 uprising of the Polish army against Russia. What had started as a protest against forced conscription into the Russian army had expanded to a political insurrection whose suppression and punitive reprisals resulted in the death of thousands of Poles as Czar Alexander II showed the world that Russia, despite the setback his father, Nicholas I, had endured in the Crimean War, was not to be messed with.

Choosing foreign exile rather than prison in Siberia, Dombrowski had brought his wife and sons to Paris. Now a Communard general, he looked a lightweight with his short stature and wispy mustache. But when MacGahan heard that Dombrowski's indifference to danger had reduced to a week the average life expectancy of his aides-de-camp, he knew this was someone he wanted to meet.

"Will you come with me?" the general asked him at their first interview on May 10. "It was a leading question," MacGahan says in his *Herald* account. The road is under bombardment, rocks and shrapnel "whizzing in every direction." Better to say yes than look a coward, however. Passing on horseback through a desolate cityscape, MacGahan fights the urge to hide from the shellfire. "General Dombrowski seemed to take it as a matter of course and I could do nothing less." Dismounting at a perimeter barricade, the reporter crouches behind sandbags and peeks nervously through the gaps. The general sits tall on his horse holding a telescope to his eye, "his head and shoulders exposed above the walls as a mark for the enemy."

The barricade overlooks a government trench three hundred yards away that is slowly being dug closer. MacGahan, never shy, suggests that if it isn't attacked, "they will be to the walls in less than three days."

The general agrees. "I am going to attempt a sortie this evening."

"Do you hope to succeed?"

"No."

This takes MacGahan aback. "Why?"

"My men refuse to go outside the fortifications unless sheltered by houses."

To which the reporter gives more advice: "Mount two hundred guns on the fortifications and pour down a storm of iron hail."

"Also impossible. I have one hundred fifty guns placed in position but only eighty artillerymen, and half of them are drunk all the time."

"So you consider the defense of Paris hopeless?"

"I do."

"Why, then, do you continue to lead the insurrection?"

The general gives a look of wonder at this obtuseness. "Because I cannot honorably retire."

Januarius MacGahan, 1871. Emerging quickly as *The New York Herald*'s top correspondent in Europe, the Ohioan was candid about the dual sense of thrill and shock that war reporting aroused in him. He never apologized for the emotionalism of his dispatches. "The truth!" he said. "And I'll tell it if they shoot me for it."

MacGahan spends the rest of his story praising Dombrowski's values of revolution and liberty. He gives as an example of the general's integrity the fact that when Thiers offered him a million francs to strip his defenses and let government troops pour through, he promptly informed his Commune superiors. Dombrowski had wanted to accept the bribe, donate it to the cause, and ambush the incoming enemy— but debate of the plan by the Commune's Committee of Public Safety took too long, and Thiers, smelling a rat, withdrew the offer. "This was another reason why General Dombrowski could not well resign," MacGahan explains. "The Commune, knowing he had been in communication with the Versailles government, would immediately suspect him. He could not abandon the cause under circumstances that might leave a stain upon his honor. He would therefore fight on to the last."

Dombrowski's resolve was matched by his cavalier style. One morning MacGahan saw enemy snipers shoot at him where he stood exposed on a rampart, bullets pocking the wall and throwing dust on his uniform: "Dombrowski took off his hat and bowed to them, for which all the Communist soldiers who witnessed it cheered lustily." No doubt MacGahan cheered as well.

While again making the rounds with the general the next day, a shell exploded behind MacGahan and wrenched his back severely. His paper played it up with a headline: "*Herald* Correspondent Wounded and Disabled." He was back in the saddle on May 14, though not for long. After "taking a bullet through my hat which almost knocked me from my horse," a shell burst caused a concussion that laid him up for several days.

His next near miss would come on May 24, though not in company with Dombrowski. By that time government troops were well on the way toward uprooting the last rebel holdouts. But instead of cheering the Commune's chastisement, the world's newspapers now recoiled from its annihilation. "The Rouge Rebellion" had become "The French Horror." And as for the young Polish general made famous in MacGahan's dispatches, he was laid out on a blue-satin bed at the Hôtel de Ville, killed in action the day before.

Charles Dickens died in June 1870, weeks before the outbreak of the Franco-Prussian War. John Russell Young eulogized him in *The Standard,* a literary journal he'd founded with a thousand-dollar loan after getting fired from the *Tribune.* Of Dickens's art, Young suggested that it was earthbound rather than spiritual: "His world was the world we live in, and although he took us into the byways of sin and misery and threw broad light into many dark depths, he never ascended. The man who sinned should be punished; the woman who fell should die." This stern worldview made Dickens more of a rigid moralist than Young would have preferred. Even so, Young concluded, "We are greatly at fault in our estimate of his labor if the time will ever come when the English world will cease to regard him with classic veneration. How much we owe this man!"

The Standard struggled. Its prospects weren't helped by its staunch defense of the scandal-plagued presidency of Ulysses S. Grant, elected in 1868. The general's towering Civil War reputation obscured his political naïveté and blindness to the opportunities for ill gain that his patronage offered; Grant's own integrity was often called into question by financial misconduct among his family and friends. *The Standard* stuck by him. Young was contemptuous of politicians and pundits determined to bring down the war hero. "What mere soldier ever held their regard?" he asked; even George Washington had seen his revolutionary stature assailed while president.

If supporting the president was hurting his newspaper, at least it led to an interesting side job. In early 1871 Grant's secretary of state, Hamilton Fish, asked Young to go abroad to conduct an overview of British-American relations. While in London that spring, he heard that the Paris Commune, whose standoff with France's Versailles government was the talk of Europe, was planning to demolish the presidential mansion of Adolphe Thiers and the Vendôme Column, Napoleon Bonaparte's monument celebrating his victories over Russia and Austria in 1805. The 144-foot column was "a symbol of brute force and false glory," the Commune said, and therefore must be destroyed. Reduced to spiteful blows rather than tactical ones, the Paris rebellion seemed on its last legs. Before it was too late, Young and some friends, like perverse tourists, "wanted to see the beautiful city in its grief and desolation. So we came!"

Delayed at the outskirts by a magistrate incredulous at foreigners trying to get *into* the besieged city, it was almost midnight on May 12 when Young checked into his hotel on Rue Saint-Augustin. He woke the next morning excited to take in Paris's fabled splendor but found "a city of death" instead, where "the only sound of life was the echo of our footsteps." But a twenty-minute walk north to Montmartre, "the worst part of the capital" according to guidebooks of the day, put him among throngs of Parisians enjoying the warm spring weather.

There were puppet shows and street performers and vendors working the crowd. Children rode swings and carousels, and boozy choirs sang "The Marseillaise" while soapbox orators proclaimed the glory of France and handed out political flyers. Young saw no hint of "ruffianism" and "the debris of human nature" that British newspapers said were rampant throughout the city. Other than a few defiant red banners flying from windows and flagpoles, he sensed mostly weariness in the air, a subdued, directionless drift: "The ship seemed to go without a helm."

At Père-Lachaise cemetery, the fighting felt closer at hand. During his half-hour visit, four red-draped hearses entered the grounds bearing Communard dead. But distant gunfire audible beyond the crooning of mourners still seemed unreal. In this third month of stalemate, rebel passions had faded. And the torpor was mutual, for government forces likewise seemed content to let the days pass. It was a letdown, really. Young wondered if Thiers would ever muster an all-out attack.

The next day he sat at a café and watched the construction of a barricade near Place Vendôme. A more casual exercise would be hard to imagine. National Guardsmen read newspapers and drank wine between jaunty demands of passersby to "stop and lift a stone" for the common defense. "It became a very sensible barricade," Young wrote, "but was night before it was finished. Two or three soldiers under drill could have built it in two hours."

He wondered how the faltering Commune might look in retrospect. Despite some deadly excesses, its ideals of "labor against aristocracy, people against kings," were worthy. Thousands of Parisians lived

Most of the barricades of the Paris Commune were constructed of cobblestones excavated from under the city streets. The resulting shallow trenches became convenient for the disposal of bodies during "Bloody Week" in May 1871.

on wages of less than a dollar a day. Rebellion was understandable under such hardship. "The world," he wrote, "may yet see there was some reason in the appeal."

On the other hand, from the government viewpoint, Thiers "was doing as well as he could." The capital had been seized in the wake of war and in defiance of a national vote. What choice did he have but to answer with force? For this the rebels had themselves to blame. "The Commune," Young wrote, "should have postponed everything to the work of rescuing the nation from Prussian occupation. That duty was immediate. Paris should have waited."

The malaise that had overtaken the Commune seemed to assure its quiet demise. Though less exciting, it would also be less violent. Nothing Young saw on May 16, when thirty thousand people jammed Place Vendôme to watch Napoleon's column torn down, contradicted this impression. In a spasm of vandalism "petulant and childish," Thiers's mansion had been razed the day before; this subsequent act was likewise more spitball than firebomb. The column featured a veneer of spiraling bronze bas-reliefs depicting Napoleon's campaigns, the metal taken from the melted cannons of his vanquished enemies. World opinion condemned its destruction as a desecration of French glory. Young demurred: "Is there really nothing better for a nation as great as France than to send her sons out to murder and devastation, and when the work is over to build a monument to assassination and misery and woe?" Napoleon was a grand figure, sure—"he knew his people's ways and whims; when to give them music, when to give them grapeshot." And the column was an impressive work of art. "But today a people have been brave enough to root out a monument to murder and say the time has come to do what statecraft has failed to do, namely to live in the world which God sent them to occupy without, of necessity, cutting their neighbor's throat."

Young conceded that his idealistic interpretation surpassed what he observed from his hotel balcony overlooking Place Vendôme; the celebration "lacked buoyancy" like much else he'd seen of the Commune. But down among the crowd in the middle of the square, MacGahan of the *Herald* had a different sense. The column was tethered with ropes and chipped at its base so it would topple like a tree—hitting the ground, it burst apart in a heave of bronze and stone. The crowd roared, *"Vive la Commune!"* and fired guns into the air. The head of Napoleon's statue atop the column broke off on impact. "The Guards spat into its face and struck it with their rifles," MacGahan wrote. People surged forward in a seething tide of red flags and upraised fists. Up on Young's balcony, hotel guests cursed the rabble. Young thought this unwarranted. The throng below seemed more feckless than malign.

With a diplomatic pass provided by the U.S. ambassador, Elihu Washburne, who'd remained in Paris during the siege, Young continued his city tour over the next few days. "I visited every part and was always received with attention and courtesy," he reported. He looked in vain for "the general pillage" and concluded that Paris under the Commune was the most orderly city he'd ever seen. One nagging concern was the welfare of Paris's archbishop, Georges Darboy, imprisoned early in the uprising on accusations that the church exploited the faithful for their alms and mindless fealty. But with Commune leaders now offering to exchange the archbishop for rebel captives, Young was confident that Ambassador Washburne could broker a deal with President Thiers. Then it would just be a matter of the government continuing to wait out the insurgency. Young wasn't holding his breath: "Thiers kept his army back. He shrank from bloodshed and street warfare. It might be weeks before the business was over." He decided to leave for a visit to Germany two days later, on Monday, May 22.

Saturday night was quiet. Early Sunday morning Young was roused by hotel personnel pounding on doors in the hallway. "The Versailles troops are in Paris! They are fighting on the Place de la Concorde!" In the time it took to throw on his clothes, cannon explosions a few blocks away began shaking the walls of his room. He found himself picturing scenes in novels where tourists caught in a war zone are forced to scramble for their lives in nightshirts and evening clothes. Rushing downstairs, he smiled at how curious it was to think of fiction in the midst of such crashing reality.

Outside on the street, people sprinted in all directions. Those with weapons made for the barricades; those unarmed and with children hid in cellars or lit out for Montmartre's sheltering hive of apartments and alleyways. Cannons thudded in the distance along with the singular rip of the mitrailleuse. "The work was being done," Young later wrote. "France and Paris were grappling, and Frenchmen were striving to do murder upon each other." His mental image of fictional scenes gave way to one of biblical wrath: "The destroying angel had thrown his wing over the beautiful city at last."

Archibald Forbes, his book on the Franco-Prussian War completed, arrived at the northern edge of Paris on Saturday, May 20. French officials had taken over the tramway between the Prussian and Communard sectors in advance of the next day's assault. Denied entry because he looked suspiciously military with his khaki fatigues and ramrod bearing, Forbes tried to sneak in on the "*cocotte* train" of prostitutes returning from work in the Prussian sector. His dislike of the French showed in his catty reference to "the frail sisterhood of Paris" but was

Napoleon's monument in Place Vendôme was hauled to the ground by the Paris Commune in May 1871. The statue of the emperor in Roman attire broke apart on impact, and seeing rebels celebrate the destruction enraged an American visitor watching the scene: "The scoundrels! I could kill every one of them."

softened by the ladies' kindness in draping him with their skirts when "the lynx-eyed *gendarme*" came down the aisle looking for infiltrators. Discovered anyway, he was kicked off the train and had to spend the night in a hayloft.

On Sunday morning he walked unhindered into the city, whose every eye was turned to the smoke and gunfire rising in the west. He dropped his gear at a hotel about four blocks from Place Vendôme and went to the Commune's war office, on the south side of the Seine, where the ease of obtaining a pass "to go anywhere and see everything" shocked his expectations of British-style red tape.

He knew from MacGahan's *Herald* reports, reprinted in London, exactly whom he wanted to see. But when he asked at a cab stand for a ride to General Dombrowski's headquarters, "No, *monsieur*, I have children!" was the terrified reply. Finally a coachman agreed to take him partway, throwing him out and almost running him over when a shell exploded overhead and blew a nearby streetlamp apart.

Forbes trotted down the street toward Dombrowski's base of operations, the Château de la Muette, not far from the Boulogne forest, from whose dense greenery came puffs of rifle and cannon smoke. Shells hitting in the vicinity barely stirred the National Guardsmen "lounging idly about the pavements." Inside the château, Dombrowski received him with a thin smile. They conversed in German. "We are in a deplorably comic situation here," the young general said.

Ignoring the din outside, he invited the Scotsman to share some salad and a cup of coffee. "Consummate coolness," Forbes wrote, echoing MacGahan. "He was the sort of man you take to instinctively."

Explosions rocked the building. A junior officer ran in with a breathless account of his unit taking heavy fire and abandoning its position despite his having beaten the men with the flat of his sword. "Dombrowski waited until the gasping officer had exhausted himself," Forbes wrote, "then handed him a glass of wine and with a serene nod returned to his salad." The general told the man to requisition a battery of cannons from the Commune's war ministry and to assemble a battalion of cavalry: "Let them be ready by seven o'clock. I shall lead the attack myself."

Dombrowski ate some dried prunes from a bowl. His orderly was refilling his coffee cup when a shell hit the roof and sent glass and plaster crashing. The spout of the pot stayed steady as the orderly poured. "The man's nerves were like iron," Forbes marveled. "The general had trained his staff to perfection."

After surveying their surroundings from a rooftop platform, which was peppered with bullets the instant he stood up to look around ("I was not ashamed to make a precipitate retreat"), Forbes returned to the courtyard to find the general preparing to fall back and leave the château to the enemy. "They may have it, and welcome," Dombrowski said, indicating that he would counterattack shortly. "Not with serious intent to retrieve this section but merely for fighting's sake." He gave that smile again. "There is plenty of fight in our fellows, especially when I am leading them."

Forbes wasn't sure how to take this. "I could not for the life of me make up my mind whether Dombrowski's cheerful words were a black joke or if the little man was in dead earnest."

The counterattack came at dusk. Invigorated by the order, the Communards moved out in a robust display owing significantly "to alcoholic influence," Forbes thought. But they broke under "hot and close rifle fire" pouring out from behind the wall of a churchyard. The staff officer he'd seen earlier with Dombrowski led a team of riflemen down a side street to outflank the shooters. The maneuver failed. The officer didn't return.

Dombrowski rode up amid blasts, bullets, screams, and curses ("a warm locality") and rallied his men for another assault. Forbes heard later that his horse had been shot from under him near the churchyard wall, and "he was last seen fighting with his sword against a Versaillist marine who was lunging at him with his bayonet."

Dombrowski survived the night. The next morning he was relieved of command by the Commune's ruling council for supposedly collaborating with the enemy. He spent the first hours afterward arranging to smuggle his wife and children out of Paris through the Prussian sector. Then he reported to the Committee of Public Safety to answer the charge.

MacGahan, still recovering from his concussion of several days earlier, rushed to the Hôtel de Ville to watch the proceedings. Seeing

The Polish freedom fighter Jaroslav Dombrowski impressed all the correspondents who covered his defense of the Paris Commune in 1871. Facing an overwhelming government force, he was fatalistic when exhorting his men into battle. "If you are not destined to die there," he cried, "you have nothing to fear!"

the proud young general plead his case to the "menacing and discontented" committee, its deliberative coherence utterly shaken by "the hail of shells pouring into the quarter," infuriated the *Herald* reporter. "It is the old story of treason. Frenchmen, if you will believe Frenchmen, are never fairly beaten. What they lose is always lost by someone else's treason." When Dombrowski's judges finally exonerated him after hours of debate, he shook their hands and strode back to the barricades. He would return the next day on a stretcher.

Forbes, following Sunday night's failed attack on the churchyard, was swept toward the city's interior with "a throng of fugitives" fleeing the enemy. Many threw away their weapons and tore their Communard insignia off their clothes. "In the extremity of panic," Forbes wrote, "men blazed off their pieces indiscriminately and struck at one another with the clubbed butts, shot and shell chasing them as they went." As dawn came up on Monday, he doubled back to make contact with government troops. Looking west down the center of a wide avenue, he waved to an approaching patrol and received gunshots in reply. "I took the hint and started off by devious paths in the direction of the Champs-Élysées."

His ears rang with shell bursts. The thick air was dusty and hard to breathe. Passing a barricade under construction on Rue Saint-Honoré near the Tuileries, he heard an order to halt behind him. A red-sashed Guardsman said to start stacking the barricade with mattresses and furniture. Forbes flashed his press pass. It didn't impress—work or be shot was his choice.

He set to it with vigor, noting that "even if you are forced to do a thing, it is pleasant to try and do it in a satisfactory manner." Released from the job with compliments for the notched gun embrasure he'd fashioned at the top of the barricade, he headed for his hotel near the intersection of Rue Lafayette and Boulevard Haussmann to find something to eat.

The boulevard was a killing zone, raked with bullets from government positions. Pedestrians huddled on each side, screwing up their courage to cross the wide space strewn with dead and wounded. With bullets "pattering like hailstones" around them, Forbes and a young boy grabbed hands and bolted from cover together. They made it, the reporter taking a round through a tobacco pouch in his coat, the boy one through his outer thigh. Heading on to his hotel, which as on any typical day was serving breakfast "with the old French *élan*," Forbes then returned to the streets to take in further sights.

He tracked the sound of gunshots several blocks west. At an embattled barricade, he saw a wave of Versaillists pour over the top and plunge their bayonets into the few defenders who hadn't fled with their comrades. He ducked behind a lamppost as rebels ran by, "pursued by a brisk fusillade that was fatal to a large proportion of them." Two men fell in front of him. A bullet clanged off the lamppost, tumbling to the asphalt a flattened disk, which was instantly grabbed by an old lady darting from a doorway. Forbes watched in dismay as she put the bullet in her apron pocket and skipped back to her protected nook, clapping her hands with glee. "One saw strange things," he marveled.

Having more than enough material, he returned to his hotel to write. Reports that Prussian sentries were shooting people trying to escape through northern Paris ended his hope of sending his dispatch by courier through there to London. Meanwhile, trapped Communards began burning their identification papers and begging Forbes to help get them a British passport, "a significant indication of the beginning of the end."

Other disturbing sights included "an extraordinary triangle of barricades" erected in confusion at a three-way intersection near the church of Notre Dame de Lorette, "thus exposing themselves to fire from flank and rear as well as from front." Figuring it would make for a good story, he found a safe spot near the church and waited for the comedy to unfold. His plan backfired when a rebel officer "noticed me, approached, and ordered me to pick up a musket and take a hand in the defense." As earlier that day, his press credentials were met with a choice of compliance or death. Somehow the sheer nuttiness of the barricade setup got Forbes laughing. The enraged officer slammed him against a wall and summoned a four-man firing squad.

The Versaillists saved him, crashing the barricade on Rue Saint-Lazare. When the hand-to-hand fighting subsided and the mop-up began, Forbes found himself a government prisoner. His pleas of neutrality brought a quick inspection of his hands "They were not clean, but there were no gunpowder stains on the thumb and forefinger," so he was released and got out of there fast, leaving behind a dozen captive Communards with hands reeking of cordite and expressions of dread on their faces. Earlier that day, Thiers had issued a decree to the city: "The cause of justice, order, humanity, civilization has triumphed. Expiation will be complete." No doubt the prisoners were wondering what "expiation" meant.

As the afternoon passed, the rebels fell back to Montmartre and the dense urban neighborhoods to the east, erecting barricades behind them with vigor more defiant than hopeful. "They were demoralized," Forbes wrote, "yet they were working hard everywhere." Most of the firing had ceased by sunset, creating a surreal impression of calm. "It was a lovely evening," he recalled. "The scene in the narrow streets off Rue Lafayette reminded me of the residential streets of New York on a summer Sunday."

People chatted outside their front doors. Children played on the barricades, their parents barely looking up when occasional gunshots echoed on the breeze. "Yet on that light wind was borne the smell of blood," Forbes wrote, "and corpses were littering the pavement not three hundred yards away." The sense of unreality was freakish. "What strange people were these Parisians!"

No reporter saw General Dombrowski die. One secondhand account had him shot through the lung on Rue Myrha just east of Montmartre and dying with a last cry that he was no traitor. Some government soldiers gave a different story, telling Forbes he'd been captured alive but badly hurt, hauled to the Trocadero near the banks of the Seine, propped up on his knees, and executed in a volley of chassepots into whose muzzles he'd stared impassively. His family made it safely to Britain.

There was plenty of death to see elsewhere. Over the next few days, MacGahan and Forbes chronicled its acceleration from tens to hundreds to thousands while still paying heed to small details that made each killing a separate saga. They wrote in lulls between chasing gunfire or dodging it and tried to get their copy out of Paris in mail sacks via the British and American embassies. Their strengths as reporters, Forbes in his efficiency and MacGahan in his empathy, rather melded as Forbes was compelled to express his shock and MacGahan to calm his emotions in order fully to describe what they saw.

John Russell Young was in Paris as a tourist. He would publish his observations of the Commune's destruction in *The Standard,* revising the day-by-day narrative to add political and philosophical context. Together with Forbes and MacGahan's, his account gave American readers a broad picture of France's infamous *Semaine sanglante,* Bloody Week—what it looked like, how it felt, and what it might mean to the progress of civilization.

It was late afternoon on Tuesday, May 23, when Guardsmen in the lobby of the Hôtel de Ville snapped to attention as Dombrowski's body was carried in. Montmartre, launchpad of the insurgency, had fallen around midday; the Versaillists punctuated their success by executing forty-nine Communists, including four children, against the garden wall at No. 6 Rue des Rosiers, where Generals Lecomte and Thomas had been shot three months earlier. The French national flag began sprouting everywhere in place of discarded red banners. Forbes was astonished at how fast the city's revolutionary fervor turned patriotic as resistance crumbled. "Where had people secreted the tricolor all these days of the Commune?" he wondered. "It now waved from every window!"

The government advance came from the west through Montmartre and from the south toward Père-Lachaise cemetery and La Roquette prison, two blocks away, where several dozen prisoners held by the Commune awaited liberation. Situated between prongs of attack, the Paris opera house became the object of heavy fighting. The Commune's fate seemed to hang on the *drapeau rouge* flying stubbornly above its ornate edifice, whose marble parapets offered an ideal spot for gunners to command surrounding streets.

From his hotel balcony, Young saw a Versaillist officer, "evidently with a Legion of Honor in his eyes," brave relentless fire to clamber up the opera house's rooftop statue of Apollo and strike down the red flag at its top. Watching the same scene from below on Rue Halévy, Forbes's jaw dropped at the officer's daredevil act. "Ha! You're a plucky one!" he thought.

Young's sympathy for the Commune swelled to pained solidarity when the tricolor was raised over the building. "We see the red, white, and blue," he wrote, "and know that Versailles has overwhelmed our poor defense and that at last the attack advances." At least the bloodshed would soon stop, he thought: "The end has come, and the morning will bring peace."

Versaillist troops poured across the opera house square. Forbes observed one of them, "a little grig of a fellow," shooting from behind a tree. Pausing to reload, he waved to onlookers in upper-floor windows. "When is a Frenchman not dramatic?" The man fell with a hole in his forehead. "Well," Forbes thought, "he had enjoyed his brief flash of recklessness."

The reporter scurried "by tacks and dodges" through alleys and back streets toward the British embassy. But the boulevards were too risky to cross. When he tried, "a shell splinter whizzed past me, close enough to blow my beard aside. The street was a pneumatic tube for shellfire. Nothing could have lived in it." On the way back to his hotel, he saw the continued outpouring of love for the liberators: "Everybody seems wild with joy, and Communist cards of citizenship are being torn up wholesale."

He collapsed into bed, waking the next day as "the aurora bloom" of sunrise came over the city. But any pity he might have felt for its inhabitants went up with the flames and smoke billowing from the great government landmarks along Rue de Rivoli, including the Tuileries, the Palais-Royal, and the Louvre. "Great God!" he exclaimed. "That men should be so mad as to strive to make universal ruin because their puny course of factiousness is done!" He didn't bother with placing blame. Maybe it was arson; maybe it was collateral damage from the government cannonade. In either case, it was just "grimy recreant Frenchmen" doing what they did.

It became clear through the morning that most of the fires had been set by desperate Communards, many of them female *pétroleuses* carrying buckets of kerosene. Forbes applauded the spread of the flames to the Hôtel de Ville, "where the rump of the Commune are cowering amidst their incendiarism." The spectacle was matched by one as damning to the other side, for on this sunny Wednesday morning began "the fine game of Communist hunting."

In writing up events later, Forbes used a frantic present-tense style to describe the rabid glee with which people, many of them supporters of the insurgency until today, collaborated with the army to drag rebel fighters from their hideouts. One victim, "a tall, pale, hatless man with something noble in his carriage," is pelted with cries of "Shoot him! Shoot him!" as he's led away.

"A Communard?" Forbes asks one of the bystanders.

The fellow shakes his head. "Questionable. I think he is a milkseller to whom the woman who denounced him owes money."

A Versailles officer smacks the prisoner with his baton. It's as if a switch has been thrown. Bystanders swarm over the prisoner, everyone wanting a piece. Forbes's biases boil. "A certain British impulse, stronger than consideration for self, prompts me to run forward. But it is useless. They are firing into the flaccid carcass now, thronging about it like blowflies on a piece of meat. His brains spurt on my boot and splash into the gutter."

He saw countless similar incidents as he walked the ruined streets now filled with happy Parisians. "The merry game goes on. Yesterday they cried *'Vive la Commune!'* Today they rub their hands with currish joy to denounce a Communist."

Many of the barricades had been built of stones scraped from under the asphalt. The shallow excavations provided convenient burial pits for the bodies accumulating everywhere. Once filled, the ditches were tamped with gravel and dirt so traffic could resume. Passing many abandoned barricades on his way to the Hôtel de Ville, Forbes knew what lay below his feet as he traversed the fresh-covered ground.

At the hotel, a handful of Communards held out against the Versaillist advance. The "chained wildcats" couldn't last much longer, Forbes knew. With gunmen outside and firebombs creating a searing inferno within, the only question was "Will they roast, or seek death on a bayonet point?" One was as good as the other to him.

Young, too, had seen the fires on Rue de Rivoli before dawn on Wednesday. Watching from their hotel roof, his friends condemned the vandalism. But he considered it from the Commune's perspective: "If we are to fall, these monuments of king's majesty shall fall with us." He counted nine buildings ablaze. Daylight brought a vision of charred ruin. "Houses had their fronts blown away," he wrote. "One had a wall cut out and the furniture appeared like a great doll's house."

Going out for a look around, he found that the greater damage wasn't physical: "This city of victory is swept with emotions so wild I cannot express them." Beneath the continued blooming of government flags, countless scenes of "expiation" played out. "When a barricade is taken every prisoner is shot," he reported. "Any man with arms in his hand is executed. When a Communist is found he is placed against a wall and killed."

A government officer got stomach pains after eating soup at a café; the entire kitchen staff was taken outside and shot on suspicion of poisoning. Elsewhere, two young women were led away under guard. The first had been found carrying a pistol. She confronted the firing squad with an expression "firm, calm, and scornful." The second, accused as a poisoner, shrieked in terror, "her eyes staring wildly around, looking for some sympathizing or rescuing face." The women's bodies were thrown into a ditch.

The policy of no quarter only prolonged the resistance. "These men sell their lives dearly," Young said of the rebels. "Die they must, for France is mad, and they might as well meet their doom with arms in their hands over the graves of their brothers as in some barrack-yard at the hands of a government shooting party." He offered, in prose, a sigh. "The fight goes on." The memory returned of his sidewalk spat with Charles Dickens four years earlier about *A Tale of Two Cities.* Young's impulsive sojourn here had shown him Dickens's Paris at last. "I can now understand what was meant by the Reign of Terror."

International newspapers condemned the Paris Commune until accounts of the rebels' widespread massacre by government forces, depicted here in an 1871 drawing from the London *Graphic,* poured in from reporters on the scene. John Russell Young wearied of trying to describe each detail of seeing civilians shot in the streets. "Events like these I might write in columns," he said.

. . .

MacGahan was with the rebels when they were driven out of Montmartre on Tuesday. Their courage edified the cause of the Commune, he wrote. But his editors trimmed this positive spin with a banner proclaiming, "The Hotbed of Communism Carried by Storm." Likewise, "Served Him Right" was their slant on his story of a Commune official bludgeoned to jelly while in government custody. And when MacGahan described a shallow trench near a barricade on Rue de Rochechouart "full of wounded persons buried alive. They shrieked and groaned dreadfully all night," his editors were unmoved: "They alone are to blame for their agony."

The reporter was adamant on the question of who set fire to the buildings on Rue de Rivoli. The *Herald* blamed the Communards, cheering Thiers's swift edict, "No mercy is to be shown the vandals." MacGahan acknowledged that Jules Bergeret, whom he'd interviewed a week earlier, indeed had packed the emperor's palace with gunpowder, exulting afterward, "The last relics of royalty have just vanished." But Bergeret wasn't the reason the rest of Paris was burning. "Government shells set fire to the city," MacGahan declared categorically.

With the self-awareness that increasingly characterized his writing, he confessed to readers his "dividing sense of danger and curiosity" at the violence. While trailing a band of rebels, he barely avoided a machine gun burst that caught them as they crossed a street. Taking cover nearby, he watched them thrash in pools of blood as soldiers took potshots at them. "One fellow had a sort of psychological fascination for my eyes," MacGahan wrote; shot through the spine, he tried to drag himself to safety before succumbing to exhaustion not twenty feet from where MacGahan was hiding. "I could not look away from him as he lay dying in agony."

The reporter contrasted his own passive voyeurism to the actions of the man's compatriots: "Two brave fellows made a rush to bring him inside the barricade in the spirit of generous sympathy, imperiling two lives to save scarcely more than a corpse, risking the chance to take his place rather than see him lie there helpless. One took him by the shoulders, the other by the feet, but the pitiless shower from across the street was too much. Both rescuers were cut down by bullets."

Such raw glimpses gave a human face to headlines howling, "True Indian Warfare in the Streets of Paris!" It was one thing to say "Insurgent Barricades Stormed in Splendid Style." It was quite another to record, as MacGahan did, the fate of a sixteen-year-old boy who'd dropped his weapon in surrender when the barricade fell. "They made him to kneel and blew out his brains," then left him with the Commune's daily flyer, *Père Duchesne,* crumpled in his mouth.

Beginning as isolated, reflex spasms, the killing of unarmed Communards soon progressed to systematic eradication at prisoner "reception centers" near Versailles. Forbes, fearing his stories weren't getting to London, had decided to deliver them himself. On his way out of the city Wednesday night, he passed long columns of forlorn captives trudging west down the Versailles road. Among them were many army deserters, distinctive in their red breeches, who'd joined the resistance in the past few days despite the certain futility. "They might as well have died fighting on the barricades," Forbes thought, "as survived to be made targets a day or two later with their backs against a wall." There were many women: "Some of them are mere girls, soft and timid, who are here seemingly because a parent is here. I marvel that they are here at all and not dead in the streets of Paris."

Young identified Wednesday morning as the moment when the rebels began to retaliate against the hostages they were holding. "You have five minutes to live," the Commune's chief prosecutor, Raoul Rigault, told one arbitrary victim. Rigault knew he was a dead man himself; he would take with him as many victims as possible. One such counterreprisal was directed at Georges Darboy, archbishop of Paris. It was carried out on Wednesday evening by Rigault's henchman, Théophile Ferré. Incarcerated since March, the archbishop was to have been released in exchange for some government-held captives. "But Monsieur Thiers declined," Young wrote bitterly, "and Darboy was left to his fate." Before facing the firing squad, the archbishop blessed the five clergymen condemned alongside him and two Communard riflemen who asked his forgiveness for taking his life. After some posthumous abuse with bayonets, his corpse was dumped at Père-Lachaise cemetery.

Word of Rigault's rogue act reached Charles Delescluze late Wednesday night. The elderly revolutionary, whom MacGahan had favorably profiled in the *Herald,* put his face in his hands. "What a war!" The next day he wrote a note apologizing for his inability to endure another defeat "after so many others." He donned his hat and coat and strolled out to a barricade, climbed to the top with cane in hand, and took a bullet in the chest.

On Friday, the pincers of Marshal Mac-Mahon's attack began squeezing the resistance into a pocket around Père-Lachaise and Buttes Chaumont, a wooded park just north. Jammed against the city walls in northeast Paris, the cornered Communards heard German accordions playing dance tunes in the Prussian-held sector beyond the perimeter. Prussian snipers shot anyone sneaking through. "Bismarck wants his money," Young wrote.

Before abandoning La Roquette prison, another of Rigault's goons, Émile Gois, took fifty inmates outside, most of them policemen, priests, and bankers. The week's blue skies had clouded and a drenching rain poured down, lending a redundant gloom to the work that followed. In front of hundreds of drunken, catcalling onlookers, the prisoners were herded into a courtyard and sprayed with shots from anyone carrying a gun. It took a long time to finish them; after the job was done, weapons were handed to latecomers who wanted to share the experience of discharging a rifle or plunging a bayonet into a human body. One corpse had sixty-nine bullets in it; another, seventy stab wounds. A fifty-first victim somehow wound up in the pile, a stray from the crowd. "Definitely one too many," Gois shrugged.

Saturday saw the Commune extinguished. One band of fighters made a stand among the monuments and headstones of Père-Lachaise. When the last ones surrendered, government soldiers found the remains of Archbishop Darboy in a ditch. A response was planned for the next morning.

Rushing back from London after three days away, Forbes went straight to Père-Lachaise on Sunday afternoon. Artillery explosions had unearthed graves and blown apart family crypts. Human bones and shattered monuments were strewn everywhere. The macabre destruction paled beside what he came upon in a natural hollow at the base of the cemetery's southeast wall. It was full of corpses: "There they lay, tier above tier, each successive tier powdered over with a coating of lime."

Limbs were tangled in rigid contortions. Faces fixed in terror stared upward through the white dusting. "How died these men and women?" he wondered. At first he thought they'd been carted here from around the city, but the surrounding clues told another story. "The hole had been replenished from close by," he realized. "Just yonder was where they were posted up against that section of pock-pitted wall—there was no difficulty in reading the open book—and were shot to death as they stood or crouched."

Père-Lachaise is today home to the remains of some of Western civilization's greatest figures, including Proust, Balzac, Molière, and Chopin (also Richard Wright, Gertrude Stein, and the Doors' Jim Morrison, among other Americans). The section of its wall where 147 Communard prisoners were shot is now a memorial known as Le Mur des Fédérés. It's a touchstone of socialist aspiration to which admirers of the Paris Commune make regular pilgrimage. No doubt it speaks to them of a dream's destruction; also, by virtue of their presence there, of something still alive.

Forbes saw nothing redeeming in the bestial horror before him: "This is the Nineteenth Century! Europe professes civilization. France boasts of culture. Frenchmen are braining one another with the butt ends of muskets. Paris is burning." Always more a chronicler than a philosopher, even he couldn't help but view Bloody Week as a verdict on us all: "We want but a Nero to fiddle." He had a job to do, however. "Here I was," he mused, "on tenterhooks, witnessing a momentous and memorable struggle; but the spectacle only useful professionally in order that I might with all speed transfer the pictures which had formed themselves on my mental retina to the columns of my newspaper. This aim, this burning aspiration, must ever absorb the zealous correspondent. We are on duty."

He turned away from the scene and walked to his horse tied at the cemetery gate. On the way he prayed, "Never again may the civilized world witness such a week of horrors as Paris underwent in those sun-shiny days of May, 1871." The prayer, as his career would teach him too well, was in vain.

Like Forbes, MacGahan almost met a firing squad at the height of Paris's midweek chaos. Leaving a café on Boulevard des Capucines near the opera house, he and some friends were arrested by a police patrol and taken at gunpoint to Place Vendôme. With prisoners being executed all over the city, Ambassador Washburne rushed to the deten-tion center on receiving MacGahan's message for help. He'd expected to find the group justifiably terrified. Instead, "both the ladies and gentlemen exhibited the utmost *sang-froid.*" MacGahan's first com-plaint was that he'd lost his hat in the melee.

His dispatch the next day begins, "The insurrection is writhing in its last agony." It confirms the death of the archbishop and other "Paris martyrs" shot alongside him, and it relates sickening rumors that Dar-boy's body was "mutilated in such a way that the savages of Patagonia would shudder at." But that atrocity, revolting as it was, "forms no excuse for the terrible excesses of the Versaillists." The government ultimately listed 867 soldiers killed. The city paid for the burial of 17,000 residents. Countless detainees died in custody and disappeared in mass graves, and countless civilians, as in every war, vanished in the fire and rubble. Most historians today agree that at least 25,000 Com-munards died and likely many more.

If the numbers are inexact, their disproportion is plain. "The truth must be told and told today," MacGahan wrote. "Here is Thiers's sys-tem of putting down a revolution—Smith burns my house and for revenge I kill Jones, Brown, Green, and their families." No doubt the Communards committed crimes, but these had sprung from individ-ual impulse rather than deliberate policy. For almost three months, Commune leaders had charge of the city and its people—and "they might have blown Paris to the skies if they wished."

Remarkably, considering its earlier implacable tone, the *Herald* came around to this view as testimonies of state-sponsored slaughter poured in. When the paper began in June to run recaps of the rebellion under the title "The Paris Massacre," it had revised its position as to who'd done most of the killing. MacGahan took credit for this change of position. "The bitterest letters against the Thiers government," he wrote his family, "are *mine*."

The *Herald* concurred. In an unprecedented acknowledgment, it published an editorial titled "The *Herald* Paris Correspondent as a Contribution to the History of the Commune." It praised MacGahan's portraits of Dombrowski, Delescluze (no longer "the last dictator," he was now designated "the old martyr of Socialism"), and even the despised Bergeret. "However great may have been their misdeeds, still, says our correspondent, there were extenuating traits in their character and in the cause they defended. Now that they have met the death they did not dread at the hands of the justly infuriated Versaillists, it behooves the historian to pass an unbiased and dispassionate judgment upon the last leaders of the Commune."

MacGahan wasn't identified by name; no way would James Gordon Bennett, Jr., have so spotlighted a subordinate. But within the profession he was now a major figure. His confidence soared, leading him to declare a new manifesto: "I changed my politics at 6:30 the Sunday the Versailles troops entered Paris." He'd been a liberal up to that moment. After it, "I was also a Communard."

He received a large salary increase, letters of credit to pay for expenses, and a note of introduction from Bennett to facilitate his "roving commission" to cover foreign affairs. The job carried the international prestige his work in Paris had brought the *Herald*. But the reporter vowed to keep his goals pure. "I have made up my mind to tell the truth as a journalist no matter how much it may seem against religion or order," he said. Bennett didn't care about that, of course. Good stories were the only requirement.

Unlike MacGahan, John Russell Young was left shaken in his values by his Paris experience. Usually resolutely positive in the lessons he drew from human calamity, the story of the Commune seemed only bleak. He was sarcastic in mocking Thiers's "holy work" of killing Communards, and his disgust at France as a whole was visceral and sour. MacGahan had deemed Paris's unhinged vindictiveness "in perfect consistence with French logic, and when this is said, *all* is said."

Young described with equal cynicism Parisians as he'd come to know them: "They had taste, they knew vintages and silks, could make coffee and salads and toothsome dishes. They were a bright and cordial people." And yet, he joked darkly, "I suggested to a friend that really France was so desperate a scandal that it should be abolished; and there might be some humane system of annual decimation, poisoning the children, and so in ten years have no more France."

Ultimately he couldn't bring himself to end his *Standard* account with anything but pity and hope: "I am confident the time will come when Frenchmen will look back with pride at the men of Paris who fought Prussia for four months after Prussia had left France at its feet, and who for two months longer held at bay the combined forces of Bonapartism, legitimacy, and reaction—dreaming a dream of liberty, equality, and fraternity and giving their lives in a desperate endeavor to make it true."

The optimism may have been strained, but uplifting finales had been his specialty ever since reporting the Battle of Bull Run ten years earlier. A better gauge of his feelings lies in his account, written several years after the Commune, of that streetside confrontation with Charles Dickens in 1867, when he'd questioned the author's portrayal of France in revolution as "a land of terror and crime and death." Visiting there at last, "I was to see the city and know the truth of the master's criticism." It was a harrowing lesson, but not a definitive one, for "France will rise again. Strengthened, purified, chastened." He wondered if the same was true for him.

His "innocent, believing days" were over. The trajectory of his career had collapsed with his firing from the *Tribune* and the financial struggles of *The Standard* ("my folly," he came to call it). Married since 1865, he had a wife and a three-year-old daughter living in New York awaiting his return; a son had died in infancy. Fearing for his ability to support them, he fretted in his diary, "I hang like Mohammed's coffin between heaven and earth, with no decisive answer from anyone on any subject."

That was about to change. His Commune account in *The Standard* would be universally praised for its "fairness, breadth, feeling, profound insight and graphic power." One of those impressed was the white-haired founder of *The New York Herald,* who lived now in stately solitude on Fifth Avenue in lower Manhattan. James Gordon Bennett the elder, once the flame-throwing scourge of Puritans, abolitionists, and liberal softies everywhere, did little these days but sit in his robe in a stuffed chair amid stacks of journals and newspapers. Described by a visitor as "very old and feeble," he read everything he could get his hands on, including, evidently, *The Standard.* He'd met Young during Young's tenure with the *Tribune* and knew all about his alleged abuse of the Associated Press and dismissal by Horace Greeley. Anyone who crossed Greeley was fine by Bennett; and as a longtime supporter of Ulysses Grant, he appreciated Young's editorial defense of the oft-criticized president. Now there was this Commune story to commend him.

Bennett's son ran the newspaper now, but the old man still called the shots when he wanted to. He would make it happen. Young belonged with the *Herald.*

5

Primitive People
1871–1873

The task was, of course, repulsive, but nevertheless had some very exciting and interesting features, combining just enough lawlessness to make it gratifying to that spirit of destruction which probably exists in a latent state in even the most peaceable and civilized of men.

J. A. MACGAHAN, *Campaigning on the Oxus and the Fall of Khiva* (1874)

On March 21, 1871, three days after Generals Thomas and Lecomte were shot in Montmartre and the Paris Commune began, Henry M. Stanley started inland from the coast of Tanzania in search of Dr. David Livingstone. The caravan included three white men and more than a hundred Africans, and flew at its head a hand-sewn Stars and Stripes that perfectly fit the Welsh-born Stanley's improvised American origins.

As mandated by James Gordon Bennett, Jr., the expedition was mounted in secrecy lest others undertake the quest before the *Herald* got a head start. Bennett especially wanted to show up Britain's newspapers. They'd honored Livingstone for exploring Africa and publicizing the depredations of Arab slave traders but lately had accepted the idea that he was probably dead; his last communication was an 1869 letter containing an ominous reference to "cannibal country." Tragic as this was, to have it disproved by American amateurs would be almost as bad.

Bennett had used Stanley before to tweak the lords of Fleet Street, boasting of the superiority of Stanley's *Herald* dispatches from Ethiopia in 1868 over anything reported in the London papers. Bennett's free-spirited upbringing in France made him contemptuous of the starched morality of Victorian England. He liked baiting stuffy Brits as much as his father had liked baiting Horace Greeley and the abolitionists.

Rumors of the *Herald*'s Livingstone quest briefly surfaced in London in June; it was the only time Bennett lost hold of the story. With timing purely intuitive, since he'd heard nothing from Stanley and had no way of knowing how he was faring deep in the jungle, he began running teasers on African affairs and the mystery surrounding Livingstone in the fall of 1871. He also published a phony claim of receiving "positive intelligence" from jungle natives. "A party of Americans," it read, "is hurrying into the interior with the object of rescuing the doctor from his perilous position." No further details were given.

British government officials took comfort in trusting that Stanley's chances of success were minimal. The Royal Geographical Society wasn't so sure. In November it began fielding proposals to send its own Livingstone expedition comprised of "experienced and well-qualified Europeans." Bennett kept up the heat, in December publishing a long letter from Stanley sent the previous July and just now received by the *Herald*. It begins with Stanley thanking Bennett for his financial support and ends with his promise to investigate rumors that Livingstone was in Ujiji, a remote village on the Congolese border. "But wherever he is, be sure I shall not give up the chase," he wrote Bennett. "If alive you shall hear what he has to say. If dead I will find him and bring his bones to you."

Bennett ran an announcement the next day that threw down the gauntlet. "An African exploring expedition is a new thing in the enterprises of modern journalism. To *The New York Herald* will belong the credit of the first bold adventure in the cause of humanity, civilization, and science." The *Herald*'s British counterparts, he went on, were "too slow and too penurious" to compete. In gambling terms, he was now all in—with zero evidence that Stanley was anything but lost.

It proved a fantastic bet. After trekking 973 miles in 236 days, Stanley found the doctor, toothless and bearded, with bleeding feet inside torn boots, on November 10. His blasé greeting, "Dr. Livingstone, I presume," probably didn't happen. Though it became the centerpiece of his popular book about finding Livingstone, his consistent vagueness in confirming the quote suggests he added it after the fact. There is no doubt, however, about the two men's exchange the next morning.

Stanley: "You are probably wondering why I am here."

Livingstone: "I have been wondering."

"I have come after *you*."

"Me?"

"Yes."

"How?"

"Well, have you heard of *The New York Herald*?"

"Oh," Livingstone scowled. "Who has not heard of that despicable newspaper!"

Stanley wasn't offended; the *Herald* was famous for the human muck it so profitably chronicled. He explained the origins of his journey and the largesse of its young sponsor, to whom Livingstone, at the end of his rope and likely to have perished without the supplies Bennett had sent, wrote a long letter of thanks. Stanley remained in the jungle with Livingstone for four months, and his sadness at leaving the man he believed represented "everything that is noble and right" was eased by that letter and other personal documents given him by the doctor. They constituted the proof of success that would make his fortune.

But first he had to overcome resistance in the British establishment. When the London *Times* reported hearsay on May 2, 1872, that Livingstone indeed had been found alive, a horde of skeptics sprang up, giving ground only to the point of allowing that Livingstone, "the great traveler," if anything had rescued Stanley. When Stanley arrived in Britain in August and produced the doctor's written testimonies, some cried forgery and some wondered if he'd employed a psychic to channel the doctor's thoughts. Only after Livingstone's son pronounced them authentic did the British government endorse his feat.

A *Herald* headline declared "Livingstone Safe" the same day *The Times* broke the news. From then through the end of summer, the *Herald* ran a Stanley/Livingstone item roughly twice a week. Papers across America praised the groundbreaking story. An exception was the New York *Sun*. Just as it had pumped sales by attacking John Russell Young three years earlier, it now ran exposés of Stanley's illegitimate birth in Wales, his defection from service in the Civil War, and

Henry M. Stanley, 1872. His search for Dr. David Livingstone in the African jungle was sponsored by *The New York Herald.* The paper's resulting boom in circulation didn't diminish the jealousy of its publisher, James Gordon Bennett, Jr., when the explorer became a world celebrity. "Who was Stanley before I found him?" Bennett demanded in the *Herald* newsroom.

his incarceration on murder charges in Turkey in 1866, revelations Bennett was content to leave unanswered since they brought publicity to his expedition while conveniently tarnishing its star.

"You are now as famous as Livingstone, having discovered the discoverer," he'd telegraphed Stanley early on. "Accept my thanks and the whole world's." But as Stanley's acclaim grew and he was increasingly called on for newspaper interviews and award acceptance speeches, the publisher tired of his employee hogging the spotlight. He shot off another telegram that was decidedly less warm: "Stop talking. Bennett."

In November 1872 Stanley came to New York to give a series of lectures about his African adventure. His boss kept up the freeze between them, receiving him in his office for ten stilted minutes before dismissing him. Bennett's lowest blow, however, was to sabotage Stanley's speaking tour with an opening night review in the *Herald,* calling it "intolerably dull." He'd had only to hint to the reviewer beforehand of his impatience with Stanley's celebrity to get the desired hatchet job. Bennett cloaked his complicity by loudly rebuking the man the next day for not supporting a *Herald* colleague. "As he did," the reviewer winked later, "I could see that he was really gratified."

The success of Stanley's book, *How I Found Livingstone,* put him beyond Bennett's backbiting, a fact Bennett tacitly acknowledged in May 1873 when he hired him to cover African affairs at two and a half times his former salary. Learning that Livingstone had died in Zambia without achieving his lifelong goal of finding the source of the Nile River, Stanley resolved to fulfill the doctor's dream. He secured funding from London's *Daily Telegraph,* contingent on the *Herald* kicking in the same amount. Bennett's cabled one-word reply was a terse concession to the explorer's stature: "Yes."

The expedition, in which Stanley established Lake Victoria as the Nile's source and mapped the three-thousand-mile Congo River, is one of the great achievements in exploration; it took the lives of more than two hundred of his party and lasted three years. Follow-up explorations financed by Belgium's King Leopold II, whose colonization of the Congo killed untold millions of Africans, severely damaged Stanley's reputation. Historians have since redeemed him somewhat, crediting his eyewitness critiques of African slavery with helping to inspire British Victorians to mount a humanitarian naval campaign to intercept foreign slavers and end the trade once and for all.

Stanley's rise from workhouse orphan to wealthy adventurer wasn't enough to get Bennett to deem him an equal, and it was hard for Stanley to shed his deference to the arrogant heir. Even knowing that Bennett had undermined him in the past, he continued to bow to him long after their formal collaboration ended, going so far in 1887 as to grant Bennett's ridiculous whim to fly at the head of his African caravan the blue-red pennant of the New York Yacht Club.

Four years later, a *Herald* reporter, on orders from Bennett to provoke a newsworthy outburst from the explorer, injected an outrageous question into the middle of their interview: "Do you beat your wife?"

Stanley went taut with fury. "My God!" But then, amazingly, he smiled. Remembering his start as a reporter in America when he too had been hungry for any good story, he said to the young interviewer as he rose to leave, "I used to have to do that myself."

It was his last communication with the *Herald.*

· · ·

Few things would seem more unlikely than the friendship that bloomed between John Russell Young and the *Herald*'s seventy-five-year-old founder, James Gordon Bennett. Young's liberalism and indeed his whole being, from his condemnation of slavery and Southern secession to his love of poetry and theater, were diametrically opposed to the old man's. Summoned to Bennett's home after his return from Paris in 1871, Young found him frail but "wreathed in courtesy and good will." His reputation for steely self-interest seemed forgivable in light of his rugged climb from poverty to the pinnacle of American journalism: "He preached amid derision and contempt—preached and won." He had few visitors. Having fought the world all his life, Young wrote, "the world would not now come to his need, and he reigned apart, looking down upon it with scorn."

Young had been awed by the man at the height of his power. "There was an aspect of terror in what young eyes saw of him," he recalled, "a lawless, eccentric influence sweeping a wayward orbit." That such a forbidding figure should live out his days in serenity was fascinating. Old age had brought a calming perspective, an indifference to the noise of the "foolish fleeting hour" that Bennett once would have stoked to high volume. Ferocity had given way to a humble regard for the world's beauty and mystery. "The things we called men, and the grasshopper brawls we called events," Young now marveled, "how small and mean to one who reveled in this revelation." Whether wiser or merely mellower, Bennett seemed a changed man.

On the father's arrangement, Young met with Bennett Junior to see about joining the *Herald*. They sat down on May 3, 1872, the day after the *Herald* announced Stanley's rescue of Livingstone. It was the perfect moment for Young to pitch his idea of going overseas to profile Europe's leaders for American readers. Bennett Junior backed it wholeheartedly. "My new arrangement with Mr. Bennett leaves me nothing to desire in journalism," Young told his wife. The job came just in time. His start-up, *The Standard,* folded weeks later. In loyal gratitude, he defended his new boss against outcries over his boorish behavior. "Mr. Bennett is a man of strong character," he wrote. "He has courage, clearness, a quick mind, a thorough knowledge of his profession, generous and resolute qualities, and great independence." Modulated in Young's typical style, it wasn't a lie, and it wasn't a case for sainthood.

He'd been a few weeks abroad when he learned of the elder Bennett's death. Though not a churchgoer, the old man, after suffering a stroke that left him partially paralyzed, had summoned a minister to his bedside to give him last rites. "He was aware of his approaching death and spoke with philosophical resignation," said an aide who was there. None of his family were with him at the end. The *Tribune*, kicked around by Bennett for years, played up the fact as fitting proof that he was nothing but "a sinner dying alone."

The obituary in the *Herald* cited "allegiance to no party" as its founder's guiding principle. The paper provided no biographical data, merely reprinting bits from other journals, including Horace Greeley's contention that Bennett had been "utterly indifferent to the correctness of details provided the event of the narrative was made clear and published ahead of all competitors." This lazy use of outside material was done on orders from the *Herald*'s now official owner, publisher, and editor in chief, James Gordon Bennett, Jr., who evidently didn't care that none of the papers got right the date of his father's birth.

Six months later, in January 1873, he hosted a banquet in his beloved Paris with Young and Henry Stanley among the guests. Stanley was swamped with fans. Annoyed, Bennett heaped praise on Young, who basked naïvely in the flattery, "astonished at his appreciation and his princely way of exceeding my expectations." Young was a *Herald* man now, at Bennett's beck and call. Splitting time between the Hotel Chatham in Paris and a flat in London, where he'd installed his wife and daughter, he increasingly acted as foreign bureau chief, composing and cabling to New York each day's international "leader" of world news. Working closely with the mercurial Bennett, who was often in Europe, wasn't easy, but the even-tempered Philadelphian was better constituted than most to endure it. Bennett regularly shows up in Young's diaries in a tantrum or ill humor only to have their meeting, luncheon, or walk along the Strand or Champs-Élysées "begin in clouds and end in sunshine."

Critics called Young's *Herald* profiles of France's president, Adolphe

"Château Lafitte of the finest vintage" was how Januarius MacGahan described his Russian wife, Varvara Elaguine. Domesticity frustrated him, however, and his long absences tormented her with suspicions of his infidelity.

Thiers, and its exiled emperor, Louis-Napoleon, "not only news, but literature." But they weren't the stuff of high adventure. Bennett would need someone else to fill that role. Convinced on the basis of his Living-stone coup that he possessed a visionary knack, he eyed the badlands of Central Asia as the next international hot spot. Russia and Britain had been waging a strategic "Great Game" in the region for decades, with each side maneuvering to control the Silk Road trade route to India and the Far East. The latest flashpoint was Khiva, a sixth-century fortress on the Oxus River (today called the Amu Darya) on the south-ern border of present Uzbekistan. Its khan had been encouraging his subjects to plunder passing trade; now Russia was preparing to punish him. Military authorities had already decreed that no reporters would be allowed on the expedition, a sure sign of picturesque violence to come. Bennett decided to send his roving correspondent, Januarius MacGahan, on a secret mission to cover it.

He informed MacGahan of the assignment over dinner in Paris in January 1873. He no doubt congratulated himself on the choice after the reporter told him that he'd begun learning Russian a year earlier while in Yalta on the southern coast of Crimea, a favorite winter spot for St. Petersburg's royal elite. MacGahan had since become conversant in the language thanks to a young woman he'd fallen in love with and now was engaged to marry.

Her name was Varvara "Varia" Elaguine, and she was a blond, blue-eyed, serious-minded daughter of downscale Russian nobility. They'd met by chance on a country road. It wasn't long before MacGahan, with the Commune's lessons of life's brevity perhaps in mind, proposed a bet that she would be his wife before long. She wasn't amused. Denied the inheritance that went to her older siblings, Varia carried herself with stern self-sufficiency. She'd vowed always to be able to support herself as a teacher and never to marry a man who wasn't an equal and constant partner. In other words, not MacGahan.

He relished his freewheeling career (Dresden, Vienna, Budapest, Bucharest, and Odessa were some of his first stops after the Commune), and had long professed distaste for marriage's "chains." But Varia's blend of straitened circumstance and noble bearing gave her a soulfulness that enthralled him. She in turn enjoyed what she called his "singularity and eccentricity," though he was so unlike her imagined perfect mate that only irrationality, she wrote, could account for her feelings: "I believed in him unlimitedly, forgave him everything, loved him the way I never dreamed of loving anyone."

They were opposites in every way. His identification with Paris's socialist movement didn't hinder his partying with "the highest class, the richest people." She counted pennies and complained that his champagne tastes and the money he sent his mother in Ohio were tapping them out each month. Sexual permissiveness had thrived in Paris during the Commune. MacGahan's three-month immersion there had only amplified his avid propensities, and Varia later wrote that she was taken aback by his worldliness and physical "advances." It didn't stop her from moving into his Paris apartment four months before their marriage. "He used to put me near him and write like a machine," she recalled, "stopping just to kiss me." He gave her few presents except flowers, taking her affection for granted while obsessing about his professional future. Annoyed to stand second in his mind, "I pretty nearly hated him sometimes, but he just had to take my hands, tell me a few insignificant words, look at me with his clever, deep, gray eyes, and my doubts were relieved."

Those doubts were about his fidelity. Their marriage plans almost blew apart after he confessed by letter that "from weakness" he'd had an affair with an American girl he'd met while on recent assignment in Berlin. Reuniting with him in Paris, Varia demanded an explanation (his excuse that the girl was "sprightly" and his interest merely "sensual" cannot have sat well), after which she absolutely intended to leave him. "I do not remember just exactly the way he did it," she mused afterward. "I was in a fog. One must have known him the way I know him now to understand that he was capable of making me believe whatever he wished. I loved him more than ever."

They were married in a civil ceremony on January 22 and traveled to St. Petersburg a month later. MacGahan petitioned Russian authorities to let him accompany the military expedition to Khiva: "You know my friendly sentiments and can be sure I would do nothing disagreeable." Denied, he and Varia trained nine hundred miles southeast to Saratov, on the Volga River, where he bought field gear and weapons to protect a solo traveler in a perilous place. "Being a man of peace," he wrote, "I went but lightly armed. A heavy double-barreled English hunting rifle, a double-barreled shotgun, an eighteen-shooter Winchester rifle, three heavy revolvers, and one ordinary-looking muzzle-loading shotgun throwing slugs, besides a few knives and sabers, formed a light and unpretentious equipment." His jaunty air belied the peril ahead. "Nothing was farther from my thoughts than fighting," he said of his portable arsenal. "I only encumbered myself with these things in order to be able to discuss with becoming dignity questions relating to the rights of way and of property with inhabitants of the desert, whose opinions on these subjects are sometimes peculiar."

When Varia tried to change his mind about going, he played on her money fears. If he were let go from the *Herald* for defying Bennett, he said, he'd have no means to support her. She upped the pressure by telling him she was pregnant. He was thrilled, predicting it would be a girl they should name Mary. But skipping Khiva wasn't an option. "He was not such a man as would stop once a decision was taken," she said.

She could stay with relatives in Moscow until his return—his *safe* return, he assured her somewhat uncertainly. European travelers through the predominantly Muslim region were generally received with the hospitality to strangers dictated by the Koran. But inadvertent offenses to Islam or the local khan could be fatal, and desert bandits were not always consistent in their adherence to holy writ. MacGahan had heard tales of Westerners meeting horrible ends at the hands of natives, from scorpion pits to scimitars, private torture to public beheading, and lately they'd begun "to float in a shadowy way through my imagination."

He promised Varia he would link up with the Russian army once he was in the field. But he wrote a friend in the States what he couldn't tell his wife: "I feel sometimes as though I'm never coming back." They parted on March 27. Over the next five months, she would receive two six-week-old letters from him sent from Russian outposts between the Aral Sea and the Oxus River. Unable to reply, she couldn't tell him she'd lost the baby, a boy, in June. She blamed the miscarriage on her depression ("I was not preparing joy for him") and on her husband's boss, who seemed to take MacGahan's marriage as a personal affront. "Bennett never let him dwell anywhere in peace for any length of time after that," she wrote.

Reprising the publicity buildup to Stanley's search for Livingstone, Bennett ran hints of an intrepid *Herald* "special" venturing into Central Asia beginning in April 1873. The correspondent was said to be traveling with an American diplomat stationed in Russia. That diplomat was thirty-three-year-old Eugene Schuyler from upstate New York. Schuyler was an unpromising travel mate in that he possessed, his sister wrote in a later memoir, "a strong love of luxury and a physical timidity which made him uncomfortable when walking beside a precipice or on a lonely road at night"—not exactly someone geared to cross the southern spur of the Ural Mountains into the snowy plains of Asia with temperatures still hitting winter lows far below zero.

Day and night of the four-week first leg of their journey, Schuyler and MacGahan shared a small horse cart that was convertible to a sled or wheeled buggy depending on whether the ground was ice or slush. The straw-filled, sheepskin-lined tarantass was just large enough for them to curl up inside and escape the cutting winds of the steppe.

Such close quarters tested their compatibility. It turned out that the Ohio farm boy and the prim Ivy Leaguer got along fine.

Like MacGahan, Schuyler was a political liberal with a love for literature. (He wrote English translations of Tolstoy and Turgenev.) But their affinity ran deeper than social like-mindedness, for Schuyler too was attracted to danger. It aroused "the other side of his nature," said his sister. He split off from the southbound MacGahan on April 30 and continued west to Tashkent, Bukhara, and Samarkand, a tour he chronicled in his two-volume study, *Turkistan,* published three years later; among its conclusions was that Russia's often harsh rule of the region was still better for the natives than "to leave them to anarchy and the unbridled rule of fanatical despots."

Subjugating warrior chieftains and the nomadic bandits they sanctioned was the long-standing mission of Russian troops in Central Asia. A general summarized the textbook approach: "The harder you hit them, the longer they remain quiet." The policy translated to swaths of inflicted misery in which hundreds of thousands of natives were eliminated over the years, a tally acceptable to Westerners because the victims were tribal Muslims little known beyond their sometimes bloodcurdling cruelty toward white intruders and their centuries-old embrace of slavery. This made it easy for their would-be conquerors to deem them benighted, expendable primitives.

The Russian army's Khiva incursion had been two years in preparation by the proconsul of the Turkistan territory, General Konstantin Kaufmann. Trained as an engineer (Fyodor Dostoyevsky had been his classmate at the military institute), Kaufmann, short and nondescript, compensated for his lack of charisma by traveling with a hundred Cossack bodyguards to keep his subjects suitably awed. His Khiva plan left little to chance. Its multipronged force of 13,000 men and fifty cannons would easily overwhelm the khan's ancient, mud-walled citadel, provided it could safely cross the treacherous Kyzylkum desert surrounding the place on three sides. Kaufmann stipulated that whichever prong got there first was to await his arrival before launching the attack and grabbing the glory.

MacGahan had hoped to catch up with the northern column somewhere along its nine-hundred-mile trek from Orenberg to Khiva. But

The American diplomat Eugene Schuyler accompanied Januarius MacGahan on the first leg of MacGahan's trek across the desert in Central Asia in 1873. Their reunion in Turkey three years later would result in a collaboration that changed the face of Europe.

at a Russian outpost southeast of the Aral Sea, he learned that it had passed through weeks earlier and was possibly hundreds of miles ahead of him. His best option was to join Kaufmann's main column coming westward from Tashkent, capital of Turkistan, six hundred miles away. The quickest way to do that was to cut south across the Kyzylkum and intercept Kaufmann at the Oxus River, a course risky for an army "but simply impossible," he was told, for a lone white man. One of the largest deserts in the world, the Kyzylkum was unmapped, desolate, and home to shadowy nomads of Persian-Mongolian mix. "The Kyrgyz were hostile to Russians," MacGahan wrote, "and had the reputation of being robbers and marauders." But going around the desert rather than straight across might bring him too late to the Khiva siege. "I had already spent so much of the *Herald*'s money that I felt morally obliged to push forward."

He expected the crossing to take nine or ten days. Camels were the traditional choice for pack animals, but choosing speed over durability, he went with horses instead—two horses for his gear (biscuits, dried meat, sugar, tea, ropes and buckets for drawing water from wells, hogskins to carry the water, and a hundred rounds of ammo for each of his firearms); and four horses to carry him, two local guides, and an interpreter named Ak-Mamatoff, a hard-drinking Tartar adept at local dialects but "the most worthless, lazy, thieving, contrary old idiot I could have found."

Russian sentries shook their heads as MacGahan and his scruffy companions ferried across the mile-wide Syr Daria River that floors the last green valley before the Kyzylkum. He later attributed his own daring to ignorance: "A correspondent often embarks on an enterprise without foreseeing or appreciating half the difficulties to be encountered, and then feels obliged to put on a brave face and carry it out at whatever risk, when in his inmost self he knows that if he were a free agent he would be among the very last to undertake it." After a day's ride through windswept hills tufted green in the hollows with thorn bushes and meadow grass, they came at sunset upon a Kyrgyz *aul,* or "wandering village," comprised of half a dozen domelike tents made of patchwork felt. Smoke curled through holes at the top. At the edge of the campsite, tribesmen in leather breeches and fleece caps looked up from watering their ponies. The *aul's* bearded elder, a matchlock rifle slung over his shoulder, approached the visitors and pronounced *salaam,* "peace." Women and children watched from beside their *kibitka* tents. MacGahan's interpreter did the talking, "of which I could see I was the subject."

MacGahan was invited into the elder's *kibitka* "with the gravest politeness." Several men, swarthy and glowering, stood at the entrance. He made a quick calculation: "I knew I must adopt one of two systems in dealing with such people. Either fight them, or throw myself entirely upon their hospitality and generosity. I chose the latter." He slipped his carbine off his shoulder, unbuckled his pistol belt, and handed them to his hosts. They went to tend his horses, leaving him with two women who were cooking over the fire inside. Sitting cross-legged on the carpeted ground, he beckoned a little boy toddling nearby. The child tumbled into his arms. "The scene was a pretty one," MacGahan wrote.

Before daylight faded, he retrieved his shotgun from his packhorse and, in "a great feat" to the poorly armed Kyrgyz, shot five ducks at a nearby pond to contribute to the *aul's* supper. Sitting down with the tribesmen while the women served, he found that he'd left his utensils at the Russian outpost and had to eat his food with the blade of his knife; it turned out to be the Kyrgyz style, further warming the mood among them. As the fire died, the hole at the top of the tent was sealed, "making everything snug and cozy." MacGahan and his men laid out their sheepskins and slept on the carpet: "Thus pleasantly ended my first day in the dreaded desert of Kyzylkum."

The next few days went much the same. MacGahan's group got an early start in the predawn frost ("at this season, the nights are as cold as the days are hot") and took shelter from the midday sun in a *kibitka* of one the many *auls* they came upon. After lunch and a nap, they pushed on till nightfall, when another welcoming *aul* could usually be found. "The Kyrgyz possess honesty and hospitality," he wrote, "virtues which our civilization seems to have a remarkable power of extinguishing among primitive people."

His praise of Kyrgyz customs was matched with praise for the women. This was unusual both in its sexual candor and its flouting of the convention among Western travelers to hold in proper distaste these exotic females with their almond eyes and wide flat features. But MacGahan was charmed. "I had never in my life seen prettier or more interesting faces," he wrote. "Rich olive complexions that were perfectly transparent; their hair, black as night, hung down over their backs in two heavy braids reaching almost to the feet; and their dark soft eyes were fringed with long heavy lashes." He attributed the women's allure to an interplay of restraint and expressiveness: "In repose, they have a hard, stolid, wooden look, like the carved face of some old heathen image; but interested, pleased, or amused, their eyes sparkle and the whole face seems aglow with some strange radiance from within."

On his second night in the desert, a teenage girl sewed a button for him while he sat back appreciating "the ample amends" her physical attributes made for her coarse clothing. "Her comrades seemed to think it very funny, laughed, and made signs to me to kiss her, which I was not slow to act upon, she submitting with a very demure grace." At another *aul* the next day, a pair of sisters "saluted each in their turn by taking my hand between both hers and then laying it on her heart with a pretty modest meekness that was perfectly bewitching." Each wore a red silk tunic called a *khalat* "fastened at the throat with a coral button, but hung loose in front, exposing a chemise of white silk worn carelessly open at the bosom in a very piquant manner." Soon their "wild beauty" moved him to propose marriage to one of them.

Told he must seek her brother's permission and bestow gifts, he offered the brother a rifle and the girl a horse, camel, twenty sheep, and a furnished *kibitka* in exchange for her hand. The proposition was seriously received and brought an earnest reply from the sisters: "I would have to marry them both." Fine, he said. "It was not for me to object to so agreeable an arrangement. It would have been a pity to separate them." The matter was postponed in light of his present mission. "When I came back that way they would give me their final answer."

Starting out the next morning, "not without some feeling of sad-

Januarius MacGahan packed seven firearms and almost a thousand rounds of ammunition in expectation of a violent reception from tribal nomads in the Kyzylkum desert, shown here in a photograph taken near the time of his 1873 expedition. "But never did I meet with anything but kindness," he wrote.

ness," MacGahan and his men covered almost fifty miles on each of the next three days, sleeping under the stars due to an absence of *auls* in the increasingly arid terrain. His men had forgotten to refill their hogskins at the last well, and the lack of water soon had them parched and feverous. Coming upon another Russian outpost, they replenished their supplies alongside a thirty-camel caravan belonging to an emissary from Khiva, who'd been dispatched by the khan to intercept Kaufmann and negotiate peace terms before the general arrived and opened fire. The commander of the outpost suggested MacGahan travel with the emissary, for he was a lofty imam with a large security force. MacGahan declined. "Greatness here as everywhere has its drawbacks," he wrote. "He was such a very important man that he could not compromise his dignity by any unseemly haste in his movements." MacGahan would travel fast and light.

He and his men next entered "that part of the Kyzylkum which offers the greatest danger. Once lost in this desert ocean, you may wander for days until you and your horse sink exhausted to die of thirst." Everything depended on finding the next well, those distant, hoped-for blessings spaced at unknown intervals along ancient caravan routes. "These wells are very curious," he wrote. "Nobody knows who dug them. Centuries have gone by, and the pure, sweet waters are as fresh as ever." At a well called Kyzylkak, some Kyrgyz riders used their horses to hoist buckets of water up the deep shaft. They told MacGahan that Kaufmann's column had passed through ten days earlier. "I might now be weeks in overtaking him," he realized. "With many misgivings I resolved to go on."

He drove his men to ride all night. As dawn broke over a landscape "bare and barren, treeless and lifeless," they came on a small *aul* where MacGahan, in a surprise after the hospitality he'd met so far, was shooed away by an old woman guarding the outermost tent. Her granddaughter was giving birth inside. When the camp packed up the next morning, "I was astonished to see the girl whose youngster was born the day before mount sturdily on her camel with her brat in her arms."

Kyrgyz migration seemed mindless to him; the *auls,* with their herds of sheep, crisscrossed one another's grazing grounds in an eternal back-and-forth. MacGahan asked a village elder the obvious question: "Why don't they all stay home?"

"Our fathers never did. Why should we not do as they have done?"

This made sense, sort of. If you insisted on making your home in a desert, MacGahan reasoned, moving constantly was as logical "as any other mode of life."

To save time, he decided to quit the caravan route for a sheep path leading directly to Khiva. "No white man had ever been this way before," he noted, and as far as his interpreter was concerned, no Tartar was about to go now. MacGahan didn't debate it: "I drew my revolver and ordered Ak-Mamatoff to mount and proceed." Complying at once ("he had probably not looked for such energetic measures on my part"), the fellow showed no hard feelings, evidently figuring his little mutiny had been worth a try.

Troubling to everyone was the loss of one of the horses, which on day fifteen buckled to the ground: "It was useless to urge him further, and taking off his bridle we left him alone in the gloom of the desert." The decision cast a pall, as "there was something fearful in the necessity which compelled us to work a poor willing beast to death and leave him alone to die." Two days later the situation was critical. The men led their horses on foot through knee-deep sand as heavy as mud. They traveled by night to avoid the blazing sun. "Vegetation has entirely disappeared. Side by side with us move our own shadows, projected long and black over the moonlit sand like fearful specters." At six in the morning on May 16, they ascended a ridge overlooking an immense plain. Through his spyglass, MacGahan saw a glitter of bayonets and a mass of soldiers in the white summer uniforms of Russian infantry. After seventeen days and five hundred miles, "Surely it is Kaufmann," he thought.

But it was only a rearguard force under the command of a "despot colonel" who refused to let MacGahan continue his trek without General Kaufmann's approval. This was obtainable only in person. "He is too busy to answer letters," the colonel said.

MacGahan almost laughed. "I cannot see him without his permission, and I cannot get his permission without seeing him."

"Yes."

Trusting "the proverbial good luck of the war correspondent," Mac-Gahan resolved to press ahead illegally. He told his men they would slip away after nightfall. Their refusal didn't surprise him, and "I had to acknowledge their objections were well-founded." A bribe of a hundred rubles each changed their minds. Riding out at midnight, he felt an exhilarating freedom. "With all its fatigues and dangers," he wrote, "there is something overpoweringly attractive in the desert that only those who experience it can understand."

Soon they were again enduring bitter thirst and sand so soft their horses sank to their bellies, causing another one to drop dead. Grabbing sleep when he could, MacGahan awoke in starts, momentarily thinking he was at home in Ohio or in a Paris hotel rather than covered in drifting sand under a vaulted sky. He'd been told this part of the desert was called Adam-Kurulgan, "fatal to men." "The name is well-chosen," he thought.

Furious at MacGahan's disobedience, the colonel he'd defied sent twenty Cossack horsemen in pursuit. They quickly turned back, though not before encountering one of Kaufmann's couriers on his way back to Tashkent. The Cossacks told him about the American *molodyetz* ("brave fellow") who was attempting to link up with the general. When the courier got to Tashkent and spread this news, Eugene Schuyler heard it with a smile. "MacGahan's ride across the desert," he later wrote, "was being spoken of everywhere in Central Asia as by far the most wonderful thing that had ever been done there, as he went through country which was supposed to be hostile, knowing nothing of the roads or language."

Meanwhile, sedition was brewing in MacGahan's little company. Tired of the bitching, he reminded them of the bonus he'd paid them and the provisions he'd shared in equal portion. "I was in every way good-natured except in the way of getting forward," he wrote. "On that I was inexorable." In the end they shrugged and mounted up pleasantly. "Although they regarded me as one possessed with an itinerant demon, they only said 'Allah is great' and liked me none the less."

On day twenty-eight, MacGahan smelled, then saw the first evidence that he was closing on Kaufmann. Bloated and rotting in the heat, dead camels from the Russian caravan littered an increasingly worn trail along with discarded equipment and campfires gone to ash. There were dead horses with their tails clipped off, a sign they'd belonged to enemy warriors; the value of animals killed in the khan's service was reimbursed if their tails were brought in as proof. "We advanced cautiously now," MacGahan wrote, "surveying the ground from the summit of every little hill to avoid falling in with any wandering bands of Khivans."

At sunset the sky turned reddish gold above a faint shimmer just below the horizon. It was the Oxus River, smooth as a lake. At its swampy edge the travelers quenched their thirst but otherwise weren't much uplifted: "What shall we see in the morning? The white coats of the Russians or the tall black caps of the Khivans?"

They slept in a hollow, clutching the horses' reins. Waking before dawn, MacGahan was filled with wonder at the vista before him. "I could hardly believe I was really looking on that river which stretches its mighty course from the mountains of India to the Aral Sea. It seemed more strange when I thought how few of my race had seen it." Another thought struck him: "Where is Kaufmann?"

They followed the course of the riverbank. Five Khivan horsemen rounded a bend up ahead. MacGahan shouldered his rifle and fired from the saddle. The riders wheeled to a narrow neck of the river and splashed across. That evening as he and his men bedded down, they saw a large band on the far shore watching them through the twilight. "Our nerves are strung to the utmost pitch," he wrote. "The enemy has but to cross the river to find us."

His men wouldn't stand watch. "In five minutes they are sound asleep and I am left alone with the murmur of the river, pacing up and down." Heat lightning flashed, illuminating the night before cutting out and "making the succeeding darkness ten times more sinister."

A mile out the next morning, they came on a smoldering campfire. A succession of blasts rolled up the valley—the unmistakable roar of cannons. The river veered south while the gunfire issued from somewhere ahead. With muttered complaints, his men followed MacGahan across the bluff toward it. They glimpsed a handful of riders who wheeled away at the sight of them. "It begins to grow exciting," MacGahan thought.

From the crest of a ridge, they surveyed the terrain and saw "something that gives us pause." At least a hundred horsemen were visible in the distance. "This looks bad," he told himself. "If Kyrgyz, they are friends; if Khivan, then our position is as bad as could be."

Two riders peeled off and headed toward them. "Matters are now coming to a crisis," MacGahan realized, but "there is no cover within two or three miles that would tempt a rabbit." He ordered his men to dismount and ready their weapons—though it seemed hardly worth it, as "none of them can be counted on to hit anything farther than ten feet."

His plan was to kill the two riders and make a run for the Russian line on their horses, surely faster and fresher than his crew's emaciated beasts. He scanned his men's faces to gauge their resolve. All looked shaky except his old nemesis, Ak-Mamatoff, who, to his surprise, looked "perfectly stolid, as though this were a matter of utmost indifference to him." The remorse MacGahan felt for imperiling him was eased by a sense that he was quite content to die: "I had made life a burden to him by dragging him here, and the sooner he got rid of his existence, the better."

Lying prone behind a cluster of thorn bushes, MacGahan asked his men if they were sure the riders were Khivan. "Yes," they said. He cocked his rifle and sighted his target.

A moment later he was embracing the strangers in delirious relief; at the last instant, his men had recognized them as Kyrgyz scouts in the Russian service. Galloping with them toward the cannon fire, he had to smile at this turn of events. After thirty days pursuing Kaufmann, he'd found him at the very hour the siege was starting. "If I had the selection of the moment when I should arrive, I could not have chosen a more favorable one than the present," he rejoiced. "The exciting scene before me was well-calculated to put a war correspondent in good humor."

· · ·

A hundred and fifty years earlier, only 40 Russians out of a force of 4,000 survived an expedition to Khiva. Their captured commander, a Muslim-born convert to Christianity named Alexander Bekovich, had received an apostate's punishment of being publicly stripped, beheaded, and stuffed with straw for display. MacGahan expected a similar reception now. But Khivan resistance amounted to little more than harassment; once Russian cannons came into range, the khan fled his palace without a fight. After two days in hiding, he returned to negotiate terms of surrender with Kaufmann. The thirty-year-old Asian towered over the diminutive general and dropped to one knee before him. It was "not a posture of humility," in MacGahan's view, "but rather one of respect."

Kaufmann saw it differently, enjoying the show of submission. "Well, Khan. I have come to see you at last."

"Yes. Allah has willed it."

"Allah had nothing to do with it. You brought it on yourself."

Between drags on a water pipe, the khan wrangled with Kaufmann over the financial penalty he owed the czar for allowing the raids on Russian trade that had forced this punitive action. The raids weren't his fault, he said. They'd been committed by a rogue Turkoman tribe, the Yomuds, who thanks to their ill-gotten gains were far better able than he to pay the czar in full. Conquer them, the khan said, and the money would be there for the taking.

Kaufmann bought it. "Hoodwinked," MacGahan thought. The khan wanted to destroy the troublesome Yomuds, "a better, braver, and nobler race," and now the Russians would do it for him.

During the army's several weeks' preparation for this second operation, MacGahan observed the daily life of the town. The bazaar teemed with carpet sellers, silversmiths, horse dealers, and slave traders. A constant flow of Persians snatched from the western frontier passed through auction markets to be bought and sold; the men, women, and children were deemed subhuman heretics for practicing Shia Islam rather than the majority Sunni version. Afghans, being largely Sunni, ought to have been exempt from such treatment, but under Khivan torture, they could be induced to convert and then be legally sold as slaves for having renounced the true religion. European captives were highest prized ("the khan generally kept them for himself"), while Jews enjoyed the perverse dispensation of being considered too lowly even to be kept as slaves, "owing to the contempt in which they are held by Muslims."

Khiva's many mosques and madrassa schools, which MacGahan likened to stern Catholic monasteries, were especially perplexing to him. Their construction varied from nondescript clay to gleaming edifices of brilliantly colored tile, but inside he found a grim conformity. "Lean and withered," he wrote, "the mullahs go prowling about with faces lighted only by the fires of bigotry and fanaticism. Years pass in their dark little cells learning the Koran by heart without even understanding it, poring over it to the exclusion of every living human interest." He wondered if perhaps as much as their hermetic faith, it was their headgear, globular turbans of thickly wrapped muslin, that impaired them: "The sight of one of these mullahs plodding through the dusty streets in the broiling heat of the noonday sun supporting this monstrous superstructure on his head is enough to make one shudder at man's inhumanity to himself."

Local tastes in entertainment were almost as jarring. He disliked

"Great mud walls, high and battlemented with heavy round buttresses"— Januarius MacGahan's description of Khiva in 1873 matches this modern view. Disappointed in his first impression, later seeing the ancient fortress under moonlight made it seem magical and, typically for him, romantic.

smoking hashish: "A very few whiffs were sufficient for me. I was glad to return to my cigarettes." And an outdoor performance at the home of an Uzbek merchant featuring two adolescent boys dancing a fable of sensual love definitely took him aback. He found it "degrading—but done very gracefully and with much seeming intelligence." Toward the end of the performance, his host took the boys "caressingly" on his lap and gave them hits on his hookah. This was a long way from Pigeon Roost Ridge. "The torches casting a fitful light on the nodding branches of the trees overhead, the wild faces around, and these children enacting a love scene," MacGahan wrote, "made a strange and picturesque tableau."

The local suppression of women irked him for selfish reasons. Forget, he wrote, "feasting your eyes on a female face. Enveloped in her long robes, the black veil covering her face like a pall, you catch only the occasional gleam of a bright eye as she glides past. Men's faces, nothing but men's faces—this becomes, after awhile, one of the most disagreeable features of Khiva." Comparing his yearning to meet a pretty girl to a desert traveler's yearning for green grass and flowers, he took matters in hand by sneaking into the royal harem when the khan and his entourage were away from the palace. He'd earlier got a peek inside while interviewing Russian soldiers who were guarding the harem gate, and had glimpsed children and unveiled women weeping in apparent dread of execution or enslavement. The women ranged from "sweet young girls of fifteen to toothless hags apparently a hundred and fifty." One stood out. "She was about eighteen, with a clear rosy complexion and large dark eyes. Her quiet firmness, tranquil air of authority, and noble appearance convinced me that she was the sultana of the harem."

She'd noticed MacGahan as well and gave him a beseeching look. "I never in my life so much regretted my ignorance of an unknown tongue," he wrote. He couldn't get out of his mind the image of her standing strong "in the midst of enemies of her race and religion with weeping women and children relying upon her for protection. I determined to communicate with her and help her if possible."

Returning after dark, he located a stairway leading up to the parapet that ran along the top of the battlement. Voices of Russian sentinels wafted from the observation tower. Below, Khiva's rooftops and minarets shone in the moonlight, "no longer a real city, but a leaf torn from the enchanted pages of *The Arabian Nights*." Peering down into a courtyard, he saw a woman flit through a doorway. There he "descended and found two passageways, one leading to the main gate and the other apparently to the interior rooms of the harem."

He moved through a series of windowless chambers in the pitch black, afraid to draw attention by lighting the candle in his pocket. He thought the place might be a dungeon till he remembered there was no such thing in Khiva, whose authorities, he'd observed, "cut off people's noses, ears, heads, whip them, stone them to death, but never imprison them."

His foot caught the edge of a raised curb. Lighting the candle, he found he was teetering at the lip of a deep pit that was either a well or some kind of latrine. He retreated into another room that had a pile of loose dirt in one corner. He picked up a handful, holding the candle close. It was gunpowder—"enough to blow the whole palace to atoms." He ran out of the room and groped his way down the corridor until he came to a locked door. He slumped against it, collecting his wits, at which point "I began to look on my adventure as the most ridiculous thing I had ever attempted. I had narrowly escaped death twice, and that was enough for one night."

He became aware of female voices on the other side of the door, "laughing in the gayest manner, like a bevy of schoolgirls having a night party unknown to the matron."

At his knock, they went silent. Then someone spoke the cadence of "who's there?"

"Aman," he replied, pretty sure it meant "peace be with you."

There was laughter. *"Aman?"*

He said it again. Bolts rattled, and the door swung open. Eight women "in strange costumes" regarded him with amused unsurprise, "as though they had expected me."

He stepped inside and turned to the woman who'd opened the door: "It was she, the one that had attracted my attention at the gates of the harem." He ventured, *"Salaam."* Getting a smile but no answer, he tried another word, *"chai,"* for tea.

She took his hand and led him across the courtyard to a room floored with pillows and lighted with lamps along the wall. Handing a teapot to her attendants—all of them, as best he could tell, "exchanging remarks about my personal appearance"—she helped him wash his hands in a basin and placed before him a platter of bread and apricots. "She wore a short green jacket," he noticed, "and a long chemise of red silk fastened at the throat with an emerald and open at the bosom. She knelt on the ground watching me with her brown eyes in a way that was exceedingly embarrassing." In his usual way, he was already smitten.

He established that her name was Zuleika. *"Ursus ma Yakshe?"* he asked. Do you like the Russians?

She made a face. *"Yoke."* No.

"Min Ursus yoke," he said quickly. I'm not Russian.

Zuleika and her attendants giggled. "Yes. We know."

He stayed two hours, "conversing principally in signs." Finally Zuleika, "my fair conductress," led him outside to the stairs ascending to the parapet. At the top he turned and gazed after her—"she kissed hands to me and disappeared in the dark corridor." Their fleeting contact, as unlikely as any imaginable, was over.

The next morning it was discovered that the sultana and the khan's many wives and children had escaped the palace sometime that night. Kaufmann was furious. Guards at the gate swore they must have got out through a sewer, "a task somewhat difficult," MacGahan thought, "seeing that no such thing as a sewer exists in Khiva." He wondered if he'd aided the escape unwittingly; perhaps seeing him sneak in under the noses of tower sentinels had emboldened the women to take that way out. Thinking it prudent to keep quiet, "I did not report my adventure to Kaufmann."

He concluded his observations of Khivan life with an interview of the khan, conducted through an interpreter. The ruler showed great curiosity about him, beginning with his origins. "America," the reporter explained.

"Not English, then?"

"Much farther away—over a great sea, four hundred days' march by camel."

They were in the palace's rather shabby throne room. It featured none of the carpets, tapestries, fine porcelain, precious stones, or pots of silver and hashish that MacGahan had seen in the harem; he suspected the khan was playing poor in order to support his claim that only the Yomuds could afford the czar's penalty. Puffing his hookah, the khan leaned in and inquired under his breath about American weapons, "what they cost and whether it would be difficult to get some." He asked MacGahan to draw a map of Europe. The reporter explained about the recent Franco-Prussian War, the fall of Louis-Napoleon, and the huge indemnity Bismarck had extracted from France. The khan, in his present circumstance, could relate: the story of the indemnity "touched him dearly."

He was curious about America's political system: "What astonished him most was that the American khan reigned only four years and that another was then elected in his place." Even a commoner like me could become ruler in America, MacGahan explained. The khan gave a skeptical look, "as if the eventuality was not likely to happen."

Asked about the notes he was taking, MacGahan said they would be soon published on the other side of the world. He did his best to describe oceangoing ships and an international telegraph system that "could send a message from Khiva to Bokhara in five minutes." This brought another guffaw—"I think he looked on me as a great liar."

In fact, it would be almost two months before MacGahan's Khiva dispatches began appearing in the *Herald,* after going by courier to Orenburg, by train to St. Petersburg, and by cable to New York. Bennett's Central Asia kick of six months earlier had cooled by that time. Relegated to a corner of the paper's international page, the dispatches were compressed to kernels, with few of MacGahan's detailed impressions. But he had reason beyond the *Herald* to continue his study. In July he'd received a letter, forwarded from the American Geographical Society, asking him to submit a paper on Central Asia. His youthful ambition to write a great book immediately revived.

The campaign against the Yomuds, spearheaded by Cossack cavalry and backed by machine guns, artillery, and tube rockets, began five weeks after Khiva's surrender. MacGahan believed Kaufmann had been tricked into doing the khan's dirty work. The task force commander, General Golovatchoff, agreed; he delayed advancing into Yomud territory to give them time to escape. The Yomuds were the largest of the region's Turkoman tribes, numbering almost sixty thousand people. Their central village combined *kibitka* tents and mud enclosures indicating transition from a nomadic to a settled life. Their arms consisted of swords, scythes, and matchlock muskets. When the first squadrons of Cossacks swept in and began torching the thatched roofs and piles of grain, terrified families piled their possessions onto horse carts and fled: "Five minutes afterward, the entire country was on fire." A soft rain pushed the smoke to ground level, where it hung in the air and turned the flames dark red. "This was war as I had never seen it before," MacGahan wrote. "It was a sad, sad sight."

Some Yomud horsemen approached for a parley. They couldn't understand why the Russians were attacking them. Golovatchoff recited Kaufmann's order that they pay the czar's indemnity. The riders dashed away with defiant whoops. Golovatchoff hesitated to send his cavalry after them, as the fleeing refugees were mostly women and children whom he had no wish to hurt. But after a moment, the general told the Cossacks to prepare to charge.

Each squadron formed up behind its standard bearer. The colors snapped in the wind. Horses and riders shifted impatiently. Meanwhile, "about two miles away, just disappearing over a ridge, was an indistinguishable mass of men, women, children, horses, camels, sheep, goats, and cattle, all rushing away in wild confusion." Prince Eugene of Leuchtenberg, a novice officer who anticipated great sport ahead, waved MacGahan over to join him at the head of his men. The order to advance passed up the line, and a thousand Cossacks moved out with lances upraised. Accelerating into a gallop, their thundering horses slalomed through livestock and discarded debris as they closed "like a tornado" on their quarry. Yomud tribesmen turned to confront them while their families and elderly scattered.

The first moments of contact, mingling Russians and nomads in a pandemonium of gunshots and thrusting lances, seemed almost a hallucination to MacGahan. His gaze flew among sights that became an unforgettable blur: "Here is a Turkoman with a bullet through his head; there a Cossack stretched out on the ground with a horrible saber cut on his face; then two women and four children sitting in the sand, sobbing piteously and begging for their lives." He called *"Aman"* to them, as if hearing "peace be with you" might console them in this chaos. He pulled up his horse to slow the impressions assaulting him. As the fighting moved away, dozens of Yomuds lay lifeless on the ground. One imperceptibly raised his head. "It is well the Cossacks have not discovered their trick of feigning death," MacGahan thought.

Not far away at least a hundred Yomuds were trying to escape across a marsh. Mothers carrying small children struggled in the chest-high muck to keep their bodies as shields between their children and the enemy. A "villainous-looking brute" among the Cossacks couldn't resist squeezing off a round to try to hit one of them. MacGahan lashed his face with a riding crop. As the man skulked away, MacGahan again called *"Aman"* to the terrified women. They didn't acknowledge him.

He watched them grope through the swamp toward the far bank.

Sketched by Frank Millet, these Russian Cossacks wear white summer uniforms and carry cavalry lances. At Khiva their instructions were to kill all the enemy, "whether they resisted or not," take everything of value, and burn the rest. "The Cossacks executed the order with a right good will," MacGahan wrote.

Twilight dimmed the sky. He reined his horse away. Russian policy was to spare women and children but to kill all the men. MacGahan watched four dismounted Cossacks methodically hack a young warrior to death in front of his family: "He has been beaten to his knees. He utters no word of entreaty. After what seems an age to me, he falls prone with a terrible wound in his neck."

Tube rockets shrieked overhead and exploded on the marsh's far bank. MacGahan heard screams within the billowing smoke and "looked in vain for the women and children I had seen in the water." He rode frantically along the shore until the haze thinned to reveal no Yomuds there. The fact was inescapable: "frightened by the rockets, they had thrown themselves in the water and drowned."

This opening engagement of Kaufmann's incursion ended after sundown in a lamplit medical tent. A Yomud boy was brought in with his scalp slashed to the bone. As the doctor dressed the wound, "his mother watched with wild, eager eyes. To her primitive mind, it was scarcely credible that the same people should first try to kill and then try to cure her son." She kissed the surgeon's hand. MacGahan later saw her in the desert with her son and infant daughter in a state of aftershock: "Near an overturned cart lay the wreck of her worldly wealth; not far away the dead body of her husband; and disappearing in the far distance, the routed ranks of her nation. She stood a picture of ruin and despair."

The next morning Prince Eugene, shaken by the previous day's one-sided slaughter, received "without any degree of zeal" orders to resume the destruction. By evening a long swath of country three miles wide lay charred and smoldering. The Cossacks had found most of the Yomud villages already abandoned. MacGahan was moved by their forlorn traces of daily life, "the marks of children's feet, the remnants of household work. Here they had lived in peaceful contentment, as isolated from the outside world as an undiscovered island in the South Pacific. But the torch was applied, and they learned all too dearly something of the great outside world."

The Yomuds struck back the next day. A swarm of riders charged the Cossack camp but fell back after losing a dozen men. The attack was a diversion; as it was occurring, a Russian observation post two hundred yards forward was overrun, its soldiers left naked and head-less for their comrades to find. MacGahan was grimly impressed: "It speaks well of the skill and audacity of the Yomuds."

When General Golovatchoff came up with his main force of infan-try and cannons, his hesitation in carrying out Kaufmann's order gave way to cold resolve. Three a.m. reveille called the army to march west, where the Yomuds were known to be massing. Sunrise streaked the sky behind the Russians, the receding night still dark in the direc-tion they headed. The air hummed with "strange agitation, almost electric." A riderless horse, its white flanks matching the Russian uni-forms, appeared out of nowhere and careened madly among the ranks, putting everyone on edge with its strange symbolism.

The Cossacks galloped out a half-mile ahead, creating a careless gap into which thousands of Yomuds suddenly charged with piercing shrieks. They penetrated the Russian ranks. Fighting became hand to hand. Golovatchoff went down with a shoulder wound, his chief of staff with a bullet in the brain. The confusion worsened when the returning Cossacks barreled into the mass of infantry. MacGahan compared the moment to "the ominous threatening atmosphere said to precede an earthquake; a low frightened murmur within the uproar, like the commencement of a cry of despair—we are on the verge of panic."

Breathless and disoriented, he spurred his horse to the edge of the melee. He realized he was on the enemy side of the field, with Yomud riders bearing down. He emptied his pistol at them and wheeled behind an infantry company deploying nearby. Exhilaration came over him as he realized he was momentarily safe.

"Fire!" came the order. Volleys erupted into the faces of the oncom-ing riders. Then "as if by magic the darkness rises and discloses the Yomuds flying over the plain in full retreat leaving behind broken bod-ies strewn about in great numbers." MacGahan wasn't alone in strug-gling to absorb what just had happened. "We were awed at the danger we had so narrowly escaped."

A native lay dead at his feet. He was barefoot and clad in a thin shirt. His hands clutched a hewn stick with a blade tied to one end. It was sobering to consider his desperate bravery in attacking armed troops with such a primitive weapon. "They were by no means an enemy to be despised," MacGahan thought.

At least one Cossack, stepping among the dead with his bayonet fixed to his rifle, perceived it differently: MacGahan "could see a wild scared light in his eye that reminded me partly of a crazy man, partly of a frightened child." The Cossack saw a Yomud twitch and slammed the bayonet into his chest. MacGahan's horrified gasp startled the man, who "slunk away without a word." The Yomud convulsed in the dirt, blood streaming from his nose and mouth. MacGahan "turned away sick at heart. The poor fellow was past all human aid."

Golovatchoff sent a detachment to sweep around to strike the Yomuds from behind. He ordered cannon shells lobbed in the general direction "as a signal" to give an idea of the enemy's whereabouts. The shells struck a ravine where several hundred families were hiding. Scores were blown to pieces along with their carts and belongings. Flushed from their shelter, the survivors spilled headlong across the plain, fleeing the pursuing Cossacks. Some stayed put, "either because they had no horses or because they trusted too much the clemency of the Russians." It made no difference—"they were overtaken and cut down."

The carnage was awful enough; "everywhere were bodies, bloody and ghastly." Worse was the sight of women and children watching while swarming Cossacks finished off their husbands, sons, and fathers. "They looked like poor dumb animals," MacGahan thought. "They expected to be treated as they knew their men would have treated the vanquished under like circumstances."

One woman sat on the ground cradling her dying husband. "She had no dread of the Russians," he wrote. "Grief had banished fear." Another looked up from the infant she held in her arms, threw back her shoulders, and raised her chin in defiance at the Cossack standing before her: "with closed eyes she waited, refusing to acknowledge the saber she expected would cut off both their lives together." The Cossack walked on. "Cases of violence towards women were very rare," MacGahan later said of the Russians in Khiva, a contrast to what he'd seen in France in 1871. "Their conduct was infinitely better than that of European troops in European campaigns."

Surveying the smoldering battlefield, he became expert in the demeanors of children who'd just seen their parents slaughtered. Some gave wrenching sobs, some looked merely bewildered, some watched the ongoing pillage with placid curiosity. He carried some injured orphans to the medical tent and placed others with random mothers who might care for them. One child wouldn't let go of him once he took her onto his saddle: "I cut a ridiculous figure riding along with the little barbarian's arms tightly clasped around my neck and her little queer-shaped head, covered in dust, lying on my breast." He freed himself and gave her to "a young and pretty woman with a bleeding face, torn robe, and woeful countenance that told its own story." He pressed some money into her hand. "She flung it back."

Moving out with the Russian troops, he took in a last sight. Three Yomud adults lay dead on the ground. Six children were nearby. The eldest, about eight years old, was already "engaged in making up a bed for them under a cart with bits of cotton and worn-out rugs, all that was left of their *kibitka*." MacGahan went over and offered him money. The boy turned away. "I have no doubt his little heart swelled with rage at the sight of me," the reporter wrote. "Twenty years hence, some white men will probably feel how well he learned to hate them."

The remaining Yomuds had dispersed. Rather than chase them around the desert, Kaufmann decided to use their example to pressure other Turkoman tribes to come up with the czar's money or endure the same fate. The £42,000 price tag was higher in comparative terms than what Bismarck had charged the French in 1871: "There was not enough coin in the country to pay this enormous sum, so they brought in horses, camels, and carpets to eke out the amount." It fell to the women to square the account. Heirloom bracelets and necklaces of beaten silver were laid out for tabulation and loaded onto carts bound for St. Petersburg. Wrote MacGahan, "It is sad to think with what pain these simple objects must have been surrendered to satisfy Russia's insatiable maw."

Kaufmann's work was done. His treaty with the khan established new terms of taxation and trade and outlawed, on paper at least, slavery in the region. It gave Russia eighty thousand square miles of Khivan territory and control of the Oxus River. The khan, thrilled to have his Yomud problem rectified and the indemnity paid off, was all smiles as he waved goodbye to the invaders. Staying in Khiva an extra day, MacGahan was awakened that night by so much gunfire he thought the fighting had resumed. But it was only locals celebrating victory over "the Great White Czar."

He'd stayed behind to help a twenty-nine-year-old cavalry colonel named Mikhail Skobelev finish a map of Khiva's outlying desert and the strategic location of its wells, in case the Russians ever had to return. Blue-eyed and blond, with a luxuriant beard, Skobelev was descended from a long line of generals. Rebelling from this tradition ("family never made men great," he said), he'd longed as a youth to become a poet. While studying in Moscow, however, his carousing incurred so much debt that his father yanked him out of school and put him in uniform in Central Asia. This bumpy start got worse when Skobelev lied about fighting a skirmish while leading a scout patrol near Bokhara. "Forty brigands killed and so on," reported the army's investigator into the incident, "though afterward it appeared there were no brigands at all." The young colonel had volunteered for the Khiva mapping mission to redeem himself, going undercover as a Muslim cleric. Flouting the faith that way risked tortures so extreme (being force-fed molten metal, say) that talk went around the Russian ranks that Skobelev's native guide must have said magic spells over him. "Now his life is charmed," people said. "Bullets can pass through him without doing any injury."

As he and Skobelev rode out of town to catch up with the Russian force, MacGahan marveled at how their sense of the place had changed: "Squalidness had changed to beauty. Residence of two months had given a familiarity that threw a tinge of melancholy over our departure." The mood of their former foes was equally surprising: "No one showed the slightest inclination to molest us. We rode on with as little apprehension as if we were a column of a thousand strong."

The Russian colonel was engaging company. He spoke perfect English, carried himself with screwball gentility ("an eccentric country squire," a friend later said), cited Byron and Shakespeare as his favorite writers, and spun tales of high and low society from the opera house to the barracks, royal courts to gypsy brothels. MacGahan's soft spot for colorful characters at once got him thinking the fellow was something rare. "Although he has not yet received the command of an army," he thought, "he will probably be heard of more than once in the future." The first indication of the prophecy's truth would come when Mikhail Skobelev received the Russian Empire's highest award for valor, the Cross of St. George, for his feat in mapping the Khivan wells. He would win the medal twenty-eight more times before he turned thirty-five, MacGahan cheering him all the way.

6

Pure and Savage Freedom
1872–1877

Existence under such conditions became intolerable. Life became
a blank, a thing not to be accepted as a gift. He determined to fly.

J. A. MACGAHAN, *Under the Northern Lights* (1876)

The doings of one correspondent in Central Asia were far from the
only thing on the mind of the owner of *The New York Herald*.
James Gordon Bennett, Jr., was now in his early thirties and eager
to put his stamp on the enterprise still identified with his late father.
He wanted the *Herald*'s success to be news in itself; his competitors
preferred to make him the story. But exposing his "amorous escapades,
sporting ventures, and brainless antics in high and low society" was
just the first salvo on the editorial pages aligned against him. Often
the criticism reached for themes of cosmic moralism that cast young
Bennett, like his father, as an agent of darkness bound to suffer one
day for his present good fortune.

The *Herald*'s competitors had painted Bennett Senior's lonely death
in 1872 as a validation of lifelong wickedness. When they described
his son at the funeral standing beside the casket, glowering behind
his handlebar mustache like an outlaw undertaker, the sinister con-
notation was clear. The death a year later of Bennet Senior's wife, of
whom little was known beyond her desire to escape her husband's
infamy by living in Europe, was likewise portrayed as fitting. "The
whole middle part of her body was consumed by confluent cancer,"
the *Tribune* reported salaciously. Her two children's absence from her
bedside made for righteous fodder: "Like her husband, she died in the
arms of mercenaries."

James Gordon Bennett, Jr., 1874. When Bennett took over *The New York Herald* from his ailing father after the Civil War, the paper was netting more than a million dollars a year in income, a sum equating to tens of millions today. The young publisher spent it recklessly. "Nothing can hurt the *Herald*," he said.

Retaliation for such jibes, which surely would have come from his father, wasn't part of young Bennett's makeup. Brash in every other part of his life, he was cautious in wielding the *Herald*'s editorial hammer. "Bennett has led a sensational life," Stephen Fiske said of his friend. "He has plenty of rivals ready to make the most of these episodes. But he is as nervously fearful of exposure as he is reckless in his escapades, and to protect himself from attack he drops all personal allusions for which his father was famous and sets his peers the fashion of editorial courtesy."

The old *Herald* had ridiculed high society, printing gossip as gospel and crying "hypocrite!" at the smallest lapse between behavior and preachment. Bennett Junior's revised policy was to flatter the rich, burnish their reputations, and hype their social occasions. Topping his small list of exceptions was Jay Gould. The financier's growing collection of telegraph networks (eventually including the biggest, Western Union) enabled him to gouge the *Herald* with high fees. Bennett retaliated by forming a cable company of his own. The resulting price war drained his and Gould's coffers and turned their dislike to venomous loathing.

Bennett mocked his rival as "the gold-gobbling gorilla of Wall Street" in the *Herald* pages. Gould counterpunched through the several papers he controlled. "I have known you many years," began one of his open letters to Bennett. "All that time your life has been one of shame, a succession of debauches and scandal. And however gentlemen might meet you in their clubs or hotels, not one would allow you to cross the threshold of his residence where virtue and honor are at stake." Pleased that his barbs were irritating if hardly impoverishing Gould, whose wealth far surpassed his, Bennett replied with a wink. "The proprietor of the *Herald* lost his reputation far before Mr. Gould was ever heard of," he wrote.

His editorial caution extended to city government. Critics said the *Herald*'s soft coverage of William M. "Boss" Tweed and other neighborhood kingpins who ran New York's notorious Tammany Hall racket of graft and patronage proved that Bennett was as corrupt as they were. But his neutrality was merely prudent. The *Herald* made a lot of money printing municipal announcements, income that Bennett didn't want to jeopardize. When politicians looking for favors couldn't manipulate him, their complaints showed the advantage to objective journalism posed by Bennett's egotism: he had no agenda but himself.

He went easy on his father's rival, Horace Greeley, when the *Tribune* founder died in November 1872. Greeley had called Bennett Senior's legacy "odious" after the old man's death five months earlier—but the son took little notice. Young Bennett likewise had refrained from ridiculing Greeley for accepting the nomination of a liberal splinter group of the Republican Party to run for president late in the 1872 campaign. Greeley lost in a landslide, helping the embattled Ulysses Grant win a second term. The defeat came two days after the death of Greeley's wife, a double blow that left him in despair whose only cure, as he saw it, was to return to managing his beloved *Tribune*. He vowed that he was finished with politics and would devote himself to "the progress of science, industry, and the useful arts." There was one problem: his ownership of the paper had diluted to a minority stake. Whitelaw Reid, the editor he'd installed three years earlier to replace John Russell Young, was now in charge. He told Greeley to stay home.

Greeley snapped. The brain fever that had felled him after the Battle of Bull Run returned. He wrote mad, woeful letters cursing Reid and himself. "I stand naked before my God the most hopelessly wretched and undone of all who ever lived," he wailed. "I have done more harm and wrong than any man who ever saw the light of day." He prayed for death, and after two weeks in a mental ward, he got his wish. He'd left instructions for a simple funeral but instead received a lavish procession down Fifth Avenue. "A Great and Good Man Gone," the *Herald* intoned, a generous assessment that brought Bennett credit for rising above the acrimony between Greeley and his father. But really it was no chore since the young man didn't care one way or the other.

Greeley's death marked the end of the *Tribune's* commitment to foreign reporting initiated by Young and Smalley in 1866. The paper's partnership with the London *Daily News* had dissolved after the Franco-Prussian War. Whitelaw Reid professed disdain for the competition for international headlines ("the field for advantages in the mere getting of news is about exhausted," he said), but in reality high cable costs had forced him to scale back. Making do with reprinting foreign news from other papers, he compensated by employing "better brains" to write commentary.

One of them was the novelist Henry James, who in the mid-1870s supplied the *Tribune* with reflections from Paris. In London the perfect man for the job was already well established. Thus did George Smalley continue the transformation from bureau chief to featured pundit that Young had encouraged; it would be his chief role through the rest of his long career. His weekly "London Letter" in the paper's revived Sunday edition let him discuss whatever interested him that week in politics, culture, or business. Beyond the freedom it afforded, he liked that his column was the first of its kind—as had been, he was fond of reminding people, the *Tribune's* foreign bureau in London, a precedent "other journals have since followed," he bragged.

Insecure about his stature, Smalley was increasingly dazzled by material prizes such as social class and generational wealth, qualities as old as Britain itself. The onetime radical now had an elegant home near Hyde Park and friends at London's highest levels. His former comrades in America groused that he seemed to prefer writing about "aristocratic drawing rooms" and "great people in great houses" rather than advocate for social reform. They wondered if he was becoming a snob.

Reid questioned Smalley's partygoing and the dent it put in his *Tribune* expense account. Smalley was defensive: "A great deal of my work could not have been done without it, which is the main reason for living the way I do and cultivating a certain sort of society." Though progressive commentators may have frowned on his Tory puff pieces, they were "perennial favorites" with readers, Reid admitted. And Smalley's high salary (now that the thrifty Greeley was out of the picture) was a bargain compared to what the *Tribune* had been paying to run reporters around Europe. Reid worried that his competitors would take notice of Smalley's popularity and try to snatch him away. In the case of the *Herald* especially, with its owner's deep pockets and lust for exclusive news, it seemed only a matter of time.

But Bennett's mind was elsewhere. He'd become obsessed with the unknown fate of the English explorer Sir John Franklin, who in 1845 had sailed the Canadian Arctic seeking the Northwest Passage to the Pacific Ocean and had vanished with more than a hundred crewmen. Search parties had found only some abandoned equipment and three bodies, providing an irresistible opportunity for an outsider to solve the mystery of what had befallen the expedition—an opportunity, in short, for Bennett again to upstage the Brits as he had with Stanley and Livingstone.

Mounting an Arctic quest under *Herald* auspices wasn't easy. Ultimately Bennett would try it twice, once in 1875 with the exploration ship *Pandora,* and again four years later with the same vessel, renamed *Jeannette.* Neither would turn up a thing on Franklin. For all his trouble, Bennett got only a deserted island in the East Siberian Sea named after him and a grudging obligation to honor his pledge to the *Jeannette*'s thirty-three crewmen that their families would be provided for if they didn't come back alive. It amounted to a sizable bill, for only ten of them did.

Another whim seized him in November 1873, when Spanish authorities in Cuba arrested and executed fifty-three Americans for smuggling weapons to Cuban revolutionaries aboard a New York–based vessel, the *Virginius*. Convinced war was imminent between America and Spain, Bennett cabled MacGahan, who'd settled back in Paris to write a book about his Khiva adventure, to come to Florida to discuss plans to cover the fighting. At the last moment, Spain defused tensions with an apology and $80,000 in compensation to families of the dead, leaving MacGahan stuck in Key West. Meanwhile, Bennett pulled the same haughty routine to which he'd subjected Henry Stanley when Stanley was riding high after the Livingstone triumph. By making MacGahan sit for days outside his office, "he wanted to give himself the airs of a grand pasha," the reporter wrote his wife in irritation. MacGahan wasn't having it: "I turned in my accounts and am leaving." Bennett was impressed with this show of gumption. In the *Herald*'s year-end review of world affairs, he credited MacGahan by name for his recent work in Central Asia—the highest praise the prickly publisher was capable of.

A year later, on November 9, 1874, Bennett got so antsy to create a splash for his paper that he took a desperate leap. New Yorkers awoke to the *Herald*'s front-page array of screaming banners:

AWFUL CALAMITY

Wild Animals Broken Loose from Central Park
Terrible Scenes of Mutilation
Savage Brutes at Large
Awful Combat Between Beasts and Citizens

The issue was packed with eyewitness accounts of people mauled by rampaging creatures from the Central Park Zoo. The breakout had started when the zookeeper stuck "Pete the rhinoceros" in the eye with a stick. The keeper was driven through the wall of the pachyderm pen impaled on the prong of Pete's horn. This provoked the lions and tigers to make their getaway, "their carnivorous instincts whetted by the smell of human blood." Other cages were smashed open in the commotion. Animals raged through the streets, and dozens of bystanders ("Benjamin P. Steiner, Pedro Velasquez, Ellen Lalor and three children . . .") suffered hideous deaths. Also killed were a porcupine, a baboon, two monkeys, four sheep, a prairie dog, a woodchuck, and Pete.

Responding quickly, the *Herald* story went on, police saved "hundreds of children in the vicinity of Thompson Square from being devoured. Had the same precautions been taken on the west side of town, the American buffalo and brown bear would never have accomplished so much fearful havoc." Many predators remained at large: "There is a sharp lookout for the black wolf. He looks so much like a Dutchman's dog he may escape detection until he commits some lamentable tragedy."

The paper sold out everywhere. Shop owners stood in their doorways brandishing firearms to repel the furry horde. A representative of *The New York Times* stormed into police headquarters on Mulberry Street to protest that the *Times* had received no official details of the calamity and so was unfairly kept from reporting it. The truth came out when people calmed down enough to read the story through to its concluding disclaimer. "Pure fabrication," *Herald* editors admitted. Anticipating a backlash, they justified the hoax as a public service intended "to test the city's preparedness to meet a catastrophe." But no backlash came. On the contrary, the story amused the city for weeks afterward. It even contributed to the nation's political discourse—after an editorial cartoon used a stampeding donkey and elephant to symbolize rancor between Democrats and Republicans, those parties' perennial mascots were born.

Bennett put out the claim that he'd read the *Herald* in total dismay that morning. The *Times* didn't buy it: "No such carefully prepared story could appear without consent of the proprietor or editor—always supposing that this strange newspaper even *has* an editor, which seems rather a violent stretch of the imagination."

Strange or not, the *Herald* remained a money machine. It padded its bottom line with uncensored personal ads ("the advertisements of abortionists!" critics said) while still besting its rivals in obtaining real news. When foreign dignitaries approached New York harbor, for instance, Bennett would send ships to meet them at sea and secure their first American interview. And in 1876 the *Herald* stunned readers with fourteen columns of exclusive coverage of the death of General

George Custer and more than two hundred cavalrymen at the Battle of the Little Bighorn. After hearing rumors of the disaster from army supply officers, *Herald* correspondents out west spent $3,000 of Bennett's money to wire the news east. Though the War Department and New York's other papers condemned it as another hoax, the *Herald's* popularity soared as the inconceivable notion of the dashing general cut down by savages proved absolutely true.

The *Herald* was the first New York paper to run a daily weather forecast. Beginning in the late 1870s, it supplemented its financial pages with information on local real estate; that Bennett owned large tracts of suburban land outside the city wasn't unrelated to the paper's focus on residential development. In foreign news the *Herald* also dominated, not least because the competition couldn't afford to keep up. Yet as with domestic politics, Bennett kept a neutral position that to his detractors seemed no position at all. "My foreign policy is simply this," he responded. "If a nation is friendly to this country, I wish the *Herald* to be friendly to that nation. If a nation shows an unfriendly policy, I wish the paper to adopt an unfriendly tone. This may not be patriotism, but it is the course I wish the *Herald* to follow."

His private frolics meanwhile rolled on. Shunned by Newport's elite for riding, on a bet, his horse through the Newport Reading Room, the resort's most exclusive club, he doubled down on his sacrilege by building a gambling casino across the street. He kept on permanent retainer Howe and Hummel, a law firm specializing in beating claims of "seduction under promise of marriage," and thus armed, he cut a carefree swath through New York's demimonde of prostitutes, actresses, and showgirls. Said to have "impartially annexed" the entire chorus line of the Lydia Thompson Burlesque Company, he particularly enjoyed its principal dancer, Pauline Markham. A curvy beauty with "a voice of velvet and the lost arms of the Venus de Milo," she was known for a move called "the Grecian bend" that had something to do with ancient Greek statuary and lots to do with bending.

Bennett's lifestyle usually didn't hinder his sharp-eyed control of *Herald* operations. But in 1876 he began to slip. This especially showed in his inattention to events unfolding in southeastern Europe, where tension between Balkan villagers and their Turkish rulers fueled protests and crackdowns that reportedly far exceeded—and this was saying something—the usual level of violence there. Russia had been waiting for a chance to invade the region and annex it into a Slavic union headed by the czar. The obstacle had always been Britain and France's joint resolve to thwart Russian expansion. Only a moral emergency graver than their strategic concerns could keep those nations on the Balkan sidelines. Muslims killing Christians might be the ticket.

It was shaping up as the kind of international fracas Bennett would normally have leaped to cover. But amid fresh heights of professional and personal fulfillment, he'd become distracted, falling victim to the cliché that just when a young man has everything going for him, he risks it all by getting married. The woman's name was Caroline May. They'd met in 1875 and now were engaged to wed. His footloose existence became a gauntlet of engagement parties and seasonal balls on the arm of a pristine heiress. Friends observed that Bennett's boozing increased with each passing day of bachelorhood. They didn't see a connection, however.

Returning from Central Asia to Paris in late 1873, MacGahan set to work expanding his Khiva article for the American Geographical Society into a full-length book. The result, *Campaigning on the Oxus and the Fall of Khiva,* an engaging narrative of arduous travel, exotic culture, and colonial war, brought MacGahan renown as "the Cossack Correspondent" when it was published in 1874. But as with Henry Stanley's best seller about finding Livingstone, it didn't endear him to Bennett, who, apart from disliking his minions gathering fame for themselves, was annoyed that in four hundred pages of narrative, his name wasn't mentioned once.

MacGahan's *Herald* pay was suspended while he worked on the book. He complained to the paper's representative in London, John Russell Young, but the best Young could do was offer to serialize the manuscript as its parts were completed. MacGahan's wife counseled her husband not to sign the contract; she was sure the book's success would finally free him from the *Herald* yoke. Young was disappointed. "I knew him fairly well," he later said of MacGahan. "I liked him very well."

The book's excellent reviews praised its humanizing portrait of Muslim nomads and its denunciation of Russian brutality. "As fascinating as a novel," said *Harper's* magazine. "It is worthwhile to know what romance and adventure and personal hazard are involved in making the daily paper we read so quietly at our breakfast table." Sales were good, but the lapse in MacGahan's salary was hard to make up. And Varia's money anxieties were worse than ever now that she was pregnant again after miscarrying a year earlier. She complained about her husband's love of nightlife and generosity to his faraway family. Recently he'd declined with regret a relative's request for a loan. "I would pawn the watch Bennett is going to give me," he wrote, "if I had it." The watch never came.

He did get a medal from the Russian army in recognition of his contributions at Khiva. He wanted literary respect, however. He tried writing a play, but his attempt to dramatize his experience in the Paris Commune fizzled. Strapped for money, he finally accepted a *Herald* assignment to cover unrest in Spain, where the so-called Army of the Pretender was trying to topple the government. Glad to have him back, Bennett flattered MacGahan by giving him a byline on his dispatches.

Spain's Carlist rebellion of 1873–76 revived MacGahan's romantic notions of people versus kings, republicans versus royalists—except now his sympathies were flipped. The self-professed Communard utterly fell for the flashy charisma of the revolt's leader, Carlos VII, strutting heir to a long line of claimants to the Spanish throne. Don Carlos's case to become king was based on sketchy blood links of generations earlier, Roman Catholic stridency in the face of secular liberalism, and the age-old enthrallment of Spanish peasants by grandiose royals. "The Carlists," MacGahan declared after meeting them, "have a flag, a faith, a belief, and the republicans have not. Call it religion, fanaticism, bigotry, ignorance, the fact remains that men with positive ideas, who know what they want, usually carry the day." He couldn't have been more wrong.

Wary of his swoon, MacGahan's editors ran a disclaimer alongside his ardent dispatches: "We think our correspondent has exaggerated the significance of the Carlists." He described their woven sandals, coarse tunics, and primitive weapons with a moistly pastoral eye, rebutted charges of their assassination of local officials and put a sympathetic spin on the "accidental" execution of a German reporter falsely accused as a spy. John Russell Young, in his travels for the *Herald*, had met the twenty-six-year-old Don Carlos and found him "dullish, courteous," but the star-struck MacGahan saw a dynamo. "Young and brave, fighting an unequal fight against fearful odds, he is every inch the old fashioned hero-king."

MacGahan leased his wife a villa in Biarritz, on the Bay of Biscay between Spain and France, where he could visit periodically as she neared her delivery date. Their son, Paul, was born on August 27, 1874, with MacGahan arriving an hour after the birth. He stayed two weeks before returning to the field, his sentiments for wife and child still warm. "How I love you," he wrote Varia in October. "How I would love to see the little one." Everything would be different now, including his eye for other women: "In the past I would have seized the opportunity to amuse myself in passing; now I avoid it. When one is accustomed to Château Lafitte of the finest vintage, it is difficult to accustom oneself to the taste of ordinary wine."

In November the *Herald* published a report that MacGahan had been arrested by Spanish police and subjected to "revolting indignities," namely confinement in a latrine trench. His release came after someone he'd recently befriended, "a beautiful creature, the daughter of the proprietor of my hotel," implored the American consul to intervene. MacGahan blamed himself for the episode. To have worn the Carlists' red beret while passing through a government checkpoint, he said, "was simply tempting the devil in the shape of a Chief of Police, arbitrary and brutal as police always are the world over."

The Carlist rebellion suffered a serious blow in December, when a military coup in Madrid installed Alfonso XII, son of the exiled Queen Isabella II, on the Spanish throne. Realizing that hostilities would eventually peter out, Bennett recalled MacGahan from the field while praising his *Herald* contributions: "MacGahan has, in the service of this journal, endured more than the usual perils of a correspondent but has always come through. The star of his good fortune is not dimmed yet." But months passed without another assignment, during which time the reporter struggled to turn his Spanish experiences into a book. But he needed turmoil to make the words flow. "Home life," Varia recalled, "presented such a crushing effect on his mind that his thoughts seemed chained." He tried moving his desk near their villa's noisiest window, pacing the room and flapping his arms like an athlete loosening up; "finally he would sit down to work again and the writing would go with rapidity."

His enthusiasm for the book died with the Carlists' soon-forgotten cause. He'd abandoned it entirely by March 1875, when Bennett approached with a proposition he'd been contemplating for years. He wanted MacGahan to join a *Herald*-sponsored expedition to find the fabled Northwest Passage from the Atlantic to the Pacific Ocean, a daunting dream that had claimed the lives of countless European adventurers. Bennett hoped the eight-thousand-mile voyage from Britain to San Francisco would in the process solve the thirty-year mystery of Sir John Franklin, the British explorer who'd been lost in the maze of islands, bays, and twisty straits of Canada's Arctic Archipelago. Franklin's countrymen had been unable to determine what happened to him. Now Bennett would do it for them.

MacGahan broached the matter gingerly with his wife, posing it in terms of finances rather than boredom. "He put the question in such a way," she recalled, "that I had to confess it was impossible not to go." He got her a train ticket to Moscow with their son and headed in the opposite direction for Southampton, England, where Bennett's hired vessel, the *Pandora*, was fitting out for the grueling voyage. His wife had no illusions: "The more I lived with him, the more I loved and understood him." In his later account of the trip, MacGahan gave his unvarnished reasons for going. "A world of pure and savage freedom," he wrote—"with such a prospect before me, shall I regret the chagrins, petty annoyances, and stifling atmosphere of the world I have left behind?" Though his rationale couldn't have been pleasant for Varia to read, it told her nothing she hadn't known already. "I forgave all," she wrote.

The great challenge of navigating the Northwest Passage was that

Spain's Carlos VII wore a signature red beret that his followers—and a bedazzled Januarius MacGahan—soon adopted. The Carlist rebellion of 1873–76 sought to topple a popular republic, but more important to the left-leaning correspondent was its leader's flashy charisma. "The ladies may be interested to know he will be the handsomest sovereign in Europe," MacGahan wrote.

vessels had to sail north of the Canadian Archipelago in order to enter its waterways that wind south and west from there toward the Pacific. The northward leg, up Baffin Bay between Greenland and Canada, extended into the Arctic Circle, where sailing was possible only in late summer. Once ships turned the corner at Lancaster Sound and headed southwest, pressure was on to reach the Pacific before the return route home was frozen over. As fall approached, a skipper had to weigh his chance of success against the certainty of being trapped if he waited too long to turn back. John Franklin, before he was beset by ice in 1845, had got farther than any attempt to date. Frozen in, he'd abandoned ship and trekked overland, disappearing in the vicinity of King William Island when winter descended full force.

Led by its captain, Allen Young, Bennett's *Pandora* voyage surpassed all previous Franklin search parties but was still 120 miles short of King William Island when ice floes twenty feet thick began to close around it. "It now became necessary to decide what we were going to do," MacGahan wrote. "If we lingered much longer it would not remain in our power to choose." Captain Young gave the order to turn back.

MacGahan was crestfallen. Before embarking on the trip, he'd arranged with a London publisher to write a book about it. With no rousing tale now to tell, he tried to disguise the letdown by highlighting "the pleasant side of Arctic life—pictures hastily sketched on a voyage that was remarkable only for its dash and rapidity. I hope the reader will not be disappointed." The first part of his narrative echoes the lighter moments of his book about Khiva, especially in his encounters with native women. It turns out that Kyrgyz maidens and the khan's bewitching sultana, Zuleika, had alluring counterparts on Greenland's Disko Island and among the Eskimos of Canada's far north: "They have the darkest, demurest eyes, and the loveliest complexion ever painted by sunshine and ocean spray." The glimpses of bosom MacGahan enjoyed in Central Asia were replaced in the Arctic with alluring flashes of thigh as the girls danced "like sylphs" to the *Pandora*'s band. "The motion caused her boots to settle down," he says of one partner, "leaving just above the knee a bit of leg exposed." It was hard not to look. "You have no conception of the small space you can dance in when you have no petticoats to deal with."

Of traditional codes mandating white aloofness to brown-skinned maidens, he cautioned readers, "Do not think I have exaggerated the charms of the fair girls of the Arctic. Do not turn up your nose at these pretty little barbarians and imagine yourself superior to them." Much as he had defended Turkoman nomads, he insisted that Arctic natives often showed more cultivation than Europeans. An Eskimo man, for example, aspired to support his family and as many neighbors as possible. But "when he becomes thoroughly civilized, no doubt this barbaric idea will be duly eradicated, and his ambition will be to slaughter the greatest number."

The *Pandora*'s crew were sad to leave their native hosts to continue the voyage: "We shall never see them again, but shall not soon forget the happy mirth and smiling faces that made the dreary desolation around them bloom as with roses." In the daily journal from which MacGahan constructed his narrative, "dreary desolation" increasingly dominated the mood—and in a surprise to himself and no doubt to his publisher, he decided to make it the theme of the book. He chose a title more ethereal than heroic to emphasize the point. In lieu of great adventure, *Under the Northern Lights* would be, he hoped, great literature.

The book spends dozens of pages trying to convey the existential despair of the frozen landscape. "There is something oppressive in this Arctic universe," MacGahan wrote. "Nature never smiles here. There is only the stillness of the grave." He strove for poetry but achieved mostly a thudding bluntness: "You begin to feel that instead of the world being created for you, you are an accidental atom, an insect, and that it is a wonder you have not perished long ago." What does it matter, he asks bleakly, if men are crushed by Nature? "When the ruin is complete the pendulum will swing back again, and there will be room for another race of men who know as little about us as we know of our predecessors, who will be in their turn someday wiped out, like the sum on a schoolboy's slate." His sense of irony, useful in journalism but less so in cosmic meditation, comes across as merely caustic under the killing weight of implacable glaciers and indifferent stars. "How pleasant are the ways of science!" he says sarcastically. "How cheerful and encouraging the prospects!"

Through most of the book's composition, he remained confident that it would bring him a new career as a serious writer. Reunited with Varia and his son in Paris in the fall of 1875, while he did his last revisions on the manuscript, he urged her to spend their savings to buy furniture and rent a bigger apartment. "He said he would not go far away any more," she wrote. She was thrilled when he tore up a letter from the *Herald* asking him to join another Arctic expedition, scheduled for the following summer. "He had achieved enough to do without the slavery of Mr. Bennett."

By the time he handed the book to his publisher, however, MacGahan had lost faith in it. He wrapped up its increasingly sullen meanderings in an odd, throwaway last chapter titled "A Tragedy." It tells of a favorite sled dog of the *Pandora's* crew that gets loose after the vessel returns to its home port. Local hunters kill it and charge people "sixpence a head" to see what they advertise as a mighty Arctic wolf. The dog's canine sled partner bays in sorrow for a few days, but like any small-minded bourgeois is eventually mollified with treats from the local butcher. "He has now adopted the ways of civilization," MacGahan writes sourly, "and does not seem to regret the change." He and the dog differed in this last regard—domesticity soon began to crush

This image of the *Pandora,* from MacGahan's 1876 book about the vessel's Arctic voyage, captures the dread of impassable ice that burdened every expedition through the Northwest Passage. The vessel turned back due to dangerous conditions, and MacGahan was forced to write "a book about nothing" to fulfill his publishing contract.

MacGahan's spirit, as it had before he left on the *Pandora*. And then the reviews came out.

Saturday Review, which could make or break a book, was typical. The lyrical flights that MacGahan had hoped would give the story artistic power had fallen flat. Said the critic curtly, "In the volume with which we now have to deal, from a literary point of view, there is not much to be said. It is augmented by several chapters made up of tolerably pertinent information extracted from other books." MacGahan took it hard. Suddenly employment with the *Herald* didn't seem so bad. He wrote his mother what he was reluctant to tell his wife: "The truth is that I have had the best of luck and best kind of work on the paper. I would have no reason to complain if I could get home oftener. But we can't have everything at once. I should be content with good health, good pay, pretty easy work, and a little glory."

As if sensing from afar MacGahan's vacillations, Bennett, escaping briefly from the constraints of his engagement to Caroline May, showed up in Paris in June 1876 to push his latest idea of this time seeking the Northwest Passage from the Pacific side. "Gird up your loins!" he urged MacGahan. "If you succeed you will eclipse Stanley, Livingstone, and any former explorers whether African or Polar."

MacGahan wanted another job with the *Herald* but not that one. He referred Bennett to a recent story in London's *Daily News* that quoted a telegram from Constantinople: "Dark rumors have been whispered during the last month of horrible atrocities committed in Bulgaria. Reliable estimates of men, women, and children massacred ranged from 18,000 to 30,000, with upwards of a hundred villages wiped out." These mass killings by Muslim death squads had supposedly occurred last April, but only now were details surfacing. If true, MacGahan said, Russia would use the premise of Christian rescue to invade and take over Bulgaria. Czar Alexander was on record as calling the Ottoman Empire "the sick man of Europe." Now his massive army might have an excuse to bring the cure.

Bennett scoffed. He wasn't interested in spending big money to cover a small war that no doubt would end as soon as it started. Their ensuing argument concluded with MacGahan quitting the *Herald*.

Bennett went home to New York to prepare for his wedding and to plan the Arctic venture. Three years later his vessel, the *Jeannette*, would sail from San Francisco, only to get crushed in the Arctic ice and lose almost all its men. His marriage engagement fared much the same.

The American painter Francis Davis Millet was as suited to modern times as he was to the nineteenth century. Born in Massachusetts in 1846, he seems in no way dated today. Photographs and portraits suggest a relaxed masculinity that was complex but not anxious, fatalistic but good-natured, and driven to high achievement in two such disparate fields—fine art and war reporting—that it's hard not to imagine similar dichotomies ruling much of his life. His friend Henry James said as much when he called Millet's brilliant career "checkered, with opposites much mingled in it." Millet would have agreed. Following a brief but harrowing stint in war correspondence, he went on to have a family, achieve world renown as a painter and muralist, and acquire

Frank Millet, 1875, all his life fought "a battle of Puritan habit and aesthetic experiment," said his friend Henry James. The early experiments were artistic and sexual, but at age thirty Millet took a leap that not even his most avant-garde friends saw coming. "Great fun!" he wrote from the Russian-Turkish battlefront in 1877. "I am quite warlike now. You wouldn't know me."

an elegant Cotswold home that became a thriving salon for American artists in Britain. Yet he was always impatient for escape. Said his granddaughter, "Only in flight where movement blurred did he ever seem at ease."

Frank, as he was called, excelled in school. When his physician father signed on as a surgeon for the Union Army in 1864, Millet helped him tend Confederate prisoners in the teeming prison camp near Belle Plain, Virginia. Amputations were routine. "Went to draining wounds and picked half a cup of maggots out of a man's leg," young Frank wrote in his journal. "This afternoon we amputated five stumps and fingertips." Later some would suggest that his splashy use of red in his early paintings derived from his time in the surgical station.

In the spring of 1864, he enlisted in the army on a hundred-day term as a drummer boy. He saw no combat, but in describing regimental life, he laid a foundation for his future reporting. One day he observed three soldiers straddling a wooden pole. The first wore a sign on his back: "I stole from and abused a woman. I am a disgrace to my uniform." The second also wore a sign: "Same like." And the third: "Me too." Showing the same offbeat sensibility, Millet's journal entry on the occasion of his leaving the army and going home to attend Harvard was only this: "Today was election day. Many of our boys voted, some more than once."

A summer job after his junior year, to paint an advertising sign for a local cotton gin, sparked an ambition to become an artist. Dr. Millet endorsed his son's dream despite its taint of "worldliness and the devil" among their New England circle of family and friends. After a few postgraduate months working in the newsroom of the Boston *Courier,* the young man went to Belgium to study painting at the Antwerp Academy, solidifying a career leap whose appeal to him, he later admitted, was based mostly on its sheer unlikelihood.

He worked hard at the academy, bragging of the many more hours he spent in the studio than his classmates. Yet his success there seemed effortless. When he became the first American ever to receive its gold medal in 1873, it was almost a letdown to him. He would later observe wistfully that Vincent van Gogh, who would attend the academy a decade later, was ignored by its professors, rebelled against its rigid traditions, and went on to become an artist of true greatness, whereas Millet was merely rich and successful.

After Antwerp, Millet's life took some odd turns that in retrospect look willful, as if he sensed the smooth path of his natural ability and was determined to break free. He had two guides in the effort, American gentlemen of talent and stature, both several years older than he, whose particular quirks fitted them well to Millet's search for direction.

The first was Charles Francis Adams, Jr., great-grandson of John Adams and grandson of John Quincy Adams. Though of considerable accomplishment in his own right, Charles was quick to insist he'd never lived up to his family legacy. "It seems to have required a degree of skill on my part to escape the great opportunities fortune flung my way," he wrote in his 1914 autobiography. "That I failed, and failed woefully, goes without saying; for it was I!" Decorated for valor in the Civil War, he spoke only of his experience at Antietam and Gettysburg. "The mere utterance of those names stirs the imagination. Visions arise of attack, repulse, hairbreadth escape, carnage, and breathless suspense. There was on those occasions all of these, but not in my case." Adams slept through both battles, lulled to drowsiness

Charles Francis Adams, Jr., Civil War general, railroad president, and member of one of America's most prestigious families. In supporting Frank Millet, whose 1876 painting of Adams is shown here, he urged the painter to pursue a path of personal and artistic daring. Millet's foray into war correspondence was one result.

by the rumble of cannons while waiting for his regiment to be called into combat. Terrible history was made a few miles away while he and his men, weary from marching, gratefully got some rest: "It was not heroic; but it was, I hold, essentially war, though by no means war as imagined in the work-room of the theoretic historian."

Adams likewise downplayed his subsequent twenty years in the railroad business, including almost a decade as president of the Union Pacific, calling them "years of waste. My office became a prison house." He was relieved when Jay Gould, who controlled the company, "ejected" him in 1890. He devoted the rest of his life to supporting the Massachusetts Historical Society and his alma mater, Harvard. "Looking back, I see with clearness my limitations," he wrote. "I have accomplished nothing compared with my ancestors; but on the other hand, I have had a much better time in life. In this respect I would not change any of it."

He may have taken his underachievement in stride, but in mentoring Frank Millet, he was a taskmaster demanding perfection. He insisted that Millet aim for nothing less than artistic immortality. "By severe lessons we learn the most," he counseled the young man, posing himself as a cautionary example. "I was deficient in times of challenge."

They first met in 1873, when Adams was a delegate to the Vienna

Exposition of International Culture, with Millet assigned as his secretary. Adams took an instant shine to his assistant, whom he described as "slender, boyish, companionable." During their summer working together, he noted Millet's "dangerous facility for doing many things extremely well" and advised him that to be a true artist, the key was "striking high instead of grubbing low." Millet subsequently embraced "dear old Bohemia" in vagabond journeys north through Scandinavia and south to Italy, where he rented a studio in Venice and tried to stretch his art beyond merely popular realms. "Imitation comes too easy to me," he wrote Adams. "I have learned from you that there is more to be struck for than present gain." Adams worried about the risks inherent in the artistic manifesto he'd preached. But he believed, for his protégé if not for himself, that the less traveled road was best. He called Millet "a rare flower of peculiar grace and attraction— a New Englander but not of New England, of native growth but yet an exotic."

New degrees of exoticism entered Millet's life in the form of Charles Warren Stoddard in 1874. A roving correspondent for the *San Francisco Chronicle,* Stoddard, thirty-one, published poetry and travel journals filled with a buoyant homoeroticism that today marks him as one of the most candidly gay American writers of the nineteenth century. In describing friendships and affections formed during his travels, he used a thin code of gender blurring and coy confession ("I act as my nature prompts me") that was more playful than paranoid. He enjoyed the game of signaling male fellowship to some readers and male sex to others, depending on whether they were "respectables," as he put it, or likeminded men who might get his true meaning "as few may be able to."

Frank Millet was one of those men. He and Stoddard shared an instant recognition after bumping into one another at the Venice opera. "We looked at each other and were acquainted in a minute," Stoddard recalled wryly, adding that they then became "almost immediately very much better acquainted." The two shared Millet's flat through the winter of 1874–75, whereupon Stoddard resumed his roaming ways. Millet, if not exactly distraught (he admitted to being only "middling faithful"), missed his "companion-in-arms." He wrote

Stoddard, "Put yourself in my place. It isn't the one who goes away who misses, it is the one who stays. Empty chair, empty bed, empty house." They exchanged teasing, tender letters for more than two years before crossing paths again, by which time their ardor had adopted the decorum of conventional friendship.

The taste of outlaw independence sparked by Adams's artistic incitements and Stoddard's sexual ones made Millet's return home to Massachusetts in 1875 unbearable for him. Squeezed by "a thousand vulturous individuals who suck the vitality out of me in a thousand different ways," he longed to resume the life of a struggling, idealistic artist. His talent got in the way. Mark Twain, about to rocket to fame with the publication of *The Adventures of Tom Sawyer,* saw some murals on which Millet had assisted at Trinity Church in Boston and asked him to paint his portrait; the author William Dean Howells later called it one of the best likenesses of Twain ever done. Deluged with follow-up offers for society commissions, Millet made a break for "the old Bohemian life" and headed for Paris, taking a studio in Montmartre and hanging out with a crowd he characterized obscurely to his family as "a different set of friends."

When masterpieces didn't flow from his brush, he took another leap in 1877. His next frontier was Bulgaria, a land ruled by the Turkish sultan and coveted by the Russian czar. As tensions there grew, newspapers had begun looking for reporters to send. John Russell Young, who'd met Millet and "talked art" with him at the Vienna exposition four years earlier, recommended him to the *Herald* editors in New York.

In April 1877 Russia declared war against the Ottoman Empire on humanitarian grounds—pretense, many said—of saving Christian Slavs from Muslim persecution. Millet got an armband stamped "journalist" and went to join the Russian army massing in Romania just north of the Bulgarian border. Russian commanders welcomed foreign reporters as a means to publicize their certain glory. They showered them with field clothing, invited them to dinner in their luxuriously appointed tents, and even gave them sneak peeks at the czar's attack plan, which commenced in June when the Russian army crossed the Danube River into Turkish-held Bulgaria.

The operation went off without a hitch in a slick display of engineering and logistics. Bulgarian villagers welcomed their liberators with flowers and parades. Millet loved it. "There is style and beauty here," he wrote after dining with other reporters at the foot of an abandoned Turkish fortress. A stream gurgled nearby, and the night air was cool. A gypsy band played for them, "wild looking chaps with fiddles. We had them play their native music, which they did with unequaled spirit and enthusiasm. No music has ever touched me more."

Returning to their tents for the night, the reporters watched the unloading of wagons full of table linens and shiny utensils for the Russian officer corps. One of Millet's American colleagues, a man about his age but with a limp, a graying beard, and eyelids etched with lines, gave a dry laugh. "A fool's paradise," he scoffed. "Our path is strewn with flowers and blessed by priests, but it's all one stupid muddle."

Millet didn't understand.

The stranger explained, "Russia's professors of war have been playing cards for years—and now they'll direct an army of 300,000 stout souls." He shook his head. "I'm afraid it's madness."

Millet went to bed with an uneasy feeling. He was still getting to know the other correspondents, but this one had a vaunted reputation for courage and candor to go along with his wide experience. He was J. A. MacGahan, late of *The New York Herald,* now of London's *Daily News*—the man who'd started this war.

7

Red Hands

1876–1877

The sight of human suffering soon blunts the sensibilities of anyone who lives with it, so that he is at last able to look upon it with no stronger feeling than that of helplessness. Only novelties in horrors will excite his feelings.

FRANCIS D. MILLET, *A Capillary Crime and Other Stories* (1892)

John Robinson, manager of *The Daily News*, had come a long way from his snap rejection, six years earlier, of George Smalley's ideas about pursuing news with American vigor. The paper's rise in influence resulting from its collaboration with *The New York Tribune* during the Franco-Prussian War had positioned it as a liberal counterweight to the London *Times*, which upheld the sternest traditions of Fleet Street. When *The Times* declined MacGahan's request to work there after leaving the *Herald*, fearing his "reputation for sensational proclivities," Robinson immediately hired him to investigate the Bulgarian rumors.

Robinson's agenda was more than journalistic. His paper was a leading critic of the conservative government of Prime Minister Benjamin Disraeli, whose support for the Ottoman Empire as a block to Russian expansion superseded his distaste for the sultan's despotic rule. Disraeli's priority was to stabilize the Balkans, the eastern Mediterranean, and trade routes to India, concerns that had underscored the so-called Eastern Question for decades. Turkey was Britain's friend in that effort, he insisted, and liberal hand-wringing about its internal affairs was naïve in the face of the region's true threat—Russia.

The prime minister was a favorite of Queen Victoria's for the emphasis he placed on imperial interests; his ladling of charm and praise on the widowed queen flattered her sense that she *was* the British Empire and he its staunchest defender. Disraeli's liberal predecessor, William Gladstone, had brought ethical considerations to foreign policy that Victoria viewed as extraneous and the British public as weak-minded. Since being voted out of office two years earlier, Gladstone had watched Disraeli widen his popularity by moving to the middle of the political spectrum with reforms in health and labor. As a result, he and his liberal colleagues had struggled to find a line of attack on the conservatives. The prospect that Disraeli's Turkish friends were committing crimes against humanity was a long shot worth pursuing.

Edwin Pears, *The Daily News*'s correspondent in Constantinople, had sent a telegram about the atrocities that appeared in the paper on June 23, 1876. Disraeli had been flippant about its grotesque charges, asking why on earth the Turks would use torture when everyone knew they "generally terminate their connection with culprits in a more expeditious manner." Gladstone, a political graybeard whose dogged sense of righteousness annoyed the glib prime minister, didn't laugh. He pressured Parliament to seek an independent inquiry into the rumors.

MacGahan was already on his way to Philippopolis (Plovdiv today), in southern Bulgaria. His travel mate from the first leg of his Khiva journey, Eugene Schuyler, was there on assignment from the U.S. State Department to assess any danger to American missionaries. Together with an English government agent, Walter Baring, they rode into Bulgaria's mountain villages to find out what had happened there four months earlier. "I came in a spirit of scientific inquiry," MacGahan wrote on July 28, "and especially made a large allowance for the gross exaggerations of the Christians."

His companions hoped to cut through the hysteria and make casualty estimates based on eyewitness testimony and evidence such as burned homes or human remains. "This necessitates traveling up to fifteen hours a day over roads the best of which are nearly impassable," MacGahan wrote. But the physical strain was nothing compared with hearing the survivors' heartrending stories: "It is this that makes the task of Mr. Baring and Mr. Schuyler one which they will hardly care to undertake again."

MacGahan too was affected. "I fear I am no longer impartial," he fretted. "There are certain things that cannot be investigated in a judicial frame of mind." He wanted to stay objective, but a typical transcript from one village conveyed staggering volumes of pain:

"How many were in your family?"

"Ten."

"How many remain?"

"Two."

"How many in yours?"

"Eight."

"How many remain?"

"Three."

"How many in yours?"

"Fifteen."

"And remain?"

"Five."

He admired his companions' fortitude in taking these depositions without recoiling from their underlying frightfulness. As the estimated death toll shot past 15,000, MacGahan could stand it no longer: "I shut my ears and say, 'This is enough! I do not want to hear more!'"

Ultimately he would leave the statistics to Schuyler and Baring and play a different role. His whole career, with its interplay of curiosity, daring, and advocacy, had prepared him for it—from fighting bullies as a boy to falling into ridiculous love with impossibly foreign women; from feeling shame as he watched Communards die in the street to feeling respect for the Turkoman orphans who'd refused his pity and money. "For my own part," he wrote now, "once the enormous number killed is admitted, I do not care to inquire further. Fifteen thousand is enough; no mere increase in a statement of round numbers can add to the horror of the thing. It is only in the recital of details accompanying the butchery that the mind can grasp and understand the fearful atrocity of the business." True to his word, his next series of dispatches would offer "a recital of details" such as newspaper readers had never seen before. They were as Technicolor in a sepia age, vivid, raw, and sickening.

The stage was set on the evening of August 1. MacGahan was in

Peshtera in the Western Rhodopes, a rugged mountain range full of caves, waterfalls, and deep gorges. Dozens of refugee women from the village of Batak, a four-hour ride north, swarmed around him. Moments before, Eugene Schuyler had snubbed a Turkish "mudir" trying to forbid them from going to Batak the next morning. The official had stomped off angrily. "As soon as he went away," MacGahan reported, "what appeared to be the population of the whole town seemed to flock to the courtyard, anxious to shake hands with us." He listened with pity and some skepticism. Nothing could be as bad as they claimed; their troubles surely would pass. "Vain hopes, and, I fear, vainer promises," his dispatch concluded.

When he and his companions started out the next day, sixty women, many accompanied by children or carrying them in their arms, followed; in time a trailing throng of almost five hundred accumulated along the way. "These were women who had escaped," he reported. "They might have returned long ago, but their terror was so great that they had not dared without the presence and protection of a foreigner." Approaching Batak, a village of nine hundred homes, the women began a chilling, high-pitched wail, aware, as the riders leading them were not, of what awaited them. "Such a sound as their united voices sent up to heaven I hope never to hear again," MacGahan wrote.

At the village outskirts, his horse stepped on a human skull in the weeds. At once he began scanning the ground with alarm. More skulls, then piles of skulls and half-clothed skeletons, became visible within the tangled foliage, coming into view like a ship's wreckage emerging from a receding tide.

In the first large heap, the skeletons wore tattered remnants of skirts and underclothes. The skulls lay a distance away—more brownish than bleached, too fresh to have been fully weathered, many with long hair attached and banded with colored kerchiefs. The implication was obvious: "These women had all been beheaded."

The warm air thickened as the men spurred their horses forward. MacGahan shared his dread with his readers: "You feel it is time to turn back; that you have seen enough." But by then his readers would have wanted to know everything, and he didn't disappoint:

"Let me tell what we saw at Batak."

In his *Daily News* account, MacGahan interspersed his moment-by-moment telling ("now we approach the schoolhouse; it is beginning to be horrible") with expositions on the nature of the villagers and their attackers. The Bulgarians, he explained with not a little design, "instead of the savages we have taken them for, are a hardworking, industrious, honest, civilized, and peaceful people." Inspired by protests over Turkish taxation in neighboring Serbia earlier that spring, several villages had mounted a spontaneous rebellion, "and a more foolish one could hardly be imagined, as each adopted the mad plan of defending itself separately." Some Turkish tax collectors were killed, along with two of their wives, who were accidentally shot while fleeing in a carriage. "The Turks themselves do not claim more killed," but as a warning to other troublemakers, Constantinople decided to deliver a memorable penalty.

An ambitious local chieftain named Achmed Agha embraced the assignment. His paramilitary militia, the Bashi-Bazouk, were Circassian tribesmen driven here from across the Black Sea by the same crushing style of Russian expansion that MacGahan had witnessed in Khiva. The Bulgarians were prosperous compared to the Circassians, presenting opportunities for looting as well as murder, which, for the benefit of his British readers, MacGahan placed in the context of religious fanaticism as he interpreted it: "When a Muslim has killed a certain number of infidels, he is sure of paradise no matter what his sins may be. Mohammed probably intended that only armed men should count, but ordinary Muslims take the precept more broadly, and count women and children as well."

But this chance to collect tickets for heaven didn't explain the zeal of the Batak annihilation. The Bashi-Bazouks' loyalty to the Ottoman Empire carried a useful edge of blood hatred for all Christians, thanks to the mass graves and desolation the Russians had made of the Circassian homeland—historians estimate the number of Circassians wiped out by the Russians in the preceding decade at more than a half a million. Thus they brought an extra intensity to their work in the sultan's behalf. In a scenario that played out in more than sixty villages, Agha offered Batak mercy if its people renounced their misbehavior, agreed to pay their taxes, and handed over their weapons. Once the concessions were extracted, "it was now the time of the saber."

The Batak operation lasted four days. It could have been accomplished faster, but Agha's irregulars took their time in certain aspects. Men and boys were killed quickly, most of them stabbed, shot, or beheaded, others herded into buildings to be burned en masse, others left to bleed on the ground after having their hands and feet cut off. Infants were killed in a somewhat casual way, thrown alive onto fires or skewered on bayonets. Survivors told MacGahan that mothers had to collect the children's heads and carry them in their aprons like cabbages, to be counted by Agha in the village square.

Two hundred girls were culled out the first day and kept apart for the duration. "During this time," MacGahan reported, "they suffered all it was possible that girls could suffer at the hands of brutal savages. The procedure seems to have been as follows: They would seize a woman, strip her to her chemise, then as many of them as cared would violate her, and the last man would kill her or not as the humor took him." Hearing the same testimony from "many women who had passed through all parts of the ordeal but the last," MacGahan came to understand that only the burning desire to have their agony known could overcome their cultural shyness. The few exceptions to this wrenching disclosure alerted him to the sense of shame the women had to suppress in order to speak honestly. In a village called Avrat Alan, for example, they all shook their heads when MacGahan and the investigators asked if they'd been raped. But as the men were leaving the next day, a deputation of older women brought a letter bearing dozens of signatures attesting that although they were hesitant to admit it aloud, "scarcely a woman in the place had escaped outrage."

The victims were as young as ten years old, many of them assaulted in the presence of parents and siblings. "I should perhaps beg pardon of my readers for dwelling on these harrowing details," MacGahan acknowledged, "but I am not writing for children, but for men and women." He was writing to one man specifically: "Prime Minister Disraeli will keep prating about exaggeration. The crimes that were committed here are beyond the reach of exaggeration."

His Batak discoveries culminated at a pond behind an abandoned sawmill, "a horrid cesspool, with human remains floating about or lying half exposed in the mud." He held a wad of tobacco under his nose to mask the stench. The sight compels his report's most piercing passage as he puts himself in the place of the victims, imagining their last moments, the last things they saw: "Little baby hands stretched out for help; babes that died wondering at the bright gleam of the sabers and the red hands of the men who wielded them; children who died shrieking with terror; young girls who died begging for mercy; mothers who died trying to shield their little ones, all lying there together, festering in one horrid mass."

The shocks kept coming through the rest of the day—piles of corpses, piles of skulls, and endless tales of slaughterhouse butchery that had left the ground soggy with gore and the sword arms of the attackers dripping blood from elbow to wrist. "Horrors upon horrors," he wrote. Schuyler and Baring put the number killed in Batak at 7,000. Wondering why Turkish authorities hadn't tried to conceal the evidence in hastily dug ditches, as they had in other towns, MacGahan ventured an answer: "This village was in an isolated place, difficult of access. They never thought Europeans would go poking their noses here, so they cynically said these Christians are not even worth burial, let the dogs eat them."

He spent the night of August 2 at the nearby village of Tatar Bazardzik. There he wrote twenty-eight paragraphs in a single seething rush. A nightmarish read even today, the report ends with a vision of the female skeletons, "coolly beheaded under the smiling canopy of heaven," lying beside the path leading out of town. Its last lines again call out the prime minister: "Mr. Disraeli was right when he remarked that the Turks usually terminate their connection with prisoners in a more expeditious manner. At the time he made that very witty remark, these young girls had been lying here many days."

Before seeing Batak, MacGahan had felt uncertain about telling its traumatized survivors that times would improve, justice would come. But his sense of purpose grew with each subsequent dispatch he cabled to London. Agha and other officials who'd overseen the killing had been promoted for their good service. MacGahan vowed to bring

Frank Millet called the Bashi-Bazouk militia, a member of which he painted here, "the Ku Klux Klan of Turkey." In 1878 he brought back to Paris the uniform and weapons of one. The dagger had blood and hair on it, he wrote, "captured from an old Bashi-Bazouk who boasted to have killed with it two hundred noncombatants."

them down. "I want the people of England to understand what these Turks are," he wrote. "If we are to go on bolstering this tottering despotism, let us do it with open eyes and a knowledge of the fact; let us see the hideous thing we are carrying."

His stated goal was to shame Turkey's allies into not interceding should Russia invade. And he didn't want to hear about diplomacy— "it is utterly impotent." London's *Saturday Review,* a conservative organ, dismissed MacGahan's emotionalism as another example of "that romantic school of journalism to which the Americans are accustomed." The skepticism only inflamed him. Addressing British readers and policy makers directly, he wagged his finger like a righteous preacher rather than, as the *Spectator* characterized him, "a damned Yankee newspaper fellow" employed until only recently by the execrable *New York Herald.* "You must find another solution for the Eastern Question," he warned, "or another solution will find you."

Schuyler, no less outraged by what he'd seen, set about forming an international commission to protect the Bulgarians, rebuild their villages, and punish their persecutors. MacGahan was skeptical. "Will Mr. Schuyler succeed in having these measures carried out?" he asked rhetorically. "I do not think it. The comfortable old gentlemen who are directing the destinies of Europe are too well fed to care for these wretched women and children."

He had a different notion of what was required. In talking with his colleagues, with the Bulgarians, and even with the Turks, he was adamant: "In less than a year you shall see soldiers of the czar here." More than a prediction, it was a promise.

Emily Anne Beaufort Smythe, Viscountess Strangford, took her newspapers in the breakfast room of her home on Chapel Street in London's prestigious Park Lane district. A longtime liberal yet no fan, for personal reasons, of Prime Minister Disraeli, she particularly favored *The Daily News.* She was, at forty-one, a woman of some worldliness. Reports of misdeeds in a faraway place might upset her but would hardly floor her.

The August 2 dispatch from Batak was different. It made you participate in its revelations of mass murder and rape, crimes hardly unheard of in history but far from typical fare in the newspapers of Victorian England. Its author revealed himself in everything but name. His eyes saw, his stomach turned, his rage boiled. By the end of the piece, thousands of Britons, Lady Strangford included, shared those sensations. Within two weeks of reading the story, she'd established the Bulgarian Peasant Relief Fund and begun hitting up her friends for donations—of *cash,* she insisted, not the usual "cheap frippery, bits of soiled finery, and odd gloves" emptied out of attic trunks for the benefit of poor folks. In a month she collected £10,000, worth more than half a million pounds today, to be distributed by her in Bulgaria.

What was conventional in Emily's beauty—she was petite, with brown hair, big eyes, and regular Anglican features—gained allure by how she suppressed it. In 1876 she'd been seven years a widow. While not one to wear permanent black, she exuded, in her garb and manner, a stately withdrawal from the world of romantic projection. Her husband, Percy Smythe, Eighth Viscount Strangford, had died at forty-three from tuberculosis contracted while serving as a diplomat in Turkey during the Crimean War. They had no children. His older brother, George Smythe, viscount number seven, had died childless in 1857, so the 240-year-old Strangford line was extinct even as Emily continued to live and breathe. Knowing her legacy marked the last impression on earth of a noble Irish peerage, from the day her husband died she'd devoted herself to its upkeep.

Emily had thrown herself into social causes as a way to cope with bereavement. She'd volunteered in a London hospital, written a first aid manual for young wives and mothers, and founded a charitable society to provide nurses for the poor. The daughter of an admiral, she'd traveled widely all her life, publishing a memoir of a trek through the Middle East in her early twenties and, as a newlywed, a breezy account of what for titled Victorian aristocrats was roughing it aboard a yacht in the Adriatic Sea: "We were three ladies and three gentlemen with two tents, a cook, and two servants. The gentlemen pitched the tents and superintended the saucepans while the servants looked on and drank up the wine and brandy."

Emily's devotion to her late husband was legendary. An expert on foreign affairs, he'd panned her Middle East travelogue in 1862 as the work of a tourist-dilettante. She'd confronted him with a public scolding, after which, charmed, he'd proposed to her. When her book about their Adriatic honeymoon came out, she appended a chapter written by her husband. Titled "Chaos," it criticized British hypocrisy in exploiting Turkey's strategic alliance while simultaneously denigrating its culture and Muslim religion. "The danger with us is lest, in over-zeal for the name of Christianity, we play fast and loose with the morality of Christianity," the viscount wrote.

Emily edited and published his papers after his death. These included an influential essay defending Walt Whitman, who'd recently lost a clerkship in America due to supposedly obscene passages in his poetry. "A child of light," her husband said of Whitman. "He seeks to outrage the Philistines who stifle him and hem him in." She also assembled and in large measure rewrote the jumbled manuscript of a novel left twenty years in a drawer by her husband's late brother. The novel, *Angela Pisani,* chronicles the mortal rivalry of two aristocratic cads from the French Regency period, whose forays into adultery and murder lead not to perdition but to the protagonists' happy advancement. Emily showed it to some friends before publication. They warned her to bury any hint of her editorial involvement lest her reputation suffer. It could only be written by a man, they said, and a dead one better yet.

Ignoring their advice, she wrote an introduction acknowledging her extensive contribution—and also settling a personal score. Benjamin Disraeli and George Smythe had been close friends early in their political careers, and Emily asked the prime minister to contribute a blurb promoting the book. When he declined to link himself to the infamous viscount, who'd burned out young in a blaze of drink and debauchery, she dug up an old Disraeli quote from one of her brother-in-law's obituaries that praised Smythe's "dazzling wit and fascinating manners." The words were composed, she alerted readers now, "with the pen of a partial friend."

The prime minister's reluctance to praise *Angela Pisani* was probably wise. Newspapers were swamped with letters denouncing it as indecent. Emily told her publisher to play up its subject of "illegitimate love" to boost sales; George Smythe's widow responded with a whisper campaign among their society friends condemning her sister-in-law's scandalous morals. So for Emily, leaving England for Bulgaria in September 1876 caused no great grief.

She departed under a rain of criticism in British papers that questioned her political sympathies. "Who is Lady Strangford?" people asked. Her husband's writings were full of high regard for Muslim culture, and only last year she'd accused Britain's foreign policy magazine, *The Diplomatic Review,* of bigotry in its analysis of the Eastern Question. "Englishmen are sometimes misled," she wrote, "by the arrogant and unfounded dogma that in any and every difference between Muslims and Christians the latter must invariably be oppressed and the former the oppressors." It was suggested her relief fund was phony: "She will appear in Bulgaria as a friend of the Turk!"

Emily rejected the charge but not its premise of meeting need wherever she found it. Her duty was to humanity, "in this case to suffering Christians." When donors boycotted her charity out of suspicion that it would aid the hated Muslims as well, she shrugged it off. "I will go simply and quietly to the districts where distress has been greatest."

She arrived "dirty and so tired" at Adrianople (Edirne today) on the border of Turkey and Bulgaria in October. Preceded by rumors that an English celebrity was coming to rescue them, she was received with starry expectation by local dignitaries. "I am so completely alone here," she confided to her diary. "These men flatter me so much. If I am not careful I could get into a fine fluster and lose my head altogether."

Her guide in addressing the humanitarian crisis was J. F. Clarke, an American missionary based in Philippopolis. He'd identified numerous Bulgarian villages facing distress as winter approached. He hoped to open several clinics in the Rhodope Mountains, including one at Batak. Emily determined to go there to see the terrible inspiration behind her venture. Clarke was against it. The trip was impossible for a proper carriage as befitted "a lady of rank." She might even have to straddle a horse to cross the treacherous paths rather than ride modestly sidesaddle as a woman should. "I felt ready to cry," she wrote.

A visitor arrived—the *Daily News* reporter who'd broken the Batak story, come to pay his respects. To Emily's surprise, "He turned out to be an exceedingly handsome, thoroughly gentlemanly American." It was MacGahan, of course.

The rapport between the English viscountess and the Ohio newsman was instant. Awed by his journalistic reputation, she was shy with him at first, but "he did all the talking and I learned a great deal." An idea struck her: "A Heaven sent (I really believe) inspiration made me ask Mr. MacGahan to go to Batak also. He seemed much pleased and said yes."

Reverend Clarke resisted, but there was no stopping the persuasive MacGahan. Archibald Forbes would say of him later, "I never saw a fellow for making himself so at home among high officials; he always started into intercourse with them on the premise that they were friends." Emily likewise marveled at his facility. "Mr. MacGahan straightened things," she wrote in her diary that night. "I like him."

Over the next two months, they were together almost constantly. Neither their nine-year age difference nor the social chasm between them impeded their closeness. His easy familiarity with her, so refined in her manners and bonneted, high-collared nurse's habit, intrigued more than unsettled her. Fraternizing with an American commoner might never have done in Park Lane, but the dislocation of present

Emily Strangford was an ill fit with the starched propriety of her aristocratic friends. A gossip magazine suggested that society ladies supported her Bulgarian charity because it kept their "chief rival" in beauty and charm far away from London.

circumstance allowed new ways of being. Going by rail to Peshtera a few days after they first met, Emily became disoriented when exiting the train in a driving rain in the dark. "I could not see how to get out," she wrote. "All in a moment a strange pair of arms seized me, lifted me and carried me through seas of mud, saying, 'We will make our bow inside.'" It was MacGahan. "He is showing always in the place he is most wanted and doing the right thing."

She found him fascinating and recorded his daily habits like a naturalist studying exotic creatures. "He had been up at 3 a.m. writing and was broken down with fatigue. He has a way of saying, 'I am not tired and can try anything,' and down on the floor he lies and shuts his eyes. He talks in his sleep," she added with amusement.

She'd purchased several hundred blankets and brought them with her to Peshtera. She stood by as workers gave them out to women and children, who quietly lined up to accept them, "gaunt, emaciated, famished, with staring eyes of such gratefulness it made my heart bleed." MacGahan took her arm and led her to a pile of blankets: "He unfolded them and gave each one away, laying my hand upon each blanket." The people wanted her physical touch, he explained, for palpable caring as much as blankets would help them through these hard times. "Each recipient grasped my fingers and always cried," Emily wrote. "Sometimes I cried, too."

Still fretting about how she would manage the trek to Batak, Clarke advised her to wait until supplies and wagons could be arranged. Impatient, she "entreated Mr. MacGahan to come with me and let the others catch up."

She'd never ridden astride a saddle and "was very anxious but left that to myself about my first ride." Standing beside her horse the next morning, she hesitated nervously. Without warning, MacGahan hoisted her into the saddle from behind; she was too shocked to protest. It was raining slightly. "Mr. MacGahan put his jacket over me," she wrote, "and on we rode."

Turkish authorities, stung by the dreadful findings at Batak, had partially cleaned up the devastation since MacGahan's discoveries had come out. Most of the skeletons had been buried; residents had gathered the skulls and stored them in makeshift ossuaries. The place itself "does not seem at first a village" was Emily's first impression: "here and there a building or wall left standing half charred, the scars of fire everywhere."

Villagers welcomed MacGahan as an old friend. They guided the couple to Reverend Clarke's future hospital, a shack without staff or furnishings. MacGahan unrolled his sleeping mat on the floor for the viscountess and went to find food and firewood. He returned with a five-year-old girl in his arms, sick with fever—"your first patient."

They spent the night feeding the child soup of "horrible foul-smelling goat" and sips of warm cream. She'd improved by morning, which Emily took as a great portent for her project. The girl later became the first of six Bulgarian orphans she adopted and sent to London to be reared and educated.

Before leaving Batak, she promised its people, "thoroughly pillaged, the women so ill treated," that she would return with supplies and medicine. It embarrassed her to see them drop to their knees and touch their foreheads to the ground. "Many think it is Queen Victoria who has come to help them," she wrote.

Back at Peshtera, Emily heard rumors that vengeful Bulgarians in a neighboring town had murdered the children of a Turkish official; a witness had now come forward. "I pricked up my ears. Mr. MacGahan has been waiting to run down this story true or false." Like a schoolgirl sleuth, she ran to him with the news. "In a trice we made up our minds. We said nothing to anyone and went off to seek the village wherein this thing was said to have happened. Soon I found myself riding up a lonely hillside alone with Mr. MacGahan."

They arrived at evening and went to meet the witness. Partners now, Emily sat on the floor taking notes while MacGahan questioned the man for two hours. "I was so tired," she wrote, "but it was very interesting." Given her privileged, insular background, it was more than that. "A great leap for me," she exulted.

They found lodging for the night at a Turkish home, "beautifully clean, with a fire going." Their lack of any travel accessories except the clothes on their backs forced an unavoidable intimacy: "We got supper and lay down. My hair got very untidy—and lots else. I managed very well." Some sort of threshold was crossed. "We had a capital breakfast!" she wrote the next day.

They continued to visit villages together, MacGahan advising her in "calculating needs and monies, etc." When he left for a week on *Daily News* business, she confided to her diary that "Mr. MacGahan has helped and comforted me more ways than you could think."

Hounded by pleas for money and aid while still trying to solicit donations from Britain, she became testy and depressed in his absence. Her Bulgarian servants were "maddening," hovering about, not letting her open a door or pour her own tea. Traveling town to town with Clarke and an entourage of charity workers and government minders, she began to dread the entreaties of destitute peasants. The news of her coming "always flies before me," she complained. "It is the part I hate, everyone kissing my hand." Touring a nunnery gave her the creeps: "Such a lot of happy-looking old hags with sweetish faces—I was fearfully afraid they would hex me."

In the midst of a snowstorm on the first day of December, the door of her quarters pushed open. "In came he!" Henceforth in her diary, the oft-mentioned "Mr. MacGahan" gave way to something less formal. "I am determined to get to see all the villages while I have McG.

to take care of me." People were aghast that they meant to ride into the mountains in winter. "Wild rides are pleasant," she said, "but they would be very hard or horrid without him." On Saturday, December 3, she made a short entry: "McG. and I were glad to get away. Having no bother, only ourselves, we get on so nicely."

Not long into their excursion, she became ill with food poisoning and struggled to fulfill her expected role of angelic benefactor for the usual throng of supplicants. "I made my little speech," she wrote, "and then McG. told them to go. He is always so helpful in these situations. He took me in hand and made me a bed—such a bed—next to a huge hearth and arranged all my things and helped me to get my night things and then went to get us some dinner. I could not eat a morsel. He ate in the next room for fear of annoying me. I think it was so sweet of him."

She got worse, enduring the sort of major gastric upheaval guaranteed to erase any last barriers of shyness between them. "My good nurse," she called him. MacGahan, his field experience showing, kept a fire burning in her room with wood he gathered himself. "He was so kind to me. He found a big pan of hot water to bathe in, and something hot to drink. I was better the next day."

She wanted to continue their tour, but he knew she was too weak and the weather too harsh. Returning to her residence in Philippopolis, they talked into the evening, MacGahan "feeding me biscuit" to boost her strength. With parting words that she didn't record, he helped "my weary little body and sore limbs into bed" and headed off on his next assignment—to Constantinople, where European diplomats had convened emergency meetings to prevent war between Russia and Turkey.

Those meetings would fail. War came the next spring, by which time Lady Strangford had distributed blankets and coats to thousands of Bulgarians, rebuilt schools and lumber mills, and opened six medical clinics with doctors and nursing staffs. When she then turned her focus from Bulgarian peasants to Turkish military wounded, critics in London would mock her for now heaping praise on the Turks after raising so much money denouncing them. This concern for Muslim soldiers proved she was her husband's disciple after all, they said.

It would be interesting to know MacGahan's opinion. Perhaps the anti-Turk feelings seared into him at Batak would have lessened his esteem for her. More likely, however, he would have applauded her response to petty jibes from home about taking sides on the basis of need. "Is not humanity better than neutrality?" she asked. He couldn't have said it better himself.

"Last year was the saddest of my life," John Russell Young wrote in his diary on New Year's Day 1876. He was thirty-four. His seven-year-old daughter, Marnie, had died the previous fall. Mild fever had turned to a diagnosis of diphtheria. Last rites given on October 14 were followed by a hopeful period of brightening and then death five days later. He faithfully commemorated the date in future diaries along with Marnie's last words: "Papa, might you fix that curtain?"

His wife Rose was often bedridden with "nervous instability" dating to the death of their first child in infancy several years earlier. Young too was prone to depression and preoccupation with his health; Marnie had been a great source of uplift. Returning to the States "to commit her to the dirt with her darling brother," he and Rose toured the American South to work through their bereavement. They visited local churches, where his wife offered "special devotions" while he focused on the sermons. "Altogether southern," he said of one Savannah preacher. "Smooth, controlled, agreeable." The period of travel saw him begin regularly to write literary reviews and to seek out all types of theater, from Shakespeare to low comedy. In time, "books and acting" became as much his journalistic interest as current events.

When Bennett asked him to return to London in September 1876, Young's wife had stayed behind in New York. Arriving "miserable and despondent," he buried himself in *Herald* duties that included composing foreign news "leaders" of up to fifty handwritten pages each morning. To this he added a full social schedule in which he mixed on a daily basis with English businessmen and eminent American expatriates: "Met Henry James for lunch. In a sorry plight, down in the dumps about his book." Young lived near Hyde Park and took his mail and meals at the Reform Club in Pall Mall, unofficial headquarters of Britain's Liberal Party. The place buzzed with the political fallout of MacGahan's recent *Daily News* reports on the Bulgarian massacres. "We hate the Turks," Young said of his fellow club members. "All sympathy with the Russians."

Young's diary notes a gradual improvement in his mood: "Marnie's loss made the world very dark. The work is returning. I write with great fluency and it is generally good." There are many references to letters sent his wife but little reflection on her absence. Any need for a home life was evidently fulfilled by visiting his former colleague, George Smalley, now a respected international pundit. "Smalley has deep roots in England but is a thorough American and an entirely good fellow, the same as he was ten years ago when our success opened together on the *Tribune*." Young went on outings with the family and got along well with Smalley's wife, Phoebe, who was tiring of her husband's Tory socializing and appreciated Young's more liberal American outlook.

With news out of the Balkans in the fall and winter of 1876 pointing to war, Young wondered if he should travel to the region. When Bennett insisted he remain at his *Herald* desk at 46 Fleet Street, Young didn't complain. "I should probably not hang around London," he admitted, "but I am the hanging type." Bennett's instruction had come by wire from New York. Lately, however, the *Herald* owner had been considering moving abroad full-time and managing the paper long distance. Unsure of what his boss might be running from, Young had joked with Smalley that dealing with Bennett's volatility at close quarters in London would be "the way of the guillotine, and in no way to be desired." Fortunately, Bennett's wedding to Caroline May was scheduled for early next year. That ought to keep him far away.

But on January 9, 1877, Young opened *The Daily News* to find an alarming item reprinted from the previous day's New York *Sun*:

MR. BENNETT AND MR. MAY

Both Out of City, Probably for a Hostile Meeting

"Hostile Meeting" was the press euphemism for duel. Over the next few days Young pieced together events leading to the clash between Bennett and Caroline May's brother, Fred. "It distressed me so much I could not eat dinner," he wrote.

The episode was a lesson in one way to end a marriage engagement. Seeing no other escape, the thirty-five-year-old Bennett had opted for a single irrevocable gesture, performed at a New Year's Day party at the Park Avenue home of Caroline's parents, Dr. and Mrs. William May. The cream of New York society was there to celebrate the year in which the Mays' daughter would wed America's most famous bachelor. Bennett, the guest of honor, showed up late, still wearing the evening clothes of the previous night's revels. Circling the crowded room, he took a drink from a passing tray, slugged it down, and strode to the roaring fireplace where he undid his trousers for a good long piss. A hissing steam was the first indication that the party had taken a turn. Ladies screamed. Some men formed a screen around Bennett while he concluded his business, after which, still buttoning up, he turned to the room and gave an impish shrug. He was hauled outside and tossed into the back of a coach.

At home the next day, he got word from Caroline that the marriage was off. He ventured out on January 3 to take lunch at the Union Club. Fred May, twenty-six and determined to avenge his sister, jumped Bennett outside and beat him to the ground, *The New York Times* exulted, "with a cowhide whip." Other papers, eager to pile on, played up Bennett's meek reaction and his cowering wail from down on the pavement, "Why don't you kill me and get it over with?"

The pee scandal was nothing, but the humiliation of a public thrashing hurt Bennett's pride. To restore his name, he challenged Fred May to a duel. It was an elaborate process based on murky traditions of managed violence between disagreeing gentlemen. Negotiating through representatives, Bennett and May would use classic dueling pistols with percussion caps and smooth-bore barrels that fired a one-ounce ball, which was said to be more humane than a rifled bullet: "It kills or wounds without mangling."

In a roadside field in Marydel, Maryland, far from the antidueling laws of Manhattan, a flipped coin determined who got choice of position, up- or downwind. They stood twelve paces apart. Both men were visibly nervous, their bodies rocking to and fro. Fred's "second," a cousin from Baltimore, began the proceeding according to rule:

"Gentlemen, are you ready?'

Fred adjusted his stance. "Not ready."

A pause. "Gentlemen, are you ready?"

Fred fiddled with his pistol. He'd wanted to fight with sabers, but Bennett, an excellent marksman, had somehow got his way. "Not ready."

Another pause. "Gentlemen. Are you ready?"

They answered together, "Ready."

"You may fire on the count of three. One. Two—"

The hammer of a pistol snapped forward. *Pffft.*

Fred's cousin asked Bennett, "Did you fire?"

"I did not." Bennett displayed his still-cocked pistol. "He did. And now I claim my shot."

Fred's weapon had gone off accidentally, its cap misfiring in a dud. There was no second chance. His cousin hesitated before asking Bennett to confirm: "You claim a shot?"

"I do."

Now all nervousness was on the May side. The cousin nodded. "You can have it." He looked at Fred. "Stand up as you are." The young man prepared himself to receive Bennett's bullet.

Bennett discharged his gun harmlessly into the air. He stepped forward, shook Fred's hand, and declared his grievance satisfied. Before leaving, however, he stipulated that when an account of the duel was released to the press (this being necessary to restore Bennett's public honor), it would state that Fred had shot first and that Bennett had graciously shown mercy. The point agreed, everyone packed up and repaired to a local pub.

For months afterward, the many newspapers aligned against the *Herald* tried to puncture Bennett's slick performance. They said the correct thing to do when someone's gun misfired was to let him reload and count off the signal again. Only the discredited "Irish Code" of dueling conceded the technicality that a misfire equaled an actual shot. "In America," pronounced the Baltimore *Sun,* "any man of honor should at once hold his fire if he should hear his adversary's pistol snap." For Bennett not to have allowed Fred May another chance to blow out his brains was "monstrously unfair." But Bennett was long gone by then—as Young had feared, he'd ensconced himself in wife-less repose in hotels in London and Paris, his legend, enhanced with a duelist's dashing aura, now truly transformed from "Jimmy Bennett" to "Tiger Jim."

Bennett's new freedom, albeit based in Europe, gave him time once again to plunge into *Herald* affairs. He'd come to recognize that war was inevitable between Russia and Turkey. Young suggested he reach out to *The Daily News's* John Robinson to form a reporting part-nership. Bennett disliked the British and nixed the proposal. Young warned him that the war would be expensive to cover. Bennett still hesitated. In a telling hint of remorse over his dispute with MacGahan about the Bulgarian rumors last summer, he wired the correspondent in Constantinople asking if he would consider leaving *The Daily News* and returning to the *Herald*.

While Bennett waited through April for MacGahan's reply, Young went ahead and negotiated with Robinson. The British editor insisted that all *Daily News* material be plainly credited. After all, the *Herald* would gain the services of two premier *Daily News* correspondents, MacGahan and Archibald Forbes. Robinson considered Forbes, who'd covered famine in India and rebellion in Serbia since the fall of the Paris Commune, to be the more reliable because he was less emo-tional. "He hoped to get some good work out of MacGahan," Young wrote, "but was afraid there would be opinions only."

Young agreed to the terms before telling his boss. He pressured Ben-nett to accept by hinting that Robinson might partner with another American paper if the *Herald* opted out. Hearing nothing from Mac-Gahan, Bennett gave up hope of rehiring him and made the deal with *The Daily News*. Young was relieved: "Received a letter from Mr. B. approving of what has been done, which pleases me."

There was a reason for Young's impatience. He was suffering from insomnia, nosebleeds, and anxiety, ailments that his wife's arrival in London in February hadn't assuaged. His doctor said to take a few days off, but Young diagnosed his problem as running much deeper:

Ulysses S. Grant, post-presidency in March 1877. Grant sailed to Britain later that year to begin a world tour. Since he was no longer a head of state, Queen Victoria made sure to be out riding when he and his family called at Windsor Castle. That evening she seated Grant's nineteen-year-old son with the palace servants, relenting only after the general threatened to walk out if the young man didn't join them at the head table.

"After a man is thirty-five his game is generally made. I sometimes think I was thirty-five twenty-five years ago." Shifting to *The Daily News* the bulk of the coverage of the coming war was one step in cutting his *Herald* workload. The next step came with the arrival in Britain of Young's longtime hero Ulysses S. Grant, who'd left the White House in March after completing two terms and now was starting a world tour with his family. Young had often corresponded with Grant during the years of defending his embattled administration in *The Standard* and the *Herald*. Now, he wrote excitedly, "The General has asked to see me."

Landing in Liverpool on May 28, 1877, Grant was met by huge crowds wherever he went, his popularity based more on his Civil War triumph than on his political record. A glittery circuit of guided tours and private banquets was capped a month later by dinner with Queen Victoria. The next evening Young hosted an informal party for Grant in London. There were thirty-seven guests but no speeches—a welcome break for the taciturn general. Young had fretted over the arrangements, leaning on Smalley, "hero of ten thousand dinners," for recommendations on the guest list, the menu, and the wine, "Château Lafitte 1864." The party was a hit.

More intent than ever on easing away from the *Herald,* Young visited Paris in the summer and fall with Grant's entourage. He asked in his diary for God's guidance in living "a man's true and honorable career, with peace, love, and felicity." That winter, Grant invited him on a four-month cruise around the Mediterranean. Young hesitated on two counts: Bennett might be angry to lose him, and Young's wife was pregnant.

It turned out that Bennett saw dollars in Young's going; his letters from shipboard about the general's private side would be a sure smash with *Herald* readers. "He was very kind about my leaving," Young wrote, "and said I might draw on him for as much money as I needed, and that I should put down my expenses to the paper."

Young got Rose a flat near London's Cavendish Square and arranged for friends and servants to attend her through her delivery next March. Misgivings about leaving her plagued him, but there was no way he could turn down the opportunity with Grant.

Looking ahead in his diary, he wondered "what events these blank pages will see." As a journalist, a professional observer, it was the blankness that intrigued him. "This new adventure tears up all my roots," he wrote on the eve of leaving with Grant aboard the steamship *Vandalia* in early December, "and compels me to begin all over again."

8

Green Leaves in a Furnace Flame
1877

Nothing can be finer as mere spectacle than a line of troops moving forward with obedience and faith into battle.

FRANCIS V. GREENE, *Sketches of Army Life in Russia* (1880)

MacGahan's destination on leaving Emily Strangford in December 1876 was Constantinople, where the Conference of Six Powers was trying to broker a peace agreement between Russia and Turkey. He had another reason for going: his wife, frustrated by his inattention, had defied his wishes and gone there from Paris with their little son, Paul. The five-day reunion was uneasy. "We still loved one another," Varia wrote, "but dinners and different celebrations took all his time."

She was getting the message. "You are too accustomed to living alone," she told him, "too uncaring about Paul and me to be sincerely attached to us." When he tried to protest, she cut him off almost tenderly: "Love on your part is past. You are attached to us only through a point of honor that you have imagined yourself." They would struggle to keep the marriage together, but she'd come to accept what he, out of guilt, refused to concede, that "this style of living can't go on."

The conference in Constantinople was a last bid by Britain, Russia, France, Italy, Prussia, and Austria to persuade Turkey to grant autonomy to Bulgaria and satisfy the Western demand that the Bulgarian massacres be punished. That demand intensified once MacGahan's Batak dispatches were published in book form along with Schuyler's statistical record of the slaughter. Prime Minister Disraeli, recently made Earl of Beaconsfield by Queen Victoria, had dismissed the findings as "coffee-house babble," but their emotional power was strong. Archibald Forbes, in Britain when the *Daily News* compilation came out, observed that "men traveling in railway carriages were to be noticed with flushed faces and moistened eyes as they read it."

Carrying even greater impact was a thirty-nine-page pamphlet, *Bulgarian Horrors and the Question of the East*, authored by Parliament's liberal lion, William Gladstone. Just as Tennyson's "Charge of the Light Brigade" had drawn on William Howard Russell's Balaclava dispatch to launch a lightning bolt of national outrage over the Crimean War, Gladstone's screed, written in sickbed under high fever, used MacGahan's revelations to level a righteous blast against the Ottoman Empire and its conservative defenders in Britain. Gladstone demanded that Lord Beaconsfield redeem the dishonor of his foreign policy pragmatism and help drive the Turks out of Bulgaria, out of Europe. "This thorough riddance, this most blessed deliverance," he said, "is the only reparation we can make to the memory of those heaps on heaps of dead; to the violated purity of matron, maiden, and child; to the civilization which has been affronted and shamed; to the laws of God or, if you like, of Allah; to the moral sense of mankind at large."

Bulgarian Horrors sold 200,000 copies in a month and inspired anti-Turk rallies across Britain. It made Gladstone a fortune in royalties, vexing MacGahan's publisher, Edward Marston, who urged the reporter to write his own book about Bulgaria—and to do it fast lest public interest wane and leave a good story unread. "Witness *Northern Lights*," Marston said. But MacGahan wasn't interested in chasing fashion. He was interested in vengeance.

He watched with disgust as European diplomats bent over backward to resolve Turkey's outlaw status peacefully. Sultan Abdul-Aziz, who'd authorized the Bulgarian cleansing, had been replaced by Abdul-Hamid II. It was hoped the new sultan would accept international penalties, but he resisted. The Conference of Six Powers broke up in January 1877 with nothing resolved and Russia still not moving to mobilize. MacGahan was furious. "They are looking to patch up a peace which may last a few months," he fumed. "Then the whole dread business will begin over again."

Abdul-Hamid was counting on Russia's reluctance to test the British-

Turkish alliance with a unilateral invasion of Bulgaria. To pressure the Disraeli government to stay on the sidelines, MacGahan laced his *Daily News* stories with continual references to Batak and "the loathsome, vice-stricken leper" that was Turkey. Though Gladstone's polemic was the greater factor in swaying mass opinion, MacGahan reveled in his role. "I have done more to smash up the Turkish Empire than anybody else," he wrote his mother. "I have fought several pitched battles with the English government and the English embassy at Constantinople." And he enjoyed it: "You never thought I was such a desperate character, did you?"

In March Europe issued the London Protocol, a final demand that Turkey reform its Balkan policies under the supervision of foreign observers. When it was rejected, Britain signaled to Russia that it would stay out of any conflict as long as Constantinople wasn't targeted. Russia agreed and declared war on Turkey on April 24, sending an army to the Romanian side of the Danube River to prepare its crusade to liberate—that is, acquire—Bulgaria.

MacGahan took it as a personal victory, made sweeter by "a very polite telegram" he received from his old employer at the *Herald*. It was the wire Bennett sent during his discussions with John Robinson about collaborating on war coverage: "He asked me if I was going on with him or whether I had taken a permanent position with the *Daily News*." The query from the proud publisher was tantamount to groveling, and MacGahan enjoyed leaving it unanswered. He didn't know that Bennett soon would agree to partner with Robinson, thereby gaining MacGahan's services in a roundabout way along with those of Archibald Forbes. The reporters had worked blocks apart in Paris in 1871 and now would finally meet.

In the six years since the Commune, Forbes had come to see himself as *The Daily News*'s top correspondent. With a personality to match his appearance, "square shoulders, superb head, strong neck," he enjoyed his job as a contest above all; he'd even had all his teeth pulled and replaced with a dental plate—much easier to care for in the field. No one was better at anticipating events and getting in position to cover them—a talent he wasn't sure whether to define "as prognosis or presentiment," that is, foresight based on analysis or instinct. He expected resentment from rivals and was leery of working closely with anyone. Before leaving Britain to cover the coming war, he pressed Robinson to grant him seniority over his new American partner.

Arriving at the invasion command center at Bucharest, he asked some Russian officers where he might find MacGahan. They lit up at the mention of the *molodyetz* who'd crossed the Kyzylkum. "Do you know him?" they asked. They hugged the Scotsman with gusto. "Next to being MacGahan himself," Forbes gathered, "was to be MacGahan's friend." A British diplomat had just returned from watching war preparations in St. Petersburg with MacGahan; he told Forbes that he'd never seen a foreigner mix as easily with Russian royalty. With "absolute imperturbability," the American had flirted with the wives at court and bantered with the likes of Nikolai Ignatiev, ambassador to Turkey, and Grand Duke Nicholas, commander in chief of Russia's Army of the Danube, somehow walking a fine line, the diplomat marveled, "of jocular swagger, the quaint fun of which took from it the serious attribute of impertinence."

Bucharest had its own quaint fun to offer. The fabled "Paris of the East" throbbed with the wartime glamour of cavalry boots on parquet dance floors and sword scabbards slung over nightclub chairs. Suites at the Grand Hotel du Boulevard could be booked for an afternoon, and "fair pedestrians," as Forbes put it, lounged at every street corner: "Bucharest was a ballroom wherein Mars, Venus, and Bacchus were dancing the can-can in a frantic orgy." Amid this voluptuous swirl, a stranger stepped out of the shadows one evening ("calm clear eyes, short brown beard, and singularly small hands and feet") and introduced himself as MacGahan. They shook. "The grip was a symbol of friendship that was never to falter," Forbes wrote. As they talked and got acquainted, the Scotsman felt foolish for having worried about their collaboration. "I was not aware how sweet was MacGahan's temper," he later recalled. "He had no egotism. We never had a moment's friction."

The two discussed war plans over beers on the garden patio of the Hotel Broft. MacGahan limped badly, having broken his ankle in a fall off a horse while reconnoitering Russian positions. The hotel was a favorite haunt of the Russian headquarters staff, "youngsters as reckless as they were blue-blooded," who knocked back magnums of French champagne while Romanian Guardsmen, wary of these strutting would-be conquerors acting as if they owned the place, sized them up with disdain.

MacGahan had only one request of Forbes in establishing their responsibilities—that he cover "a certain heroic young officer named Mikhail Skobelev." Forbes hadn't heard of him, but MacGahan's memory of the man's boisterous charisma during their last days in Khiva made him sure that that was where the action would be. It turned out a great hunch. Skobelev would play key roles in the biggest battles of the war. That his gallantry was mixed with viciousness wasn't something that MacGahan, with his soft spot for larger-than-life characters, was inclined to examine. "Needful severities" was his euphemism for the devastation Skobelev wreaked that often took no prisoners and left no enemy alive on the field. To be sure, the thirty-three-year-old general expected to receive the same treatment at the hands of the Turks. "He leaned toward nihilism," MacGahan wrote. "He had superb confidence yet did not expect to survive the campaign."

After Khiva, Skobelev had remained in Central Asia as one of the czar's main enforcers. He'd led many operations against numerically superior Turkoman foes, including one in which his lone battalion left "two thousand turbans on the field of battle." Though Russian regulars usually wore white canvas uniforms in warm weather and dark woolens in cold, sometimes even in hot summer they would don winter gear before battle; so spotty was their army's medical service, they hoped the warm wool might prevent them from falling into shock should they end up wounded and abandoned. But Skobelev always wore white. He rode white or gray horses exclusively and went into battle with his rank emblazoned on his epaulets, medals gleaming on his chest, and his coiffed hair and beard "scented like a popinjay." If the enemy could spot him a mile away, so too could his men. To be in front in dazzling white gave inspiration and also a visible beacon leading to the objective. But that was only part of his aim. He longed for distinction, he admitted, "and then would die with a light heart."

Mikhail Skobelev liked culture, women, and hard partying. The youngest general in the Russian army, he commanded with brute efficiency. "The duration of peace is in direct proportion to the slaughter you inflict on the enemy," he said on the eve of the Russo-Turkish War in 1877.

His obsessive daring was rooted in frustration that he wasn't respected by his peers and especially by his father, Dimitri Skobelev, a lieutenant general who was his immediate superior at the start of the Bulgarian campaign.

The epic scale of Mikhail's carousing created wide suspicion that he'd embezzled "millions of rubles" while stationed in Central Asia. If true, he blew through it at record speed, for in Bucharest he needed his staid, disapproving father to settle his hotel bill. "He had a habit of regarding his own and the paternal purse as identical," Forbes would discover, "a view which Skobelev Senior did not share." Mikhail was most generous with other people's money. A friend recalled that he never passed a beggar without directing a subordinate to hand out a gold piece; "as he often forgot the outlays made for him, and often had no money, it naturally followed that meeting poor people was more alarming to his orderlies than meeting the enemy."

Dimitri Skobelev commanded a division of cavalry from the rugged Caucasus Mountains between Russia and Turkey. Caucasian Cossacks were better fighters than Cossacks based to the north along Russia's Don River. Don Cossacks had fought at Khiva with little distinction beyond mowing down fleeing nomads; they made fine scouts and had "a genius for plundering," Forbes wrote, but didn't care for close combat. Caucasian Cossacks, on the other hand, were fearless, charging "knee to knee as regular cavalry, against any odds." Dimitri's division included a regiment of Muslim horsemen, the Kubanskis, whose willingness to fight their Turkish coreligionists was doubted by many Russian officers. Not Mikhail. He asked his father to be allowed to lead them. His tactical role was freewheeling, "a sort of open commission to risk his life where he pleased," for which the Kubanskis were ideal. Along with tireless energy and good cheer, they brought another quality: "They kill and spare not," Mikhail raved.

In the weeks preceding the Russian army's move across the Danube, young Skobelev escorted the two *Daily News* colleagues through Bucharest's nightly mash of "princes, dukes, countesses without their counts, operatic ladies whose more probable engagements did not strain the voice, diplomats, aides-de-camp, Polish Jews, and war correspondents of every European nation." Forbes had never met anyone like the general—"it seemed he had been everywhere, seen everything, done everything, and read everything." MacGahan was amused by the Scotsman's dismay. Though indeed a Renaissance character, he told Forbes, Skobelev's greatest talent lay elsewhere: "You have not seen him fight."

Assuring readers that he would "be heard from more than once before the present campaign is over," MacGahan began composing newspaper sketches of Skobelev's past exploits. Notwithstanding his reputation as a suicidal crackpot, "it will be seen that it is not such a mad business after all. He calculates his chances at victory as any prudent general would do." Skobelev himself downplayed the prudence part. In his 1901 study, *The Varieties of Religious Experience,* the psychologist William James quotes the Russian general: "The risk of life fills me with an exaggerated rapture. I am crazy for it, I love it, I adore it. I run after danger as one runs after women. Were it always the same it would always bring me new pleasure." James attributed Skobelev's mania to "cruel egoism," a verdict he might also have applied to the boisterous young man who was James's student at Harvard at the time of the Russo-Turkish War—Theodore Roosevelt. When Roosevelt later clamored to get in on the glory of the Spanish-American War, James interpreted it the same way he did Skobelev: "Still mentally in the Sturm and Drang period of early adolescence."

. . .

"To the remains of our friend, the late Frank Millet, care of the vultures," was how Mark Twain addressed his letter to the young man who'd painted his portrait in Boston the previous year. Now working for *The New York Herald,* Millet had written the author from Bucharest in early June 1877. Czar Alexander recently had arrived with five hundred cartloads of supplies for himself and his traveling court. This "dread information" was leaked by staffers unable to hide their excitement that the czar was there to watch the invasion. "The pretense of secrecy at Russian headquarters is amusing," Millet wrote.

Twain, figuring his reply wouldn't arrive till after the shooting started, took an attitude that Millet might not be around to read it: "I write with the gravity becoming a person who is possibly addressing himself to a corpse. I have written corpses before, unwittingly, but I find a peculiar grandeur in addressing a corpse that may be decorating a field of battle."

In contrast to whatever unpleasantness Millet might be enduring, Twain assured him that he and his family were "extravagantly well, and send our love to our old friend mouldering among the other decaying heroes upon the field of blood." This irreverent tone was the right one to take, for Millet, just a few months past leaving the artistic haven of Montmartre, had become expert in war's dark absurdities by the time Twain's letter reached him at the front.

Millet was embarrassed to confess the "strange and perhaps silly" reasons why he'd put down his paintbrush to become a war correspondent. One of his studio models, a Hungarian acrobat, had declared that May that he was leaving Paris to join the Turkish army. "Nothing was further from my intention," Millet recalled, "than following the example of my little circus friend." But the *Herald* pay was generous, and if Millet survived "this great gambling game," he could bank enough to support his painting career for two years. "Curiosity and a mild love of adventure" were also factors: "Although not a moment passes but I regret that I am not at my easel, I am satisfied that it was the only thing to do for me to come."

Traveling here from Paris, he'd been amazed how war fever intensified the closer one got to the front—but then once there, it turned so blasé as to seem almost "a farce." Newsmen from dozens of papers "go about our preparations as if we were to go out on a picnic and only are worried at the possibility of being beaten by other correspondents." Even artillery exchanges over the Danube "do not stir us as much as squirrel shooting in a country town." Notified of the *Herald*'s new partnership with *The Daily News,* Millet and a *Herald* colleague, John P. Jackson, reported to Archibald Forbes for assignment. Having given Skobelev to MacGahan and taken headquarters for himself, the Scotsman let the men draw lots for their respective beats. Jackson got Russia's right wing, comprising mostly Romanian troops, and Millet the left, at the eastern end of the front.

If the timing of the invasion was well known, its exact location remained secret. A quarter-million Russian troops, along with more than a hundred cannons and thousands of supply wagons, were spread out on the river elbow where the Danube turns from its eastward course along the Bulgarian-Romanian border and angles north to the Black Sea. With the czar's court established in the riverside town of Braila, rumors flew that the army would cross there. It seemed an odd choice. Since the river was in its spring flood, passage would be harder there than at narrower points upstream, due to miles of marsh created by swollen waters spilling over the banks. Perplexed reporters told themselves it must be that Turkish fortifications were lightest where the natural barrier of the river was most formidable. It would be the last time they assumed any strategic cleverness on the part of Russian planners.

Millet was at the town of Galatz (Galati today) when boats filled with soldiers launched from there on June 22. Forbidden to go along, he wrote a frantic dispatch based on details gathered from the first casualties brought back across the river. He paid a merchant traveling to Vienna to wire it to London from the nearest telegraph office on the rail line. This three-hundred-word exclusive catapulted *The Daily News* and the *Herald* to the forefront of the war's coverage, a position they would hold to the end.

The dispatch showed its author's inexperience. Treating as gospel the frazzled accounts of wounded soldiers, Millet characterized the fight as monumentally bloody: "Reports are flying about that Russian loss is heavy." A medic who'd crossed with the first wave said the Turks had "fought like tigers" and reduced his unit from eight hundred to twenty men. A squadron of the infamous Bashi-Bazouk militia was said to have butchered an advance party of Russian scouts: "They got down off their horses to mutilate the dead by cutting off their noses and ears and hacking the bodies into pieces." Despite this savage defense, the Russians secured a solid foothold. "It is difficult to account for the fact that their inferior force was not overpowered and driven into the water," Millet admitted.

Actually it wasn't difficult at all, for it soon became apparent that Turkish resistance had been minimal. MacGahan, who left Skobelev's headquarters and rushed to Galatz at the first word of the crossing, was quick to detect this reality. He and Millet ferried across the river to inspect the scene. MacGahan's dispatch put things in perspective: "It is impossible to say what the Turkish plan was, but it certainly looks as though they had no plan at all." He lavished praise on the Russian "liberators" for not defiling religious items found in abandoned Muslim homes, and ended with the image of a Russian banner waving from the minaret of a mosque, "emblematic of the long struggle between Islam and Christianity, and ominous of the end."

The Galatz operation involved only a few thousand soldiers; it was a feint to draw Turkish defenders away from Russia's main deployment at Zimnicea, fifty miles south of Bucharest. Shortly after midnight on June 26, Forbes, separated from his *Daily News* partners, stood on the bluffs above the Danube while 80,000 troops waited "in strained silence" to board barges that would take them across to Bulgaria. Then "through the sullen gloom I could discern a man in a white coat jump onto the first barge." It was Mikhail Skobelev, doing as MacGahan had predicted—rushing to the front of the action.

Gunfire from emplacements on the opposite bank targeted the vessels as they rowed across. Skobelev, the first ashore, looked back in dismay as most of his assault battalion hit the dirt in fear. "Get up, my brothers, and follow me!" he shouted. He bounded up the tree-dotted slope, losing almost half his men in the process of securing the village of Sistova (Svishtov today) overlooking the river. Within a day an entire Russian corps, including two infantry divisions, a cavalry division, and more than forty cannons, had deployed south of the Danube.

By the end of the week, construction was complete on a pontoon bridge that would be Russia's main conduit of reinforcements and supplies into Bulgaria. Three more corps came over and fanned west toward Sofia, east to the Black Sea, and south toward the Balkan Mountains. The last was the key thrust, aiming to traverse the high passes before winter, descend to the farther valley between the Balkan and Rhodope ranges, and then pivot eastward toward Philippopolis, Adrianople, and Constantinople beyond.

The army's efficient Danube crossing encouraged confidence that the campaign would be a triumphal march lasting three months at most. Not wanting to miss the fun, the czar packed up his court and rushed to join Grand Duke Nicholas's headquarters outside Sistova. Units that had spearheaded the landing assembled in review. It was time to hand out medals ("all the idiots in this army have some decoration or other," Millet wrote), starting with the division and brigade commanders. Forbes, watching from the edge of the parade ground, noted the hearty embrace the czar gave the first two generals in line.

Mikhail Skobelev was next. He stood at attention in his white uniform before his notorious Muslim regiment. The Kubanskis looked like no other outfit. Called "motley" and "sinister" by their regular army compatriots, they wore fur caps and long black cloaks over bright-colored shirts, and unlike typical Cossacks, they carried not lances but carbines, daggers, and curved scimitars stuck bare-bladed under bullet-packed bandoliers. Their flag was a square banner of yellow and red, "quite medieval in appearance," with a Cross of St. George on one side and Skobelev's initials on the other.

The czar paused when he came to the blond, bearded general. Well known as a womanizer, a drunk, and a possible thief, Skobelev had lately added to his disrepute by marrying a girl from an esteemed family in Moscow. She'd run home in tears fourteen days after the wedding. Her family was ashamed and embarrassed till she described her husband's vile desires that had compelled her to flee, after which they forgave her with open arms. No one divulged the details behind her revulsion, not even Skobelev, who only shrugged that in all honesty he couldn't blame the girl one bit.

The czar, fifty-eight and more than twenty years Russia's absolute ruler, knew all about the scandal. Would he now overlook his distaste and reward Skobelev's Danube heroics? Forbes saw his expression waver; indeed, "all the men watched the little scene intently."

The czar walked on—no embrace, no medal. His back was already turned as Skobelev bowed respectfully after him. The episode confirmed what a Russian prince had earlier told Forbes: "Skobelev is an officer with whom, in peace, no one would shake hands." But Forbes saw it another way: "It was a flagrant insult in the very face of the army, but Skobelev took it in proud silence that seemed to me very grand." Henceforth the Scotsman would join MacGahan in his devotion to the young general, leaving only Millet to make the case that Skobelev, while indeed a phenomenal warrior, was totally nuts.

The Russo-Turkish War of 1877–78 is best understood by its nine-month toll of 170,000 dead—not counting 50,000 Turkish prisoners who died in Russian captivity, and not counting many thousands of civilians. Its military lessons are mainly of ineptitude and have no more eloquent expression than the number of soldiers killed, one-third by bullets, bayonets, and shrapnel, the rest by disease, hunger, and frostbite.

Russia's original plan was sound, addressing the natural obstacles of rivers and mountains and also the powerful fortresses manned by the Turkish army at key junctions inside Bulgaria. Beyond its perimeter, each Turkish fortress had a network of redoubts built of rock or earthworks and connected by trenches to a central stronghold. From these outlying emplacements defenders could deliver crossing fusillades over open fields or down steep escarpments against the oncoming enemy. The four largest fortresses—at Varna, Rustchuk, Silistria, and Shumla—comprised the so-called Quadrilateral, which Russian strategists chose to bypass rather than try to destroy. Another smart move was to deploy 70,000 soldiers on Turkey's Caucasus border to threaten a second front and prevent Turkish reinforcements from shifting west.

Unfortunately, Russia underestimated the number of Turkish troops already in Bulgaria by almost a hundred thousand. Light resistance at the Danube belied the 250,000 defenders who were dug in at various overlooks awaiting the Russian push into the mountains.

Relative to the opposing armies in the Franco-Prussian War seven years earlier, the Russian military was like the Prussian in its professional officer corps built on traditions of pride and obedience; but unlike the Prussians, most of the rank and file were completely inexperienced. The Turks in turn were like the French in trusting that their poor training and disorganized command structure would be compensated by superior weapons, especially the American-made Peabody-Martini rifle that was accurate at far longer range than the Russian Krinkov rifle and thus a sure bet, the thinking went, to decimate enemy assaults long before bayonets came to bear in close-quarter infantry combat. "The Russian carried a weapon sighted at 600 yards," Millet explained. "He met the Turkish bullets at 2000 yards and marched steadily up to his own distance before he fired a shot. This tries the nerve."

Also like the French, most of Turkey's generals were sycophantic political "pashas" who ran their commands like private armies geared to win the sultan's favor, with little loyalty or coordination among them. Two whose mutual dislike was legendary were thirty-nine-year-old Suleiman Pasha and a Prussian-born mercenary known as Mehemet Ali. Each would be promoted to supreme commander during the course of the conflict, and each would be fired in disgrace. Their refusal to support one another in battle added tens of thousands to Turkey's casualty rolls and deeply impaired the war effort.

On the Russian side, personal rivalries were less a factor in the leadership's poor performance than the decision-making gridlock that set in once Czar Alexander planted himself at headquarters. With their emperor looking over their shoulders, Grand Duke Nicholas and his staff began so much to fear making wrong moves that they made few moves at all. Caution ruled every deliberation. As this paralysis filtered down through the ranks, complacency among field commanders clashed with a martial reflex just to do something now and then. Often the result was an impulsive frontal assault on a marginal target at astronomical human cost. Millet, writing to Mark Twain after several months covering "this diabolical war," described the Russian situation with fury: "Everything has been mismanaged to a criminal extent. Imbecility reigns. The poor, patient soldiers, the devoted officers of the line, the gallant colonels and brigadiers, have to go up and be slaughtered because a stupid major general is taking his tea in the middle of the day and has given the order without the very slightest idea of the state of affairs. It is too much for human patience to stand. I fear I should go mad."

Standing out from the many poor generals were three of high ability. Skobelev was one; crazy as a loon, he was decisive, flexible, and adored by his troops. (Millet, a quick study in military arts, put it this way: "It would be embarrassing if every general were a Skobelev, but a few scattered through an army are of real value in warfare.") Skobelev's colleague, Joseph Gourko, thirteen years older and a notch higher in rank, succeeded through an opposite style, gruff, terse, and dogged in gaining objectives step by step. They had one equal on the Turkish side, forty-five-year-old Osman Pasha, a veteran cavalryman who led 40,000 men in a gutty defense against an overwhelming foe; their superhuman resilience under a long and merciless siege was due almost entirely to Osman's inspiration, and therefore, like Robert E. Lee, he earned a beloved national stature that was unrelated to winning or losing.

To go along with its three best generals, the Russo-Turkish War featured three main battlegrounds. The first was Shipka Pass, four thousand feet up in the Balkan Mountains. The second was the fortified town of Plevna (Pleven today), located in northern Bulgaria between Sofia and the Danube. Scenes of constant fighting through the summer and fall of 1877, both these battlegrounds became symbols of boneheaded leadership as Russian and Turkish commanders fixated on structural objectives—a mountain path, a stubborn fort—rather than maneuver around them.

Following a period of deep winter at the turn of the year, when hunger and cold far surpassed combat in devastating both armies, the war's third major killing ground was the Maritsa River valley, a hundred mile plain extending eastward out of the Rhodope Mountains toward the Turkish-Bulgarian border. Two Russian spearheads, one led by Gourko and the other by Skobelev, converged on the valley in January 1878, driving before them a ravaged enemy abandoned by its leaders. Turkish soldiers and refugees mingled in panic. Two correspondents were there to report it—Millet and MacGahan—down from more than eighty at the start of the war. "Fever, wounds, and various disabilities had spared only this small portion of our corps," Millet wrote. "We made the whole campaign and know more about it than the rest."

Their horses labored in slush and mud churned by the fleeing multitude into a ghastly mash of "broken carts, piles of bags and clothing, and frequent bodies." Only weeks before, the reporters had been caught up in the fever of climactic events. "Russians and Turks making for the same point—it was the wildest excitement!" The excitement curdled in the Maritsa valley. "I gave up counting the dead noncombatants," Millet wrote. "It was the most horrible experience of the war."

The Turkish army, in eight months of trying to dislodge Russian and Bulgarian defenders from Shipka Pass in the Balkan Mountains in 1877–78, suffered 30 percent losses— a casualty rate exceeding the American Civil War. This period illustration depicts what must have been a constant stream of Turkish wounded being carried down the rugged slope.

. . .

"The Turks so far have shown themselves as feeble against regular soldiers as they are ferocious in fighting women and children": that was
typical MacGahan, reporting in the heady first weeks after Russian
forces crossed the Danube at the start of the war. Always quick to
invoke the Batak atrocities, he put the Turkish practice of killing prisoners and enemy wounded in the same category of savagery. Millet
was more pragmatic: "The Turks rarely gave quarter. It was just this
little throat cutting trick that made the campaign uncomfortable."

The two Americans were separated through most of July, Millet on
the quiet eastern flank, MacGahan riding south into the Balkans with
Joseph Gourko's advance column of 16,000 men, including Skobelev's
Kubanski regiment. Still nursing a broken ankle, MacGahan operated
out of a wagon to which he tethered a spare horse to carry him close
to the action. Forbes later described MacGahan's driver as "a forlorn
wandering Jew ever in vain search for his meteoric master. For all I
know," the Scotsman joked, "Isaac and their wagon may be haunting
Bulgaria to this day."

On July 19 the Kubanskis conducted a reconnaissance probe of
Shipka Pass, a ten-mile-long trail along the ridge of a mountain range.
They found only "fires yet burning, rations half cooked," left by Turkish defenders who'd abandoned the place hours earlier. They also found
a large number of Russian POWs captured in earlier skirmishes. "All
were headless," MacGahan reported. "Nearby was the pile of heads."
Among the dead was an emissary of Grand Duke Nicholas seized under
a flag of truce. "It is believed by those who have seen the body that he
was first mutilated and afterwards killed."

Forbes, hearing of this at headquarters, denounced it as an outrage
against civilization. Feeling obliged to write something momentous to
compensate for his distance from the action, he pronounced General
Gourko a military genius: "He has crossed the Balkans! He has burst
open the door that closed Turkey against invasion. I can recall no expedition more brilliant, more successful. Stonewall Jackson's raids must
henceforth resign their pride of place." In fact, Gourko had already
reversed direction after his troops were needed in reinforcement sev-

enty miles northwest, at Plevna. Descending from the high ground through forest terrain thick with Turkish irregulars skilled at "Indian fighting," in MacGahan's phrase, the general moved slowly as supplies dwindled and casualties piled up.

He'd left 4,000 Russians and Bulgarians behind at Shipka Pass. The Turkish commander, Suleiman Pasha, moved to retake it from the south with almost 40,000 men. It was a mistake. Suleiman's colleague, Mehemet Ali, was sitting with a large army east of the Balkans more or less out of the action. Had the two bypassed Shipka and jointly attacked the Russian army's Danube supply lines, they could have cut off the invasion force inside Bulgaria as winter fell. But the pashas' acrimony killed any cooperation. For the next three months Suleiman hurled repeated assaults against Shipka, suffering enormous casualties while inspiring national legends of resolute courage on the part of the Russian and Bulgarian defenders.

The reporters were elsewhere. The same day that Skobelev entered Shipka Pass, Osman Pasha, the most capable Turkish general, completed a forced march of 30,000 men from eastern Bulgaria to Plevna, which was garrisoned by 3,000 Turks facing imminent attack. That attack came at five the next morning. The confident Russian commanders didn't bother to reconnoiter the battleground and had no idea that Osman's arrival had hugely upgraded Plevna's defense. After a perfunctory one-hour artillery bombardment, 6,500 Russian infantrymen set out "like a promenade." By midday, half lay dead or wounded in the fields surrounding the town.

Plevna was only a three-day ride to the Russian supply bridge over the Danube, lending some logic to the Russians' decision to take the town at all costs. But since Osman, facing severe shortages of ammo and food, could likely have been pinned down while the bulk of the Russian army continued south, the Plevna campaign was really Shipka Pass in reverse. Pride more than reason compelled the siege, which ultimately required more than 100,000 Russian troops and lasted months. And this time it was the outgunned defenders on the Turkish side around whom legends arose of astonishing endurance and bravery.

Ten days after their first repulse at Plevna, the Russians tried again. Skobelev rode ahead to take part, leaving MacGahan behind with

Gourko's plodding column. Forbes, traveling with headquarters, got to Plevna in time to see Russia's commander on the scene, General Baron Krüdener, conduct a long bombardment prior to attacking with 30,000 troops. It didn't help. Krüdener lost a quarter of his men before sounding retreat—2,500 killed outright, the rest hacked to death where they lay wounded on the battlefield after dark, their cries for mercy filling the air until eventually silence fell.

Forbes's description of standing helpless through the night listening to those cries is one of the most affecting dispatches of the war. "How miserably raw and chill struck the bleak morn just before dawn!" he wrote. "What must have been the suffering of the poor wounded nearby, weakened by loss of blood, faint in the prostration which inevitably follows a gunshot wound. Yet happy were they in comparison to their fellows who had littered the battlefield, butchered in their helplessness by the Bashi-Bazouk." Krüdener's inability to muster fresh soldiers to conduct a rescue was heartrending. In penance, he stood on a moonlit ridge as enemy snipers shot at him. "No one dared say to that stern chief, eating his heart in the bitterness of his disappointment, that it was tempting fortune to linger longer on this exposed spot. There was no force available to save the wounded. It was only humanity which so long detained the general in this position."

The Scotsman's next dispatch was datelined August 3 from Bucharest, where "malarious fever" had forced him to go to recuperate. The fortunes of war had reversed. "One bad day and lo! the scene changes. The sunshine is overcast by black clouds; the advantages of the Russians crumble like burnt-out tinder." MacGahan echoed the pessimism when he got to Plevna a week later. After touring Russian positions semicircled around the town, he wrote a bitter eight-thousand-word indictment of Russia's prosecution of the war, now at a standstill, and its loss of so many fine soldiers, "killed as uselessly as if they had been simply led out and shot by their comrades."

A few weeks earlier his wagon had tipped into a ravine, and he'd broken the same ankle injured last spring, leaving it swollen and purple. A British military advisor with Gourko noted MacGahan's "indomitable resolution" in coping with the injury, but the reporter finally was forced to return to Bucharest to reset the bone. His wife and son were at a local hotel, installed there by MacGahan before the invasion. He stayed with them while he convalesced, writing all the while. "He composed easily and rapidly in a clear flowing backhand," Varia recalled, "and the sheets fell from his pen and fluttered on the floor like leaves."

Frank Millet showed up at the hotel unannounced. He'd changed considerably from the novice with a shiny press brassard who'd come to see a war. Now he resembled a haggard, unshaven Cossack in a torn cloak and muddy boots. "Notebooks, sketchbooks, writing materials, and toilet articles were stowed away in a dispatch case," he wrote in self-description, "which with field glass and revolver I carried as a soldier carries his kit." A silver-handled riding whip called a *nagajka* was draped over his shoulder. A Cossack major had given it to Millet in exchange for Millet's recipe for cooking turtle, which the major and his fellow officers had previously thought impossible, indeed vile, to eat.

Millet had recently experienced his first mortal near miss, ambushed while crossing a cemetery with an infantry battalion. Explosions and bullets had doused him with dirt and chipped the tombstone he'd hidden behind as if struck by a sculptor's chisel. "I am unable to chronicle the exact incidents of the first few minutes," he wrote candidly. "My fear was so overpowering that my actions were controlled by instinct rather than reason."

Falling back under fire, he'd come to a makeshift triage facility where Russian wounded lay bleeding. "The surgeon and his assistant looked like butchers," he wrote. "Everything we possessed in the way of flannel or cotton was made into tourniquets, but scores died for lack of these simple appliances." One image so moved Millet, he sketched it in his notebook: two Cossacks bringing their captain to the rear after rescuing him from enemy capture. "Grievously wounded as he was, and stripped stark naked by the Turks, they had borne him through a cornfield on a small cart." He'd died on the way, and when Millet found them they were discussing "with patient pathos" whether to bury him or return to the fight.

An artist first and foremost, Millet routinely drew soldiers, villages, landscapes, and peasants, and he made countless compositional stud-

Frank Millet illustrated his later essays about the Russo-Turkish War. This one from *Harper's* magazine recalls his encounter in the summer of 1877 with two Cossacks hauling their captain, his body stripped and hacked by the enemy, through a cornfield back to safety. The officer died on the way.

ies of, say, the line of a horse's jaw, tilted stones in a graveyard, or the braiding of a flogger's whip used to discipline army malingerers. Noticing this, Frederic Villiers, a young battlefield illustrator for the London *Graphic* who'd gone down ill that fall, asked Millet to take his place in sending the magazine images from the front. Mailing them to London added to "the fat salary" Millet enjoyed. He wrote Mark Twain in October 1877, "If you have seen *The Graphic* you have doubtless seen many of my sketches without knowing it, for we who do the work never have our initials put on." Despite their anonymity, his contributions were unmistakable in their artistry and predicted his later success as a painter and muralist whose work is today displayed in museums around the world.

Millet decided to take his account of the cemetery skirmish to Bucharest for transmission. The Danube was seventy miles north, Bucharest sixty miles beyond that. Carrying barley for his horse and a crude map, he started out before dawn. He came on a Turkish soldier lying in the grass, "his brawny chest half bare, his shirt matted with blood." A swarm of flies formed a living pelt across the man's face and in the seeping wound in his side. His mouth and nose crawled with insects, yet he breathed. "My struggle between pity and selfishness was brief," Millet confessed. "I hardened my heart and, ashamed of my inhumanity, rode on without attempting to succor the poor wretch, too much concerned for my own safety to risk a moment's delay." The memory haunted him. "There is no more disturbing spectacle than a solitary victim away from the dramatic surroundings of the battlefield. I almost felt as if this wounded man and I had been carrying on the war between us."

Pausing to lunch on some "putty-like ash cake," he looked up to see two brightly clad scouts of the dreaded Bashi-Bazouk riding toward him down the trail. From there it was a race along a winding brook that finally Millet resolved to jump, steering his mare toward it, clutching her mane, and closing his eyes: "With the ease of a steeplechaser she took the leap in stride. The Circassians drew up at the brook, unslung their rifles and wasted cartridges at me."

Resting briefly at a Cossack outpost, he forced himself to leave its safe confines. "My ambition for adventure was fully satisfied," he admitted. "I left the camp with reluctance, the certainty of scoring an excellent beat outweighing all fainthearted arguments." He reached the Danube at sunset, left his horse with a farmer as collateral for a rowboat, slogged through a swamp at the opposite shore, hitched a ride on a Russian military wagon to the rail line, and hopped a train for the last forty miles to Bucharest, finishing his dispatch on the way. After cabling it to London, he immediately went to rejoin his unit at the Bulgarian front. There he was told that negative news out of Plevna had led the Russian high command to revoke all press passes. So he returned to Bucharest in the belief that his stint as a war correspondent was finished.

MacGahan, when Millet came to his hotel to inform him that they'd been shut down, laughed at the notion. He knew from long experience of Russian bureaucracy that the edict would never be enforced. Though his ankle was far from healed, he immediately set out for Plevna with Millet. Stopped at a Russian checkpoint south of the Danube, he rebuffed an officer demanding they turn back.

"I beg your pardon," MacGahan said, "but I don't believe you're in the military police."

The man blustered, "I'm an infantry colonel!"

"Then you have no authority in this case. *Au revoir*. See you in Plevna!"

The reporters drove in MacGahan's wagon to Skobelev's sector outside the besieged town. It was Millet's introduction to the young general, and like everyone else, he was bowled over by Skobelev's dizzying exuberance. MacGahan had brought food and liquor from Bucharest in expectation of what Millet later confirmed was "a merry night." Joining the party was an American lieutenant, Francis V. Greene, attached to Skobelev's command as a military attaché. Greene filled in the reporters about General Krüdener's second attack on Plevna, which had been disastrous except for Skobelev's brief success early in the day. Skobelev had crashed through the Turkish perimeter with six hundred riders and four cannons and established a bastion inside the town. Hanging on for four hours, he'd withdrawn under heavy fire, losing half his men, many while retrieving wounded comrades from enemy hands.

Back within Russian lines, his white uniform filthy from battle, he'd stomped to the tent of the general who'd failed to send him reinforcements and asked with icy sarcasm if the general would mind if Skobelev rode back into Plevna "and held it until further orders."

The general, a prince named Schahovskoy who was prepared neither for command nor for the day's devastation, regarded him with dismay. "Go where you want," he sneered. "Get killed where you want." The prince's contempt for the social pariah was blatant, Greene told the reporters, but Skobelev took it in stride:

"Thank you, Excellency."

Turning to leave, Skobelev remarked that at least his "unequal fight" in Plevna had saved Schahovskoy's brigade from being outflanked and annihilated. The prince gave a grunt, "like a bear with a sore head," which was something less than gratitude.

At the end of August Skobelev went off "to feel the enemy" by reconnoitering supply routes to Plevna that were not yet under Russian control. MacGahan and Millet, obliged to check in daily with

Grand Duke Nicholas at his nearby bivouac as a stipulation of remaining on as journalists, ran through the mud of the previous night's rain to find the forty-six-year-old commander standing inside the flap of his tent in a dressing gown and slippers. "I suppose you want to go with Skobelev," he said in impeccable English.

They nodded.

The grand duke made the sign of the cross. "Go where you please, and God bless you." The gesture gave them free rein through the rest of the campaign.

Skobelev's knack for finding the hottest fight failed him in this case; no sooner had he left camp than Osman Pasha stormed out of his Plevna emplacements and struck the heart of the Russian line. Coming in two waves about twenty minutes apart, the attack left more than 2,000 casualties. MacGahan got close enough to hear Turks shouting *"Allah akbar!"* as they came, and afterward counted six bodies per every ten feet at the edge of the Russian breastworks.

Hopelessly undermanned, the attack was puzzling coming from so skilled a fighter as Osman. When Millet and MacGahan caught up with Skobelev the next day and described what had happened, the general wondered if it was a feint disguising some other deployment—potentially to the village of Loftcha, a trading hub eighteen miles south of Plevna on the road to Sofia. He would take a detachment to investigate. "Do any of you fellows care to see the fun?" It was a rhetorical question. "If so, saddle up!"

Skobelev made a confession to MacGahan as they rode together: "I've a good mind to desert and join the Turks. Our soldiers are beyond all praise, but the Grand Duke has no more notion of running a campaign than I have for calculus." The facetious comment was subversive in its candor. It opened the door to military discussions between the two men that would continue regularly in the months ahead. Many of MacGahan's subsequent stories featured specific critiques of the Russian performance based on inside information from Skobelev: "All those in high command are very old men whose whole lives have passed in one occupation: card-playing. True generalship consists in adapting existing means to required ends. In this the Turks have excelled. Put a Turk in a ditch, give him a gun, a sackful of cartridges, a loaf of bread, and a jug of water, and he will remain there a month under the most dreadful fire. But Russian generals have no grip of battle and are unwilling to fight with anything but the army of their dreams."

At the outskirts of Loftcha, Skobelev saw that some of his men had already arrived and at the sight of the village had sprinted up the rise toward what appeared to be an abandoned redoubt. Suddenly rifle fire poured out, along with torrents of grapeshot. Skobelev spurred his horse, trailed by a dozen Kubanskis. Millet assumed he wanted to lead the charge, but MacGahan shook his head. "Our fellows have got the fighting madness," he explained. "Skobelev is trying to stop them."

The general, his white uniform "making a splendid target," galloped through the ranks waving his sword. His horse tumbled to the ground, its foreleg snapped by a bullet. One of Skobelev's three companion riders (nine had been shot by this time) gave up his mount. This second horse went down. "The bullets must be falling like hail," MacGahan wrote. "A roar rolls down the hollow in one continuous crash of thunder. I said to myself, 'He has got it this time.'"

Skobelev survived unhurt. He found a trumpeter to blow retreat and, screened by smoke, led his soldiers down the hill bearing their dead and wounded. He'd guessed from the volume of enemy fire that it was hopeless to continue forward; Osman had secretly shifted a full division to Loftcha to protect his Plevna supply line. The next day Grand Duke Nicholas moved 20,000 men and fifty cannons into place to take the village. Eight hours of bombardment were followed by all-out assault. Skobelev, his prestige rising, was given the left wing at the head of 9,000 men. His objective was the strongest outlying redoubt. Forbes had recovered from his fever and was there to watch: "The Russians hung somewhat around it, for it was a grim and formidable obstacle. Suddenly we heard a great cheer. A broad back in a white coat was seen to rush up the sloping face of the Turkish work. A swarm of dark-clothed men followed their guiding spirit, and the redoubt was carried at dusk after a hand-to-hand struggle in which perished all its defenders and many of its assailants."

When Forbes and the Americans clambered up the fortification, they found dead from both armies mingled in heaps. "Skobelev stood panting in the heart of the slaughter leaning on his bloody sword, great smears of blood on his coat," but the general wasn't finished. He ordered his Kubanskis to do what they did best and hunt down the fleeing enemy. "Pursuers and pursued were co-religionists," Forbes wrote, "but there was no pity in the hearts of the Cossack Muslims for the Ottoman followers of the Prophet." The killing—done by hand for the most part, with lances and swords—was vigorous and complete. Three thousand retreating Turks never reached Plevna.

The next evening, hosting a dinner in his imperial tent at army headquarters, Czar Alexander raised a toast. Less than three months had passed since he'd snubbed Skobelev on the parade ground at Sistova. Now he hailed him as "the hero of Loftcha!" Forbes pondered the satisfaction Skobelev surely took from this turnaround: "It is not given to many men to earn a revenge so full and grand."

Skobelev was elevated to a rank above his elderly father, Dimitri, which amused Mikhail no end: "Poor Papa! With all the horses killed under me, he little knows how much money he'll have to fork out to replace them." Now the tab would include some new uniforms befitting Mikhail's rank. He gave his father the bad news when the old general came to congratulate him two days after Loftcha. Dimitri was uneasy in the raucous salon that was Skobelev's field quarters, in a farmhouse just out of sight of the Plevna redoubts. MacGahan was there with Millet, Forbes, and Greene, along with several Cossack officers known as unsavory blackguards. "Skobelev himself owned that they deserved the appellation," Forbes wrote.

Told of his son's latest money requirements, Dimitri crossed his arms and announced he wouldn't pay. Mikhail threatened to pull rank and have him jailed for insubordination. The moment was tense until smiles broke out. Father and son embraced. Dimitri wept in pride, and afterward Forbes observed him sitting in the corner with a dram of *vodki* watching, "with complacent contentment, the rapid play of the younger man's handsome features as he conversed."

With Osman's breakout thwarted, the Russian army, replenished with reinforcements, was ready to hit Plevna again. MacGahan was skeptical, gauging the grand duke's huge advantage in manpower insufficient to dislodge Osman from the defenses his men had been bolstering nonstop since the last attack five weeks earlier. The town bristled with fortified fire positions overlooking killing grounds as bare as mown meadows. On the eve of the initial bombardment, Nicholas and his staff reviewed the Russian ranks. Tens of thousands of infantrymen cheered their leader. MacGahan frowned. *"Morituri te salutant,"* he thought to himself. Those about to die salute you.

The siege guns opened fire on September 7 and continued for four days. During that time, MacGahan and Millet scouted the front for the best place to watch the assault. The redoubt on Krishin hill southwest of town was the most heavily defended, but it lacked the usual network of secondary emplacements that elsewhere made attacks difficult to sustain due to cannon fire and fresh counterattacks issuing from each successive redoubt—in other words, take Krishin, and the path into Plevna was open. "It is the key to the position," MacGahan said as he gazed through his telescope. "And it's in Skobelev's country."

The general was aware. "If I can carry and hold that redoubt," he told MacGahan, "and if reinforcements are sent when I ask for them, we may drive Osman out of Plevna. But everything turns on coordination, and this, as you know, is not our forte."

With artillery pounding continuously, Skobelev's time was filled with reconnaissance probes and arranging his units for the attack, keeping horse-drawn cannons and infantry reserves poised to support the front rank. Most of his 18,000 soldiers were recent conscripts with no combat experience. "I don't expect you to be madly brave," he told them. "That is stupid. I only want every man to do his duty."

Forbes came from headquarters to visit Skobelev's sector. "When he had a quiet hour he spent it with MacGahan," he wrote of the general. "They would talk over Balzac's novels, as much engrossed as if there was no such thing as Plevna in the world."

Millet, more ambivalent toward Skobelev than his colleagues ("I hate deliberate swagger," he said), recalled as "strangely jolly" the days preceding the ground assault. The rumble of cannons created a sort of insulation in which they passed the time at Skobelev's quarters. "He made us quite at home with him. He enjoyed our startled looks when a stray bullet from the Turkish works would whistle through the tent just over our heads."

Outside, sappers extended trenches into no-man's-land to shorten the width of open ground between attacker and defender. Millet noticed that they'd taken all night to push out a few yards. "Not much to accomplish," he remarked to Skobelev.

"Young fellow," Skobelev said with a smile, though at thirty-three he was only three years older than Millet, "don't you like night work?"

"I only wonder why they work in darkness rather than finish the project more quickly by day."

"We are here within range of Turkish cannon," Skobelev explained. "Had we set about entrenching in daylight, it would have made things very unpleasant." He put his arm around Millet. "I'm a humane man. It's my misfortune and sorrow that sometimes I cannot avoid getting my soldiers killed. But I do spare them when I can."

After morning chapel services ("the Russians preface every act, great or trivial, with an appeal for Divine aid," Millet wrote), the attack kicked off under a shroud of drizzle at midday on September 11. The regiments marched forward in precise columns with banners high. They were to hold fire until they were two hundred yards from the enemy, shoot once, and then rush up the long incline, the glacis, that ascended ramplike to the lip of each redoubt.

Telescopes in hand, lying prone on the crest of a hill, MacGahan and Millet enjoyed a perfect view. They squinted through the rain to take in the vast tableau. MacGahan picked on some grapes to calm himself as the Russian columns glided toward the high escarpments looming at the far end of the field. White smoke spewed from the Turkish side as thousands of rifles let fire. Seen from a distance, the Russians faltered with a sort of undulating ruffle, as if hit by a sudden headwind. Whole blocks of men went down, many from terror rather than injury. In this first taste of combat for most of them, "they were shriveling up like green leaves in a furnace flame," MacGahan wrote. Swept by successive volleys, they clawed the ground for cover and hid behind dead bodies, shooting wildly without effect. MacGahan muttered to his colleague, "When they begin to hang like that, there's not much more to be said."

Activity sounded behind them. Skobelev was committing his reserves. "His finger on the pulse of battle," MacGahan wrote, "he'd discerned the symptoms of wavering. This situation could not last."

The general would lead the next wave. He called to MacGahan as he trotted past, "Wish me good fortune, old friend."

"God bless you," MacGahan said.

The reporters crawled forward. To the north, they saw tides of dark-clad Russians roll up the slopes of distant redoubts, only to recede every time. One dense pod of men cut through a cornfield trying to go around an emplacement. Enemy gunners poured down fire from above. "Did but one bullet in ten find its target, none of those gallant fellows would return," MacGahan wrote. "While waiting to see them emerge from this little hollow, my excitement was so great my hand trembled."

Amazingly, the detachment came out the other side of the corn-field and dashed up the less-defended rear of the redoubt. The daring maneuver surprised the Turks. "A rush might do it," MacGahan thought. "Victory was almost within their grasp." It didn't last: "My heart sunk within me. I saw that all this bravery, all this loss of life, would be useless." To his dismay, the Russian reinforcements coming to help were paltry: "Two battalions! They might as well have sent two men." Those holding the redoubt against counterattack had no chance and "were left to die, overwhelmed, broken, vanquished. It was sublime, and it was pitiful."

Skobelev meanwhile had rallied his men and stormed the Krishin redoubt. Accounts by MacGahan, Millet, and Lieutenant Greene concur that only his inspiring example saved the operation. His horse was killed, his sword broken, every one of his staff members shot, but he was the first man up the Krishin glacis and the first to jump into the enemy trench. "Having seen as much as I have seen," MacGahan wrote, "I thought it beyond flesh and blood to break the Turkish fire. Skobelev proved the contrary, but at what sacrifice! In that short rush of a few hundred yards, three thousand men had been left on the hillside."

Evening fell. Skobelev sent word to headquarters that his hold on the redoubt was precarious and he needed reinforcements. Commanders up the line had lost almost 18,000 men without taking one objective. None were inclined to renew the battle at Skobelev's side.

Throughout the day, Osman Pasha had taken advantage of the Russians' poor synchronization and shifted his forces to meet each onslaught. Seeing Skobelev's vulnerability at Krishin, he brought in

Frank Millet here depicts one of General Skobelev's notorious Kubanski Cossacks escorting a Turkish prisoner. Skobelev called it "a sad necessity" to execute prisoners when their care and detainment hindered a unit's ability to fight. "They are shot, but they are not beaten," he said. "Only ruffians and good-for-nothings are capable of such atrocities."

thousands of troops from positions elsewhere. Skobelev knew what was coming. Designed to repel frontal assault, the redoubt had no back wall, just an open portal leading to Plevna's central fortification two miles away. He dispensed shovels to his exhausted men and spent that night driving them to bolster Krishin's rear defense. Where they were unable to build breastworks of dirt and rocks, they fashioned low protective walls from the stacked bodies of Russian and Turkish dead.

Despairing of any response from headquarters, Skobelev rode out the next morning looking for help. He left in charge "a stout officer" named Gortalov with but one mission: "Remain here at any price."

"Remain or die," the major saluted.

Skobelev returned a few hours later to find smoke billowing over Krishin and gunfire crackling in the air. He charged ahead, MacGahan wrote, "but was met by a stream of his own men flying back." Not even he could turn them around this time—"they were worn out, hungry, and dying of thirst and fatigue."

The entire Russian detachment at Krishin would have been wiped out by the Turkish counterattack but for Gortalov and a handful of men holding off the enemy hand to hand while the bulk of their unit escaped. From a distance, Skobelev saw the major in silhouette atop the redoubt. A half-dozen Turks had impaled him on their bayonets and were holding him aloft in display to his retreating comrades. His body writhed. They threw him down Krishin's front slope and raised a victory flag.

MacGahan visited Skobelev in his tent that night. "I never saw such a picture of battle as he presented," he wrote. "His white uniform was covered with mud and filth, his face black with powder and smoke."

The general's broken sword lay beside him. The silk band of his Cross of St. George was twisted and grimy around his neck. He spoke in a hoarse whisper. "My command is half-destroyed, my regiments gone."

Seeing his friend's bloodshot eyes, MacGahan wondered if he'd been crying.

Skobelev put his head in his hands. "I did my best. I could do no more."

The "great assault" of September 11–12 left 20,000 Russians dead or wounded. "To find a parallel," MacGahan wrote, "we must look at the hard fought battles of the American Civil War, Shiloh, Antietam, and the Wilderness." The Turks suffered only 5,000 casualties, but this meant stalemate rather than victory—they remained surrounded, cut off, and facing an army that soon would swell with tens of thousands of new troops.

For more than a month, MacGahan had been saying that ground assaults on Plevna were futile and only a methodical siege could force surrender. His advice had been ignored: "The generals complain that they did not understand the Turk would fight so hard. They might as well say they did not think the Turk would shoot with bullets." Now the Russian command agreed. It brought in Edward Todleben, a fifty-nine-year-old army engineer who'd designed the fortifications at Sebastopol in the Crimean War. Mild and dignified, the professorial Todleben studied the situation at Plevna and laid out a construction schedule of progressive emplacements to encircle and strangle the town. Meanwhile, Skobelev and others would harass the Turkish perimeter, keeping Osman's defenders under sleepless strain for however long it took to break them. The process combined engineering, artillery, and mobile operations in a tactical compression whose essence was simple—"the argument of starvation," MacGahan said.

Turkish lookouts discerned from activity on the Russian line that they were being enclosed. Osman rushed a courier to Constantinople asking permission to quit Plevna and withdraw southwest to Sofia, where Mehemet Ali had shifted his army. The sultan said no. On October 26 he changed his mind and sent word to Osman to get out of there—two days after Todleben's cordon of mortar batteries and 120,000 dug-in troops had been sealed tight.

The siege lasted into December. For the journalists, MacGahan wrote, "It is a kind of monster picnic." They enjoyed comforts of warmth, food, liquor, and genial company while a few miles away thousands of Turks systematically died.

Millet left in November to join Gourko's army in its blockade of the Sofia road. MacGahan stayed at Plevna with Skobelev, who continued to star in his dispatches, his gallantry matched with private glimpses when the action slowed: "The break in the monotony of our existence always comes from Skobelev, who is one of those restless spirits that cannot keep quiet." The general was often cynical about the war, saying that all the medals handed out by the czar would be better stuffed down cannon barrels and fired at the Turks. He would race about with his Kubanski posse, dismount, grab a shovel, and dig a trench alongside a prison detail that was being punished for thieving or drunkenness. He might quaff a bottle of wine and declaim Shakespeare in his quarters, and the next night sleep under a freezing rain with a canvas stretcher for a bunk.

Fatalism ruled his self-view. Even the nightmare of September's "great assault" became, in retrospect, an abiding matter of faith. Sometimes he and MacGahan talked about it. "Why didn't they send you reinforcements?" the reporter asked one evening.

When the question had been put to Skobelev right after the battle, he'd responded bitterly that his fellow generals' neglect had been personal. "Napoleon was grateful to his marshals when they gained him a half hour's time to effect victory. I won days for them, and they didn't support me." But now he was calm. "Who's to blame, you ask?"

"Yes. Who?"

Skobelev shrugged. "I blame no one. It was the will of God."

• • •

It ended just after noon on December 10, 1877. Osman Pasha emp-tied out his stores and distributed a handful of bullets and three days' rations to each of his soldiers still able to carry a weapon. From a peak of almost 40,000 last fall, his army had lost half its men to ill-ness and hunger, and thousands more to Russian arms; the rest were walking skeletons with only patchwork clothes and woven sandals to repel the winter cold. Todleben's siege had turned Plevna into a place of desolation. Osman's sudden breakout with his pitiful remnants was more a dying spasm than a coherent operation. A month earlier, he'd turned down Grand Duke Nicholas's request of him to surrender and spare further loss of life. "My honor forbids it," Osman said, "until all means of defense are exhausted." That moment had come.

His column, making for a bridge across the Vid River west of Plevna, was deluged with fire the moment it appeared in the open. Horses and cows were used as shields; once these were gunned down, the Turks were exposed to perfectly sighted artillery fire that had been months in preparation. With a guttural howl, they swarmed over the first Russian emplacement they came to, plowing through metal gusts of grapeshot and overwhelming the resistance by sheer sacrificial mass. MacGahan, riding to the sound of guns, arrived in time to see the onslaught: "They poured into the battery, bayoneting the officers and men. An entire Russian regiment was in an instant overthrown and annihilated."

Frenzied by their triumph after months of being trapped, the Turks bludgeoned to death every defender, evidently forgetting, MacGahan wrote, "that they had come out to escape Plevna and not take hold of a battery." With few officers and no plan, each Turkish soldier had to gather himself and take in the truth of what lay ahead. This was only the first in Todleben's concentric series of fortifications designed to bleed dry any breakout attempt with multiple murderous obstacles. The Turks roused themselves from soul-deep exhaustion and lurched forward. A hundred Russian cannons erupted "with terrible execu-tion" from the surrounding hills. The ground churned with explo-sions and flying debris. The Turkish column was engulfed in smoke. Its advance slowed to a crawl.

After three hours, the Russians ceased firing: "The smoke lifted, and

there was silence." A white flag fluttered above a cluster of rocks where
many Turks had taken cover. At the sight, waves of Russian cheers
wafted down the valley, "a joyous shout that echoed off the sullen
cliffs overlooking the scene." MacGahan was on horseback alongside
Skobelev and his staff. The general rode forward waving a white hand-
kerchief and pulled up midway across the Vid bridge about seventy-
five yards from a mass of enemy eyeing him with weapons in hand.
Two Turkish horsemen came out and spoke with Skobelev through an
interpreter. "Osman will be coming out," the general told MacGahan
when the reporter rode up.

"We should salute him," said one of his aides. "He made a heroic
defense." Their horses scuffed and snorted, steam spilling from their
nostrils in the cold air.

Skobelev nodded. "He's the greatest soldier of the age. I will offer
my hand and tell him so."

The officers all agreed, "and the butcheries of Russian wounded by
the Turkish army were forgotten"—by them, if not by MacGahan.

In the long minutes of waiting for Osman, the reporter took in
the vision of an obliterated army. Six thousand Turks had fallen that
morning. Dead animals, shattered wagons, and broken bodies lay
everywhere "The ground was bloody and ripped to pieces, telling
how these unfortunates had met their fate." He saw four solders lying
under a tarp staring at the sky. Alive but wounded, "they suffered with
calm fortitude which brought tears to my eyes."

Shouts erupted. "There he is! He's coming!"

But the approaching rider wasn't Osman. It was a startlingly young
officer with fair skin, blue eyes, and a red fez. He introduced himself in French as Osman's chief of staff, Tefik Bey. "Osman Pasha is
wounded."

"Not severely, we hope," Skobelev said.

"I don't know." The young man spoke in a halting whisper. His lis-
teners leaned forward, their politeness strained by excited impatience.

"Where is he?" Skobelev asked.

Tefik pivoted in his saddle and pointed to a stone cottage in the
distance behind him. There was a pause. MacGahan began to think
the man was in shock. Thousands of Russian infantry had come down

from their emplacements and stood opposite thousands of Turks across the river. "The situation was critical," MacGahan wrote, "yet possessed an amusing element that was also embarrassing."

"Is there anybody you'd like to see?" Skobelev offered helpfully.

No answer. Was this Tefik empowered to surrender Plevna or not? He seemed content to sit in silence as two armies stared at him.

Skobelev tried again. "With whom do you wish to speak? Is there anything—" He stopped midsentence and snapped at MacGahan in English, "What the devil is the matter with his man! Why don't he talk?"

One of Skobelev's aides spoke up. "Osman has made a brilliant defense. We admire his character."

"A great general," another added.

Tefik wasn't listening. He gazed down the Sofia road beyond the bridge, where the Turks had been aiming but would never reach. Many high-ranking colleagues had joined Skobelev by now, all hoping to share in the epic occasion. It occurred to MacGahan that if the enemy opened fire, a huge portion of Russian command would be wiped out.

Czar Alexander's representative arrived. He asked Tefik if he had authority to negotiate surrender. The young man seemed to take in the matter for the first time. He shook his head, reined his horse around, and trotted back to Osman's stone shack. The czar's people followed him.

The matter in his superiors' hands now, Skobelev walked his horse across the bridge. MacGahan went with him. Russian medics had begun to tend the enemy wounded. A teenaged soldier was polishing his rifle while the wound in his gut was examined. "He evidently takes pride in his gun," MacGahan observed, "for it is very bright and clean. He has put it carefully under him so it will not be taken away." MacGahan conferred with the medic about the boy's condition. Not good. "He will not live till night."

Osman signed an unconditional surrender that afternoon. Afterward, his foot injured by shrapnel, he draped his arms over two assistants and limped to a waiting carriage. He was bearded and strongly built, "with a sad, endearing, thoughtful look out of his black eyes," MacGahan wrote.

Grand Duke Nicholas rode up with his entourage. He dismounted and went to Osman. "I compliment you on your defense of Plevna. It's one of the most splendid military feats in history."

Osman shook off his helpers and accepted Nicholas's hand. Dozens of Russian officers chanted "Bravo!" Osman gave a nod and got into his carriage, his dirty blue cloak a humble contrast to Nicholas's glittery tunic. Osman was bound for Russia, where he would be detained until the end of the war. But for now his carriage turned for Plevna—he'd requested of his captors to spend one more night in his usual tent.

That evening MacGahan and Skobelev found the Turkish aide, Tefik Bey, wandering on a road outside town. Skobelev insisted he join them at his quarters; after hesitation, the young man agreed. He hardly touched his food but did sip some vodka. His spirits lifted a little when Skobelev proposed a toast to Osman. When one of the guests addressed the general by name, Tefik's expression came alive. "You are Skobelev? The White Pasha?" It was the Turks' nickname for the crazed commander often seen in the midst of fighting.

"I am."

Tefik smiled. "That was a very good attack on Krishin in the fog and rain. But you didn't get it all."

Mikhail Skobelev and Januarius MacGahan were among the Russian throng saluting the Turkish commander, Osman Pasha, after his surrender at Plevna in December 1877. Skobelev wept to see his great foe humbled by injury. "To me, he is Osman the Victorious."

"I didn't want it all."

The two men laughed—a strange meeting of minds that isolated them from the others. "After this momentary fit of sunshine," MacGahan wrote, "Tefik Bey lapsed into melancholy." Skobelev too became gloomy, slumping in silence beside his former foe. He turned everyone out and gave Tefik his bed. "Skobelev then passed the night in a hut of one of his officers," MacGahan wrote. "And so ended this eventful day at Plevna."

MacGahan returned to Bucharest a week later, stricken with the pestilent fever that had afflicted Forbes and many other reporters. "Thin and tired," a colleague described him, "wearing the sheepskin coat of a Bulgarian peasant." His ankle remained unhealed, and illness drained him. Cumulative traumas were taking their toll.

His Plevna dispatches were triumphs. To satisfy reader demand, *The Daily News* had published popular extra war editions throughout the fall, his contributions singled out for excellence. "Those who had the good fortune to read Mr. MacGahan's *Campaigning on the Oxus and the Fall of Khiva*," said one commentator, "will not need to be told that the courage and determination which carried him across the desert of the Kyzlkum have been conspicuously manifest in Bulgaria; nor will his power of description and keen insight be subject of surprise." The acclaim did little to raise MacGahan's spirits, however. He wrote John Robinson, "I who have been lucky all my life, who never undertook anything without succeeding, have failed most miserably during this campaign." He hadn't failed, of course. It only felt that way.

The previous September he'd spent two weeks with his family after the disastrous "great assault" at Plevna. He'd kept to the hotel with Varia and their son, unwinding in the domestic cocoon that had unnerved him in the past but now gave welcome respite. He wasn't alone in needing time to recover. Even the blustery Skobelev had been shaken by that ordeal: "Until then I was young, but I have come out of it an old man." The general consoled himself with alcohol and "the lionesses of Bucharest," to little avail. "I drink and drink, but it grows before me. I see that breastwork of bodies, and Gortalov thrown into the air on the points of the bayonets. Dreadful!"

MacGahan's affection for his family had never been deeper than during that September visit. The same held true now when he rejoined them for the Christmas holidays—enjoying nights out with Varia, playing with their son, and hosting reporters and Russian officers at their hotel. "They came often to see him and stayed for hours," she wrote. MacGahan's closest friends weren't among the guests. Forbes, felled again by illness, had been "invalided" home to Britain. Frank Millet was in the field with General Gourko. And Skobelev was leading an operation to relieve the beleaguered defenders of Shipka Pass. Returning to action was a blessing for the general. "I can't sleep," he said. "Screams still ring in my ears. I forget more easily when at my duties."

MacGahan was content for the moment in Bucharest. His dispatches, reflecting on the fall campaign and the strategic outlook ahead, were milder than his earlier editorials furiously denouncing Russian ineptitude and Turkish atrocity. From outside the redoubts of Plevna, he'd described Osman Pasha as "a monstrous spider inside his web." But seeing the man's dignity in surrender and again later when Osman, still nursing his injured foot, passed through Bucharest on his way to Russia had opened his mind to the humanity of even the Turks. "He was carried up to his room at the hotel in an armchair," he wrote. "A little Romanian girl met him upstairs and gave him a bouquet of flowers. He lifted her up and kissed her."

The MacGahans rang in 1878 sleigh riding together. Varia, fed up with her husband's restlessness, had all but ended their marriage last year; now she was more in love than ever. "We talked nonsense," she recalled, "laughed like crazy, galloping through the streets, and stopped at midnight at a confectionary shop to eat pastry while he added to it a bottle of wine."

It was understood that he would return to the front after the holiday; his work was a mission more than a job. But he'd begun to wonder if his health setbacks didn't signal some dark cloud gathering. "I have been pursued by a fatality," he'd written John Robinson the previous fall—yet clearly the pursuer was he. Millet had noted his friend's growing resignation on a night that fall when MacGahan had declined to move his position after an artillery shell exploded nearby. "Lightning never strikes twice in the same place," MacGahan had rationalized. And at a time of constant peril from midnight sorties of knife-wielding Bashi-Bazouks, he'd curled up in his wagon and gone to sleep. "I'll take what comes," he said.

Millet spent New Year's in the wintry forests outside Sofia, which Gourko was preparing to attack with 80,000 men. The crusty general had a graceful touch and marked the passing of the year by distributing bits of chocolate to his staff from his private stash in a tin box his orderly carried. "Russians are very fond of sweets," Millet wrote, "and we had eaten nothing but captured Turkish rice since Christmas."

Skobelev meanwhile was closing on Shipka Pass. With typical heedlessness, he and his Kubanskis had far outstripped the main column. All night long on New Year's Eve, they stoked dozens of campfires to give enemy scouts an inflated impression of the size of their force. It was anxious work, but it had the effect of distracting Skobelev from "the terrible impressions that torment me," he said.

As all that was occurring, John Russell Young, on hiatus from the *Herald* while he toured the Mediterranean with General Grant, was at sea somewhere between Malta and Egypt; next on the itinerary were the Holy Land and Turkey. The trip was going well but for Young's seasickness. "I never saw water too calm for my nerves," he wrote. "I prefer a hansom cab. I felt like saying to General Grant the other evening when he was talking about his generals, if I could only command an army in a hansom cab I could do wonders."

Young lately had been troubled by dreams about his pregnant wife in London. Thoughts of Rose alone on New Year's dampened his enjoyment of the shipboard celebration that night, and after brandy, cigars, and a brief round of Boston at the card table with the Grants, he retired to his cabin. As was his habit, he made a note in his diary: "At 11:30 I turned in, thinking—well, what did I think? The year goes, as thousands have gone before, and our days go on and on, and the last meditation on all is silence."

With that, he closed the book on 1877.

9

The Pause of an Instant
1877–1890

It was humble work. I have seen nothing of it in canvas or stone, and somehow it has never found a note in the trumpet of fame. It meant everything to be the stricken hero away from home.

JOHN RUSSELL YOUNG, *Notes and Queries* (1892)

In the weeks leading up to Osman's futile breakout from Plevna, Turkish attacks had repeatedly tested the Russian blockade of the town's southern supply lines. Dozens of Russians had died in skirmishes every day. Frank Millet, leaving the Plevna siege to find more action elsewhere, had first caught up with Gourko's army during one such engagement. He was riding with a stocky Greek servant named Paulo, "so loyal, he sleeps in the doorway to protect against intruders." Winter snowfalls had begun. While sewing sheepskin linings into their jackets one afternoon, they heard gunfire coming down off a ridge. Leaving his horse with Paolo, Millet clambered up the steep forest slope. He came to a surgical station, where medics with their "ghastly array of instruments" were treating incoming wounded. "As I hurried past the bodies of Turks and Russians, I could trace by the footsteps and pink blood in the snow the story of the fight."

It was dusk when he entered a clearing, only to realize he'd wandered into the fire zone. Diving behind a tree, he was told by troops crouched around him that they'd been driven from their emplacement at the top of the ridge. Now they were trying to rescue the wounded, "thirty or forty of whom lay on the slope within hearing." Turkish fire pinned them down. As night fell, gunshots yielded to the windy hush of the forest. But it wasn't entirely quiet; for the rest of Millet's life, "a blustery winter evening brings that scene back to me with oppressive reality. I hear the faint cries of the wounded and the stifled groans of friends powerless to help them." Daybreak told the gruesome tale. "Not a wounded man was alive on the snowy slope above. In the fog and darkness the Bashi-Bazouk had crept down and cut off their heads."

The Russians retaliated with a crushing attack the next day. Millet couldn't see the action through the woods but heard it well enough, "as plainly as if across the street came the crack of rifles and Russian soldiers yelling." The sounds were clear in their meaning:

"Let the poor devils go!"

"No! Kill them!"

And in Turkish, "Enough! Enough!" followed by screaming cries for mercy. "Then all was still again," Millet wrote.

Descending from the hilltop, the Russian detachment passed the bodies beheaded the night before. "They could be seen for many days until a charitable snowfall gave them a winding sheet."

Millet and Paulo wandered off in search of a hut to sleep in. Going by foot through the knee-deep snow, leading their horses by the reins, they became disoriented in the dark as they moved along the edge of a ravine. Millet "saw a ruddy light among the trees below and stepped toward it." He slipped, lost hold of the reins, and tumbled down the slope, collapsing in a heap fifty feet from a crackling campfire tucked against "a little amphitheater" of sheltering pines. Three Bashi-Bazouks, weapons in hand, horses tethered nearby, dozed beside it. It was a moment beyond fear: "Everything was so vividly impressed on my mind that I can never forget the slightest detail of it." He'd seen what these men did to captives, yet even in terror he cast a painterly eye on the scene: "The curious little copper kettle gleaming in the firelight, the boots of the prostrate men reflecting the glare from the glowing coals, the shaggy cloaks snow-covered except where the radiating heat had melted the flakes as they fell, the tangle of branches sharply defined overhead as a red tracery against the mysterious gloom of the stormy sky—every feature is as fresh in my memory as if I had looked on it only yesterday."

He eased his revolver from his belt and backed into the darkness beyond the firelight. Somehow he found Paulo and they scrambled out of there, eventually coming to a forest trail. Then they "saw a twinkling light ahead and heard the cheery sound of Russian singing. Soon I was being hugged and tossed in the air by jovial companions." News from Plevna had just arrived—Osman had surrendered. It brought great hurrahs from the men, not least because it meant they could leave their icy confines and start moving again. Heading out with Paulo the next day, Millet gazed up the ravine behind them. A curl of smoke sifted through the treetops—the Bashi-Bazouks' campfire. He spurred his horse forward, grateful not to be lying there in separation from his head.

He came upon a touching scene. It was a soldier's burial deep in the woods. Two Cossacks prayed beside the grave they'd dug for their friend. They reacted shyly to Millet's intrusion; he put them at ease by removing his hat in respect. "Between them," Millet wrote, "a long low mound disturbed the rounded outline of the hill, and a rude cross made of branches added its unexpected silhouette to the shapes of the men, seen as irregular masses against the deep crimson of the western sky."

The graceful ceremony clashed with what he saw when passing through Plevna a few days later on his way to rejoin Gourko: "On a plain outside town are bivouacked at least 15,000 Turkish prisoners, fighting for bread, miserable beyond description, in the cold, with hundreds of unburied dead around them." The Russians, with barely enough supplies for themselves, admitted that feeding captives wasn't a priority; throwing loaves of bread into a pack of ravenous Turks was the best they could do under the circumstances. Ultimately almost all the POWs would die in custody, killed by neglect as surely as if murdered. Russia's honesty about its failure didn't pardon the result, Millet wrote: "Any excuse can have no weight against the total human suffering that resulted from characteristic Russian *laisser aller*."

Thousands of Turkish sick and wounded remained inside Plevna. Only after several days did Russian officials begin inspecting the mosques and other buildings housing the invalids. Millet was there when they opened the doors. His dispatches carry the same trembling outrage MacGahan had felt over Batak and William Howard Russell over the medical crisis in Crimea. "Plevna is one vast charnel-house surpassing in horror anything that can be imagined," he wrote. Inside these makeshift wards, the stench of pus and excrement was overpowering. Bodies covered the floors, the tangle thickest near the doors and windows where victims had crawled to get air. Stepping gingerly through the foul gloom, Millet heard cries for water. He gave a heel of bread to two skeletal men slumped against a wall. Later he found them dead with the bread uneaten.

His reports conclude with a mass burial of Turkish dead. Manpower shortages forced the employment of Bulgarian laborers to collect corpses from the fields and hospitals and haul them to "the common ditch" for disposal. It was an opportunity for easy revenge. The Bulgarians didn't bother about living or dead, bodies warm or cold— everything was piled into the carts. "I have seen this myself," Millet wrote of the burial teams. "One says, 'He is still alive!' Others cry, 'Devil take him! He will die tomorrow anyway. *In with him.*' And the living goes with the dead, and is tumbled into the grave."

Millet screamed at the gravediggers to no avail. He ran to find Mikhail Skobelev, who immediately put forty men under Millet's direction. The reporter led them to the site, and "with drawn revolver and whip in hand, I forcibly took possession of three Bulgarian oxcarts." He spent the day organizing Russian burial details before leaving to catch up with Gourko.

The memory of Turkish wounded buried alive would color his reporting for the rest of the war. "A race without heart," he called the Bulgarians. With Forbes in Britain and MacGahan still with his family in Bucharest, Millet was for the moment his paper's only man at the front. His description of "the final act from the drama of Plevna" shocked readers, brought scandal to Russia's military administration, and tilted *The Daily News* away from the exclusively pro-Russian stance dictated by MacGahan. International sympathy began to extend to all the war's victims regardless of religion or nationality. As the war turned in favor of Bulgaria and against the Turkish occupiers, Millet stood out in denouncing both sides' reprisals as equally barbaric and shameful.

Rejoining Gourko's army, he worried that his graveyard exposé wouldn't sit well with the dour general, whom he'd always tried to

Frank Millet saw countless burials while covering the Russo-Turkish War in 1877–78. One of them, encountered while riding along the Russian line in the Balkan Mountains, touched him so deeply, he drew it from memory years later. "All that friendly hands could do to honor a victim of the fight had been done by his two comrades," Millet wrote.

avoid out of worry he was being allowed to tag along only by bureaucratic oversight. When Gourko summoned him a few days later, he feared the worst. The general was holding a newspaper when Millet entered his tent. "I believe you are the correspondent who wrote the dispatches about Russian treatment of the prisoners at Plevna," he said.

Millet gulped. "I can't deny it."

"Then I wish to say that I approve entirely of what you wrote. It bears the mark of truth." Gourko let his meaning sink in. "I've ordered correspondents away many times, but as long as you stick to the truth, you're welcome in my army."

Millet rode at the general's side after that, promoting him in his dispatches as an alternate hero to MacGahan's flamboyant Skobelev. Previously Gourko had come across as humorless and dull. Millet saw humble warmth, and his fond depiction in his dispatches says as much about him as about the general. No less a fighter than Skobelev, Gourko was calm, persistent, and encouraging. In a grueling winter campaign that every day brought death quite apart from Turkish bullets, those qualities, wrote Millet, "are simply sublime."

General Joseph Gourko was methodical and relentless, like a Russian Ulysses Grant. As Turkish resistance crumbled in 1878, Frank Millet was struck by Gourko's intensity when telling his men not to mistreat prisoners or pillage local towns: "He has a thrilling sternness to his voice when he chooses, and he gave this order with as much earnestness as an order to charge."

Sofia was the western terminus of a rail line running from Philippopolis. Though not operational during the fighting, the track still offered a guiding path through the mountains. Clearing out the enemy would let the Russians use Sofia as a launch point for the final phase of the campaign. Unsure how strong Turkish resistance would be, Gourko decided to deploy his artillery on the high ground overlooking the town. The four-mile ascent was sheer ice. Horses had no traction. Sixty men, their hands frozen on the ropes, hauled each cannon step by step as sappers hacked a trail through the trees and underbrush.

Gourko organized a system in which squads took turns between the ropes and a warm fire. Millet thought the progress needlessly slow until the general, his beard crusted with icicles, corrected him: "These men have stood the long siege at Plevna, and now without delay or rest have made a difficult march here only to find a harder task before them." Gourko remained in the saddle till the last cannon was in place. Only then did he dismount and "without distinction of rank" wedge in among his soldiers. "He scooped a place in the snow, lay down with his feet to the fire, and went to sleep."

The Turks ultimately put up little defense, evacuating Sofia after two days of fighting. Gourko sent a cavalry brigade to nip at their heels and gave the remainder of his army three days' rest with a warning, on pain of death, not to loot or pillage. After the frigid mountains, Sofia was "a veritable Capua" whose citizens opened their homes to their liberators and to Millet, who thought it "an indescribable pleasure to sit in a chair at a table in a warm room and write at my ease."

Five thousand Turkish wounded, "such as could walk," had fled hours before the Russians arrived. "Of their fate there is little doubt," Millet wrote. "The majority will die from cold and hunger, the route of retreat paved with their corpses." Sofia's army hospitals were grim warehouses, many of the patients murdered in their cots by Bulgarians when the Turkish forces pulled out. "This is not a subject I care to linger over," he continued wearily. "It is becoming monotonous to chronicle instance after instance of neglected wounded, of long unburied dead, and of pestilential hospitals; but it is such a prominent feature of this war that one is forced to describe it in order to do justice to the situation." He blamed stupidity more than cruelty: "I firmly believe that if the Russians had recaptured their own wounded, they would have acted no more promptly."

Gourko tried to help. After inspecting the hospitals, "entering rooms where his aides would not go, examining typhus wards and passing among the corpses with the same fixed expression with which he rides into hot musketry fire," he sent men to clean the facilities and deliver rations, astonishing the Turkish patients that "this leader of dogs and assassins" should care for them at all.

Surprisingly, the hospital treating the worst cases was the cleanest and best organized. Gourko's advance scouts had got off on the wrong foot when they'd first gone there, kicking in the door and knocking the cap off the director's head because it bore the red crescent of the Turkish medical corps. She'd refused them entry till their commander offered a personal apology for the insult.

The director was Viscountess Emily Strangford. She'd come to Sofia from southern Bulgaria the previous fall in the belief that as the war turned against the Turks, it would be they and not the Bulgarians who would most need her help. She'd since become devoted to them. Her hospital housed almost two hundred, their wounds so severe that often all she could provide was a dignified death. "They say I am mother and father to them," she wrote. "I grieve for them like old friends. They are so gentlemanly and patient, much pleasanter to nurse than any Englishman of their rank." For her, four nurses, and one volunteer surgeon, it was grueling work. Disease was always a danger; 10 percent of the war's medical personnel died of illnesses contracted in the sick ward. Friends had begged her to get out of Sofia before the Russians came. She wasn't worried. "My name is well known," she said, "and I am a woman and I do not think any Russian officer would interrupt my work. Whatever happens, I cannot desert my men."

A visitor from London had been amazed at Lady Strangford's insistence on upholding appearances despite cannon fire in the distance and the groans of patients in wards adjacent to her living quarters. One evening at dinner she was offering the visitor a spoonful of cream when a painful coughing sounded in the next room. "Oh, dear," she said. "I'm afraid the bey's abscess has burst again."

She and a nurse went to tend the man. After they returned to the table, another nurse offered to pass some melon pieces among the soldiers in their cots.

"Oh no," the viscountess said. "Enough of them have diarrhea already." Whereupon she served after-dinner coffee to her guest.

Her affection for the Turks carried a reciprocal distaste for Russians. Expecting them to commemorate their success with a mass at the cathedral next door to the hospital, she vowed to "put cotton in my ears when they sing the *Te Deum* in celebration." Gourko's visit to her facility, his apology for the behavior of his men, and his promise to post a guard so her work could proceed uninterrupted brought a mixed reaction. "We are the greatest possible friends," she said of the general. But later she told an interviewer that, in the beginning at least, he'd behaved like a brute: "He spat at me and swore at me."

"Gourko spat in your face?"

"He spat somewhere. I saw him spit somewhere."

"And he swore at you?"

"Dreadfully."

"What did he say?"

"I don't speak Russian. But some things are easy to understand."

Millet, as impressed by Lady Strangford's pluck as by Gourko's vigilance, downplayed the dispute. "There was some difficulty at first," he wrote, "but everything has been amicably settled." Gourko, he assured readers, was respectful, "which I'm sure she appreciates." As for the feisty viscountess, "the fact that she remained at her post at a time when her sex and her position were not the least protection need only to be recorded to be admired."

The Russians marched out of Sofia the second week of January. "A more dramatic scene cannot be imagined," Millet wrote. "Batteries of artillery, the caissons and gun carriages piled high with forage for the horses, alternated with masses of infantrymen trudging through the deep snow, their heads enveloped in pointed hoods and their legs and feet wrapped with straw and rags." They were in Philippopolis six days later. "Crossing the great Balkan range in severe winter weather, driving the enemy before it, occupying the city after a series of bloody engagements—it is one of the most brilliant feats of the war." Eight months after Archibald Forbes had anointed Gourko a great general, Millet backed up the claim. Yet his first dispatch from Philippopolis confessed to smaller concerns: "If I were to write on the subject which at present interests me most, it would be an essay on the luxury of a bed."

He would have no rest. Adrianople, the last major town before Constantinople, was a hundred miles away, at the far end of the Maritsa valley. Chased from the west by Gourko and from the north by Skobelev, whose forces had blown through Shipka Pass and poured down the mountain like an avalanche, the remnants of Turkey's huge Bulgarian force streamed eastward toward sanctuary beyond the border. With sympathy for the Turks that was rare among the reporters, Millet admired their attempts to mount defensive stands despite months of crippling defeat. "No justice will ever be done to the heroism of their last resistance against such great odds," he wrote. "They were defending their homes and religion against an invader who in their eyes represented everything that was cruel, despotic, and despicable."

The desperate courage of many Turkish soldiers contributed only in part to the carnage of the war's last days. Fleeing alongside were tens of thousands of civilians, "the whole Turkish population of Bulgaria, led to desert their homes on account of fear of the invader and by command of the pashas, who ordered the people to accompany them in retreat." Families pushed laden oxcarts through the snow while fighting raged around them. Stragglers were jumped by local peasants wielding farm tools and kitchen knives, avenging the massacres of the previous April. The harassment intensified as word spread of the refugees' helplessness. Marauders tracked them like packs of wolves. Bodies accumulated "with terrible wounds in the head and neck, mutilated and disfigured, women and infants, children and old men, fallen in the fields by the roadside half-buried in the snow or lying in pools of water in the ditch."

Millet came upon a wagon with young and old scattered around it. Most had been killed with axes, the patriarch with a scythe: "It was a pitiable sight to see the grey-bearded Turk lying with his open Koran splashed with blood from gashes in his throat." Bulgarian youths picked through the clan's belongings. "Who did this?" Millet asked.

"We did. We and our friends." Their manner was "effusive," their grins "fiendish."

He rode on, steering his horse around corpses littering the road. His descriptions seethe: "Crowds of Bulgarians swarmed in this great avenue of desolation, choosing the best of the carts and abandoned possessions. Bundles of rags and clothes nearly all held dead babies. Tiny hands and feet, innocent and peaceful baby faces, caught the eye in every wayside pool. But these scavengers would drive the carts across the heads of dead women and old men without even a glance of curiosity at the bodies."

Memories of the experience would stay with Millet all his life. He later took time from his painting career to publish essays and short stories about it. The stories are bleak ("a hue of ashes where the rosy tinge of life had been"), while the essays convey, often with dark humor, his wonder at finding himself in a combat zone instead of an artist's studio. In addition to written recollections, he gave lectures about the Russo-Turkish War. He usually opened with an apology to his audience that it was "ancient history," its names obscure, the nations involved little understood by Americans. He was restrained about the worst details, since "they were brutal and sickening—too brutal to speak of, too sickening to think of even at this distance of time." Yet for all its horrors, he said, the experience had tested his mettle and showed him the grandeur of common soldiers on both sides. "They have no poets to tell of their noble deeds and unparalleled endurance," he said. "They went into the war impelled by the noblest of purposes, ignorant of diplomatic tricks and the unscrupulous devices of politicians."

Skobelev entered Adrianople on January 24. MacGahan was a day behind him, his progress hindered by the rickety wagon to which he lashed himself with leather cord to keep from falling out. For the third time in less than a year, he'd broken the same ankle. Combined with constant fever, it left him sallow and pinched with pain. Like Millet, he'd seen dreadful sights on the ride into town. The worst was a little Turkish girl lying in the snow. Climbing down from his wagon to help her, "I laid my hand on the little face and it was hard and cold as ice." It lingered with him beyond countless other horrors he'd witnessed: "The imprint of her icy face remains on my hand as distinct as when I first touched it." Even for him, sectarian vengeance—she was a Turk, after all—could no longer justify such cruelty.

Hearing of Gourko's approach from the west, MacGahan marveled that the general had managed the feat after resting his men, "half-starved, half-frozen," in Sofia for only three days. Skobelev had covered the last 250 miles to Adrianople in twenty days, leaving the land scorched and plundered. "It will be many years before it recovers," MacGahan wrote. Skobelev's troops, thanks to MacGahan's coverage, shared the luster of their commander. After one engagement, the reporter had toured a surgical station. A soldier about to have his leg amputated refused anesthetic. "No chloroform?" MacGahan asked.

The man shook his head. "Just a pipe and tobacco." In explanation he added, "I ride with Skobelev."

Pronouncing the war "virtually over," MacGahan closed his dispatch of January 26 by admitting, no doubt reluctantly given his pro-Bulgarian sentiments, that much of the current killing was by Christians against Muslim civilians: "English friends of the Turk could not do better than organize some system of relief for the fugitives now arriving in Constantinople by thousands." Beyond hunger and injury, disease would spread as the weather warmed, insects would swarm, and latrines would turn boggy and putrid. "The mortality will be terrible," he wrote.

A cease-fire was imposed at the end of January. Peace talks progressed quickly over the next month as Russia sought to consolidate its gains before the rest of Europe stepped in to limit them. Britain was in a state of alarm that Russian forces were now outside the Ottoman capital with nothing to stop them from seizing it; a fleet of British warships was sent to the Dardanelles, the strait linking the Aegean Sea and the Sea of Marmara south of Constantinople. But Sultan Abdul-Hamid just wanted all the foreigners to go home. Signing away Bulgaria to Russian control was fine by him. Many of his generals shared this view. "They did not seem much distressed by the misfortunes of their country," MacGahan marveled. "They spoke freely of the ups and downs of war, and appeared to regard it as an interesting game of chess in which their side happened to lose."

He warned *Daily News* readers that if the sultan didn't come to terms, Russia would resume the campaign and prosecute it without mercy. That was Skobelev's preference, he added, clearly enjoying the dread this provoked in Britain's conservative circles: "In the case of declaration of war by England, Skobelev can throw four divisions on the heights above Constantinople in forty-eight hours."

Millet, reunited with MacGahan and Skobelev after two months apart, got an earful from the young general on the same subject. Due to sensitive peace negotiations, Russian military were not permitted inside Constantinople until a treaty was signed. This rankled Skobelev, who grabbed Millet one evening, donned the reporter's coat as a disguise, and went with him for a secret stroll through the city; the escapade gave him bragging rights as the only Russian soldier to enter the Turkish capital during the war. He shared his future hopes with Millet during their jaunt: "He wanted Russia to conquer the world, beginning with the absorption of the Ottoman Empire, extending to the conquest of India, and ending with piratical designs on England and Europe." Maybe this was Skobelev's usual guff, but Millet wasn't sure: "I would have dismissed it as utter moonshine had I not been a witness to the previous months, when he rose from an inferior posi-

Januarius MacGahan (left) and
Frank Millet, 1878. The photograph
shows their contrasting conditions
at the end of the Russo-Turkish
War. Millet wears a Russian medal
and press brassard while sporting
his *nagajka* whip draped around his
neck. MacGahan, seated due to his
broken ankle, looks stiff and gaunt,
with bone-thin fingers and wrist.

tion to become the hero of the war. Whether a madman or a genius, he
was the practical hand which Russia held on Turkey's throat."

More bloodshed was avoided when the Treaty of San Stefano was
signed on March 3, 1878. Turkey gave its eastern territories of Arme-
nia and Georgia to Russia and granted independence to Bulgaria and
to several smaller Christian republics, including Serbia and Monte-
negro, rendering them Russian puppet states in accordance with the
czar's Pan-Slavic dream. When *The Daily News* published an account
of the signing, which took place at a seaside village outside the capital,
John Robinson praised its American authors: "The following letter,
the joint work of two correspondents who have contributed narratives
of some of the most striking episodes in the war, brings the history of
the struggle between Russia and Turkey to a close, with the description of a scene no less picturesque and romantic than important for its
historical interest."

The dispatch is restrained. After seeing firsthand the war's human
cost, MacGahan and Millet might have been forgiven for reaching for
cosmic meaning. Instead, they constructed the piece for suspense, with
units from both armies, "scarcely more than a rifle shot away," standing in formation outside the cottage where diplomats finalized the

treaty's details. "One o'clock passed. Two o'clock passed. Rain fell, but they remained at their posts." Finally Ambassador Ignatiev emerged in the late afternoon and saluted Grand Duke Nicholas: "I have the honor to congratulate your Highness on the signature of peace."

It was dusk when Russian troops passed in review before the high command on their way to bivouac for the night. The Turks watched them go. "Like true soldiers," MacGahan and Millet wrote, "they had learned to respect and esteem each other, and welcomed peace as an honorable finish to a war they cared not to prolong." As the Russians paraded away, the reporters listened to the slow fade of boots tramping in lockstep down the road. The grand duke and his generals—except Skobelev, who'd pointedly declined to attend—lingered behind, sitting on horseback in silent contemplation as darkness fell. Only at that moment in their dispatch did MacGahan and Millet shift their prose to the present tense for its simple last line:

"So ends the war of 1877–78."

While steaming through the Sea of Marmara on his way to Constantinople, John Russell Young had stood at the *Vandalia's* rail and gazed on Turkey's coastline with mixed emotions. Like everyone in General Grant's touring party, he was anxious to learn how the last days of the Russo-Turkish War had played out. He also carried an irrational dread that a tragic telegram awaited him about his wife in London: "I look with trepidation upon land, lest I may have news." In an ongoing ritual of penance for leaving Rose during her pregnancy, he was constantly vowing to quit drinking and smoking in order to be a better husband when he returned to her. But it was impossible in the constant round of banquets and late-night card games with Grant. "I have made many resolutions of this kind," Young wrote in his diary, "but cannot control my poor human nature."

The *Vandalia* had docked at San Stefano on March 1, two days before the treaty signing. At a shipboard reception that evening, Eugene Schuyler of the American legation explained to Grant that peace talks were at a final stage, and the president should continue to Constantinople to be greeted by Turkish officials. Schuyler apologized that Turkey's recent defeat "perhaps tended toward diminishing the usual pomp and ceremony which belong to Oriental receptions." Grant was relieved to hear it. Young explained to Schuyler, "General Grant, with his dislike of grand reviews and military displays, is pleased that he will escape the usual round of warlike pageants that await him in every port."

After dinner, three Americans came to pay respects—MacGahan, Millet, and Lieutenant Greene. Conversation went late as Grant sought their impressions of the war and the Russian military. "Grant is very strong in his ideas against the Turks," Schuyler wrote in his journal afterward. It was a *Herald* reunion for the reporters and Young, who found Millet looking vigorous but his colleague in bad shape. Schuyler concurred: "MacGahan is full of interesting accounts of events and people, but he has suffered much in the campaign and is very lame."

Two nights later General and Mrs. Grant were at Schuyler's residence in the Pera section of Constantinople, on the north side of the Golden Horn inlet dividing the city, where most Europeans lived. News arrived after midnight of the peace signing at San Stefano. Grant had almost gone to bed too soon to hear it. Staying up late for tea didn't appeal to him until Schuyler offered "whisky toddy and cigars." When the Italian ambassador burst in with word of the treaty, everyone enjoyed another drink and a laugh that they should learn of the war's official end before the British, who'd been obsessing over it for weeks.

MacGahan and Millet visited the next afternoon, recounting the previous day's scene at San Stefano. The rain clouds had parted as Grand Duke Nicholas announced the signing to his troops, MacGahan told Grant: "I must say that the peace was not greeted with anything like the wild excitement caused by the czar's proclamation of war last April. These men were worn out by cold, hunger, and fatigue." This aroused Grant's memories of the exhausted mood at Appomattox after the Civil War. When the reporters had gone, he and Young reflected on the parallel state of the Turkish capital. "Everywhere," Young quoted Grant later, "are strong and fallen men desolated by a dreadful experience."

The *Vandalia* left Constantinople with Grant's touring party on March 6. In Greece two days later, Young received a telegram from

Rose: "My little daughter is born!" They would name her Catherine, "the crowning mercy of another little one to replace our dear Marnie." It was the start of a positive period for him. Rejoining his family in London, he met with James Gordon Bennett, Jr., while there. The publisher praised the accounts of Grant in repose that Young had been sending the *Herald*. He suggested Young expand them into a book about the tour, which shortly would continue to India, Burma, China, and Japan. "I always wanted to write a book," Young admitted. "I never felt I had anything to say or that there were not a thousand people who could not say it better." The first of two volumes, *Around the World with General Grant*, would appear the next year to wide popularity. Soon afterward, however, the pages of his diary would go dark as he mourned the death of both his wife and his newborn daughter from sudden illness.

On leaving Constantinople that March morning in 1878, Young hadn't minded that it was one of Grant's briefest ports of call—the place was depressing. "Some cities have the great misfortune of being situated in positions which seem to attract strife," he wrote. "Here sooner or later will swords be crossed and shots fired, until the Bosporus becomes the dividing line between races of a different creed." Millet shared Young's impatience to get out of there. With the war over, newsmen were pouring into Turkey acting as if they'd never left. "I was disgusted with the bluster of some correspondents," Millet wrote Mark Twain. "It made me hate the trade."

Millet said goodbye to Skobelev and Gourko and arranged to meet up with MacGahan next summer in Paris, where he planned to resume painting and MacGahan to write a book about the war. He then packed his gear, sent *The Daily News* his last expense sheet, and started for Paris in mid-March. He took along his servant Paolo and several trunks of Turkish and Bulgarian clothes, rugs, and jewelry. He also packed four medals for valor he'd been awarded by the Russians. He joked about their significance: "When I get to believing, as I always have and do yet, that I am a confounded coward, I can refer to this proof to the contrary. What a consolation for old age! Just imagine being able to answer a chap who calls you a poltroon, 'No, sirree! Just go to St. Petersburg and search the military archives!'"

MacGahan, after his brush with mortality at the Paris Commune, had found himself drawn to the security of wife and family. Millet made the same leap a year after the Russo-Turkish War, marrying Elizabeth "Lily" Merrill, twenty-four-year-old daughter of an established Massachusetts family with roots dating back to the Pilgrims. He'd been friendly with her in Paris before the war, but only on his return did he succumb to what he called the "malady" of her appeal. He'd always found women attractive if not quite compatible, favoring as an objective ideal "an intelligent, capable, sensible girl with a face and figure to stimulate the ambitions of a worn and weary painter." That was Lily. A later portrait by John Singer Sargent captures a woman of dark eyes and creamy skin whose beauty conveys the ingrained privilege of her Boston lineage, stately and casual both.

The spontaneous sexual rapport Millet had experienced with Charles Stoddard in Italy three years earlier was, for the moment anyway, put out of mind; likewise any liaisons he'd enjoyed since, including "a first-rate young Greek" with whom he'd claimed to be "spooning frightfully" in a letter written to Stoddard in June 1877. In a similar sort of conventional anchoring, his artistic goals pulled back from the rarefied aesthetic preached by his mentor, Charles Francis Adams, to ones more accessible and lucrative.

After enduring the hardships of war, he wasn't inclined to sit in a garret creating high unsalable art. He would feed popular tastes with genre paintings that captured everyday life in agreeable narratives of work, domestic routine, and family relationships. Later he moved on to public projects, decorating lobbies, ceilings, and interior facades of civic buildings across America, from train stations to city halls. He worked tirelessly on multiple projects, eventually managing a virtual industry of assistants. Within a decade he was well on his way to wealth and fame. "Keeping the market supplied," as he put it, was a far cry from the avant-garde trailblazing of French impressionism, which he came to admire. Perhaps in atonement for compromising his ideals, he gave financial support to students and struggling painters through academies, guilds, and art societies in Europe and America.

He and Lily kept homes in Massachusetts and New York while basing themselves near London in the picturesque Cotswold village of

Broadway. They had three children, losing a fourth to diphtheria at four months. Millet traveled frequently while his wife, their grandson later wrote, "quietly raised their family in England, allowing her husband many of the joys but few of the responsibilities of married life." Their home, Russell House, was the vibrant center of an artist colony that included three of Frank's best friends, the American painters Edwin Abbey and John Singer Sargent and the British-born Alfred Parsons, whose work was said by another friend, Henry James, to present the exact image of idyllic English country life that Americans romantically imagined.

Millet undoubtedly had discontents. It was said he and Lily respected each other but didn't really get along. But like the "mad career" he professed to be unable to stop, his flawed marriage provided him with stability, financial freedom, and social status. Not much of a churchgoer, he often gave a notably secular blessing at the family dinner table (when he was home) that hints at his inner view of his marriage, his work, and himself: "We shall have to do today a lot of things we don't want to do, so let us do them with the best possible will."

Monitoring the Russo-Turkish War from Prussia, Otto von Bismarck hadn't worried about it until Britain actually seemed poised to intervene to defend Constantinople. The chancellor didn't want to choose sides in a shooting war between Russia and Britain, the great powers to his east and west. He preferred to keep alliances flexible while consolidating the still young German empire.

The Treaty of San Stefano didn't help matters. Bismarck shared the British view that it overly penalized Turkey and overly rewarded Russia, especially in the treaty's double move of expanding Bulgaria far beyond its former borders and then handing this new "Greater Bulgaria" over to Russian control. To restore balance, Bismarck called for an international conference in June 1878. There, thanks to his backroom machinations beforehand, Germany, Austria, France, and Britain came in with unified demands that Russia scale back its winnings and chop Bulgaria to half the size stipulated at San Stefano.

MacGahan received instructions from John Robinson in May to make preparations to cover this upcoming Congress of Berlin for *The Daily News*. He wouldn't have missed it—it would close the curtain on the Balkan saga to which he'd devoted the previous two years. The Congress was scheduled to begin on June 13, the day after MacGahan's thirty-fourth birthday. He died on June 9.

His colleagues were stunned by how quickly it happened. Once doctors got a look at his deteriorating condition, their diagnosis of typhoid, a bacterial infection transmitted by contaminated food and water, progressed in less than a week to the more dangerous typhus, caused by a lice-born parasite prevalent in overcrowded prisons, hospitals, and army camps of the nineteenth century. Typhus is deadliest when it spreads to the brain, inducing vertigo, delirium, and coma. He'd started getting chills and chronic headaches in April. "Gastric fever," he'd thought. Nothing serious.

Frederic Villiers, the young illustrator for the London *Graphic,* had recently returned to Turkey after recovering from illness. He was one of the first to voice concern about MacGahan: "He ate quinine by the spoonful." With thousands of refugees overwhelming Constantinople's sewers and fouling its public spaces, typhoid and smallpox were rampant. "The funeral dirge was heard throughout the city from sunrise to sunset," Villiers wrote. "The mosques, with their crowds of homeless and starving, were like huge, festering sores contaminating the atmosphere."

Edwin Pears, *The Daily News*'s correspondent in the capital, noticed his colleague's frailty. He hosted MacGahan at his summer home on the Sea of Marmara. "He was the delight of all our family." MacGahan's Arctic memoir, *Under the Northern Lights,* had a fan in Pears's son. The two of them, Pears wrote, "would sit by the pond in my garden and construct fleets of paper boats to amuse themselves."

Against Pears's advice, MacGahan returned in mid-May to Constantinople, where his wife and son had just arrived from Bucharest. Forever careening between affection and disregard for them, he'd been barraged with letters from Varia. They alternately condemned and forgave his failings as a husband and father—but they were consistent in

Correspondents Archibald Forbes (left) and Frederic Villiers of *The Daily News* and London *Graphic* missed much of the Russo-Turkish War due to illness but subsequently worked together in India, Burma, and Africa. "The most remarkable personality I have come across," Villiers said of Forbes. "Grand physique, great courage, and bent on adventure."

expressing the despair of a woman at wit's end. She blamed herself for "this crazy love I still have for you" and hated herself for perpetuating "this joyless, parasitic existence that brings happiness to neither of us." He owed her nothing, she said: "I gave myself to you without reserve and knew well what I was getting into. You have no duty toward me."

But reading between the lines of his few letters of reply, she'd whipped herself into anger that he was teasing her with hints of his infidelity: "The way you compare me with other women leads me to believe that you are not neglecting any opportunity to acquire all the experience possible in this connection." He'd heard this from her before and had always been able to dispel it with a joke or a kiss. But with his *Daily News* assignment to Berlin coming up, he felt at a crossroads where he must finally break with her or recommit.

Asking only temporary child support until she could provide it alone, she gave him every out: "Please don't suspect that I am engaging in some hidden intrigue. My cards are on the table." He could have ended it right there. But her stoic dismissal of their emotional ties stung him more than if she'd screamed or wept. She sought only practical aid: "I beg you to send me money to live on. I am in grave need." He'd shot back a telegram telling her to come to Constantinople with Paul.

He got them a flat in Pera and moved in with them. "For a few more days we were happy," she wrote. They slept in separate rooms; she wasn't sure if he insisted on the precaution because his ailment might be contagious or because their marriage was possibly over. On May 31 he learned that Francis Greene had come down with fever and was confined to a room at the American consulate. He insisted on keeping vigil at his friend's bedside through the night. "I asked him to be cautious," Varia wrote, "but he would not listen to that."

MacGahan returned to their flat the next two evenings, reading fairy tales to his son. "He could play and speak with Paul better than I," she recalled. "He never tired of noise and childish conversation." In the middle of the second night, he came into Varia and Paul's room to kiss the sleeping child. "I asked him to lie down in my bed," she wrote, "but he refused." They parted the next morning. Two days later he sent word that he was at the British hospital suffering from typhoid; she and Paul must stay away. From his doctors, she learned that the disease might be typhus and may have spread to his brain.

Frederic Villiers was at Skobelev's headquarters six miles away at San Stefano. The general was hosting a visiting French officer, and they were discussing the motivation of soldiers from different nations. What made the Turks so formidable, Skobelev said, was that they were always fighting for Islam. Villiers said Russians were the same, except their religion was equal parts faith in the czar and in the Orthodox Church. Skobelev suggested to his guest that the French army's religion was personal glory. "But you English," he said to Villiers, "have no religion to fight for."

"I disagree. We have the best religion of all."

"And what's that?"

"British interests."

"By God, you're right!" Skobelev leaned forward slyly. "I respect you redcoats so much, I'd like to fight you and see who'd win."

A message arrived: "MacGahan seriously ill. Unconscious." Skobelev gave Villiers his horse to ride back to the city. He told Villiers to assure their friend that he'd be at his bedside before nightfall. Villiers took off at a gallop.

Twenty-five years later, Frank Millet would write a short story in which the narrator watches a young colleague die of typhus: "They raised him in bed, thumped his poor back, and pulled out his swollen tongue." Last rites are discussed. "The Catholic friends were overruled. It was decided to consult no spiritual advisor." Hours pass. Dogs bark in the street. The patient's breathing comes hard. "We had long since stopped the medicine, and nothing remained but to ease the sufferer over the chasm." Millet's narrator moves beside his friend's cot. "There was no fear in those eyes that rolled in their hollow sockets. At last he turned toward me and said plainly, 'All right, old boy.'" His face becomes still. "The pause of an instant, while death was asserting its power, impressed me strangely—and this was no new experience for me. An awful vacancy yawned."

In the story's afterword, Millet explained that its details were "absolutely true." Did he base the scene on MacGahan's death? He'd set himself up at a studio in Paris by then; rushing to Turkey in time to attend his friend's sudden illness would have been almost impossible. Still, Archibald Forbes, who definitely wasn't there, said Millet definitely was. So did two of Millet's grandchildren in biographical sketches of him. However, Millet's many accounts of the period don't mention a return to Turkey after his departure in March. So it's likely that John Robinson's telegram to him at Montmartre was the first he heard the news: "You will be grieved to hear that MacGahan died on Sunday in Constantinople. I cannot say how distressed I am."

When giving future lectures about his youthful stint as a war correspondent, Millet always ended on a personal note: "In my reverence for the memory of him, I can but feel pained that in America his name should be almost unknown." He was speaking of MacGahan. They'd had their differences—MacGahan only grudgingly conceded any humanity in the Turks, whereas Millet, though appalled by the Bashi-Bazouk, equally denounced Russia's criminal neglect of its POWs and the savagery of Bulgarian vigilantes. Their brotherhood endured, however. "MacGahan was loyal, generous, and true," Millet told his audiences. "Those of us who were fortunate enough to know him intimately will never resign ourselves to his loss."

Frederic Villiers, breathless from his ride, got to the hospital minutes too late. Attendants had closed off the room where MacGahan lay until it could be washed and sanitized. Footsteps bounded up the stairs. Skobelev had come by train from San Stefano. He shoved aside the orderlies and went to MacGahan's bedside. He took the body into his arms, murmuring, "Dear brother, did you think I'd forgotten you?"

A hospital messenger brought Varia the news, whereupon "I lost my senses. I did not admit the possibility of death." Seeing her husband's body didn't dispel the fantasy: "I got the senseless hope that he had not died. His face was the same. He seemed to have a childlike expression, like someone without troubles." The doctor drew her away, and "I said goodbye to the dear man whom I had loved for the past seven years."

Dominican monks conducted a funeral mass the next day. Varia attended but was too distraught to accompany the coffin to the Greek cemetery outside Pera. Villiers later described a congregation that included Schuyler, Pears, Skobelev, some embassy officials, and several "brother correspondents." He went on, "When the sad procession arrived at the cemetery there was some misunderstanding about the interment—the grave was not yet dug—so the corpse was placed in the mortuary and the mourners returned to town." Early the next morning he, Skobelev, and Pears came back to lower the coffin. "Skobelev was broken down with grief and sobbed like a child. We had some difficulty getting him away from the grave."

Varia visited a day later. The cemetery was old and decrepit, "a wilderness of neglected graves half-buried in wild reeds and shrubs." Yet among its dismal monuments bloomed a bed of white and red flowers, jasmine and rose, freshly planted around her husband's plot. She asked a groundskeeper where they'd come from. The answer was a name she didn't recognize:

"Viscountess Strangford."

Archibald Forbes would always insist that in addition to the flowers, Emily Strangford provided MacGahan's headstone "with an inscription true and beautiful." He wasn't there to attend the ceremony and based this assertion on hearsay. He later wrote many remembrances of his colleague, tender benedictions not unlike the flowers sent by Lady Strangford, "his great and loving friend." Like her, Forbes wished he could have said goodbye in person. Every eulogy he wrote, he said, "puts a poor stone on the cairn to the memory of MacGahan."

After their parting in 1876, the viscountess didn't write again in her diary about the man she'd called "McG." Her entries became spotty as the war progressed. Whatever was exciting in her work was eclipsed by its terrible reality. Her advertisements for donations in British news-papers reflect the change. Early requests are for household items such as shoes and children's clothes; they give way to calls for bandages, crutches, and "apparatus for artificial arms and legs, and boots for partial amputations of feet."

Her relief effort was eventually surpassed by more established hu-manitarian organizations, including Britain's National Aid Society, the Stafford House Committee, and the Red Crescent Society (a Turkish version of the International Red Cross). Private contributions from Britain exceeded £300,000 by war's end, an astonishing sum that Lady Strangford applauded—though not without a nod to the comparative efficiency of her little group. "It is wonderful to see," she said, "though I cannot help adding, thousands have been thrown away."

In February she turned her Sofia hospital over to local control and went to rest in Vienna for two months before traveling to Turkey. Most international charities there were focused on civilian refugees, but she took up where she'd left off: "Those who have tended the brave, gentle, and patient Turkish soldier cannot be other than glad to return to such work." She announced that her specialty would be treat-ing patients with terminal injuries. Many in Constantinople's British community thought this egotistical; likewise her claim that donations to her cause had been given "by friends and strangers who care to help *me*." Tales she told of her time in the war zone—of enduring Russian bombardment, of seeing caregivers die, of tramping with the young surgeon William Stephenson through Sofia, picking dying Turks off the street and carrying them back to her hospital—were mocked as "impossible stories." Edwin Pears attended an embassy party at which a visiting English lord teased Lady Strangford behind her back for "singing the praises of the Turk." And the ambassador's wife was heard to express satisfaction that her husband, in denying some request of the widowed viscountess, was "less impressed than most gentlemen by the lady's beauty and charm."

In early May she opened a hospital and an adjacent orphanage at Scutari, on the Asian shore of the Bosporus. A short boat ride from the urban swarm of Constantinople, Scutari was where Florence Nightingale had nursed British soldiers in the Crimean War. It's also where MacGahan had wanted his wife to take an apartment when she'd first arrived from Bucharest. But Varia had demanded to be near his workplace in Pera rather than in "the wilderness" forty-five minutes away. He'd cited health concerns for her and their son. She'd suspected some other reason. Had she consented, MacGahan would have had occasion to see Lady Strangford in Scutari while visiting his family. Perhaps they met anyway. Flowers on his grave are the only indication that they kept somewhat in touch.

The viscountess closed her hospital in September 1878 and took a recuperative cruise through the Black Sea, so indifferent at this point to social appearances that telling everyone, "Dr. Stephenson accompanies me," seemed in no way indiscreet. But once back in London, she was snubbed by former friends. "Why am I so persistently ignored?" she wrote one hostess. "Is it only because I don't keep a carriage?" No explanations came, though doubtless her wartime activities made her seem strange and risqué to the ladies of Park Lane.

In 1882 she again put on her nurse's habit and headed this time to Egypt, where a coup against the British-backed regime had forced a military incursion to restore order. A British medical official toured Cairo's military hospitals and was appalled by everything he saw except at one civilian-run facility that treated British and Arab soldiers together. "I wish you could go and see Lady Strangford's hospital," he wrote the surgeon-general, "and see what can be done by the energy of one woman."

After founding the Victoria Hospital at Alexandria, Lady Strangford returned home to great honor. She received a Red Cross medal and became a leader in the Women's Emigration Society, helping poor

British women and single mothers to resettle in the colonies. On the eve of her return to Egypt in 1887, where she planned to open a hospital for British seamen, she met with her solicitor to update her will. Stipulating that her wealth be distributed among goddaughters and the Bulgarian orphans she'd adopted in 1876, she closed with a request to be buried beside her husband at London's Kensal Green cemetery with "Lord Have Mercy On Me" carved under her name. Alternatively, "should I die at a distance from England and the bringing home of my body a great expense, let it be buried where I die. My funeral is to be plain and inexpensive."

She died of a stroke while at sea a few weeks later. She was fifty-three. The vessel turned around and brought her home. The stone she shared with her husband was so jammed with details of his Strangford lineage there was no room for the plea for God's mercy she'd wanted inscribed by her name. One likes to think she didn't need it.

Mikhail Skobelev died at thirty-nine in a whorehouse in Moscow. His political enemies, of which he had many by 1882, were overjoyed. His friends tried to cull some redemption from the seamy particulars, suggesting he'd died of poisoning rather than a heart attack midcoitus. It didn't stick. Before long the impression was fixed across Europe that the great general had left a legacy that Frank Millet called, when he heard the news, "miserable, wasted, futile."

Russia's victory over the Ottoman Empire had been almost completely negated by the maneuvers of Bismarck at the Congress of Berlin in 1878. Russia took possession of little more than a whittled-down Bulgarian satellite, while Austria, for doing nothing, gained control of much of the Balkans. This outcome created a flashpoint between Vienna and St. Petersburg that led to the formation of alliances matching Austria and Germany on one side against Russia and France on the other—a first step on the way to World War I, thirty-six years later.

Skobelev criticized "old woman" Czar Alexander for submitting to the Congress of Berlin's humiliating terms. This insult, together with the general's reckless calls for war with Germany, went unpunished only because of his popularity with the Russian people. When revolutionaries carrying suicide bombs in 1881 killed the czar, the resentment of palace officials for Skobelev's seditious rantings intensified. They took satisfaction in rumors that he'd died in the arms of "a riotous carnival of *German* courtesans," for it added a gratifying element of hypocrisy to the episode's sordidness.

Archibald Forbes knew better than most that the manner of Skobelev's death utterly fit the man. On hearing speculation that the general had killed himself, he gave a categorical rebuttal: "He did not commit suicide, at all events with intent. He sacrificed his life to a paroxysm of what was his chief weakness—sensuality." He saw Skobelev once after the Russo-Turkish War, running into him at a hotel bar in Paris. Drinks and nostalgia turned the conversation to the past—and to MacGahan. "Their friendship was as the love of David and Jonathan," Forbes wrote. Often held as an ideal of affection between brothers-in-arms, the Old Testament pairing ends in bereavement; likewise that of Skobelev and MacGahan. "I loved the man," the Russian told Forbes, his face swollen with grief and dissipation, his hands shaking. Even the pride he took in his military honors had been poisoned by MacGahan's death—in which case, said Forbes, David's lament over Jonathan was apt: "How are the mighty fallen, and the weapons of war perished!"

This final image of Skobelev is included in one of more than a dozen books Forbes wrote after leaving journalism in 1880. He'd lived, he said, "ten lives in ten years." Married with a family to support, his health poor, and his skill at chasing war news no longer practicable, he built a lucrative career as a memoirist, historian, lecturer, and novelist. Frederic Villiers, whose work sketching war scenes for the London *Graphic* continued through World War I, told of once seeing Forbes come in exhausted from the battlefield, guzzle a bottle of champagne for an energy boost, then blast out two thousand words for the telegraph. He was a machine, Villiers said—the most competitive reporter in the world. But William Howard Russell gave the most lasting judgment on his rival. The old *Times* correspondent simply threw up his hands: "The incomparable Archibald!"

Forbes dreamed of writing great literature. So had MacGahan—and so did the American diplomat Eugene Schuyler. After the Russo-

Turkish War, Schuyler wrote translations of Tolstoy and a biography of Peter the Great while at embassy stations in Italy, Romania, Greece, and Egypt. His investigation with MacGahan into the Bulgarian massacres in 1876 remained a permanent torment. "How I wish all those hideous scenes would pass," he wrote.

Schuyler got married less than a year after seeing Batak. His wife accompanied him through his subsequent postings, parting briefly in the summer of 1890 when he was in Egypt and she remained at their home in Italy. He churned out a hundred pages on local irrigation systems before turning to dreary reports on agriculture and education. Frustration with his duties depressed him: "I feel desperately like writing novels, plays—but no time." He came down with malaria in June 1890 and died en route to rejoin his wife. He was fifty. He'd always asked to be buried wherever he fell—the Protestant cemetery on Venice's island of San Michele was therefore the spot. As for many in journalism, the military, and the Foreign Service, where Schuyler last laid his head was home.

That didn't hold true for MacGahan. In 1884 the Ohio legislature persuaded the U.S. government to send a navy vessel to Constantinople to retrieve his remains from the churchyard in Pera. State Department officials and representatives from the city's newspapers met the steamship *Powhatan* in New York. The casket went by train to New Lexington, Ohio, where it was buried under a stone declaring MacGahan "Liberator of Bulgaria."

Varia, now going by the Anglicized "Barbara," attended the Ohio ceremony with Paul before returning to Brooklyn, where she'd moved after her husband's death. Never marrying again, she became a leader in New York's Russian community, writing for newspapers in America and her homeland. She saw her son through Columbia University and into a successful career as an electrical engineer. Paul later recalled his mother as "strong and positive," with a fond but sober view of her seven years as MacGahan's wife. "Maybe," she said, "our young enjoyment of life was all the keener spurred on as it was by the sense of ever-present danger, by the intense suffering and death that had hemmed us all in." Varia was the realist, MacGahan the restive dreamer. Opposites attract, the saying goes. Also, war is an aphrodisiac.

10

Our People
1884–1912

Glad are we all to meet you here,
In our own proper atmosphere . . .

FREDERIC VILLIERS, *Peaceful Personalities and Warriors Bold* (1907)

The New York Times, reporting the arrival in port of the vessel bearing MacGahan's remains in August 1884, can perhaps be forgiven for misstating his name as James rather than Januarius. That the *Herald* also got it wrong, calling its former star correspondent "John" in his own paper's obituary, is harder to accept. But the error was symptomatic of the *Herald*'s expedient priorities during forty years of absentee management under James Gordon Bennett, Jr.

The publisher's excesses never slowed. His former four-in-hand races outside Manhattan now took place in Paris. At least once he misjudged the height of an archway and almost beheaded himself as he sped under it; he was found unconscious the next morning sprawled stark naked on the cobblestones. Showgirls and courtesans passed in parade, though in his first year of exile his steadiest companion was a pet mule he led through Paris with a sign in French around its neck: "This donkey is the most sensible American in Paris." Bennett's withering cruelty to servants and underlings was offset by huge tips, often thousands of dollars, dropped like pennies into their palms. One of his girlfriends, an actress named Camille Clermont, called him an outright barbarian yet didn't hold it against him. "He had not been tenderly reared," she said.

He conducted *Herald* business from bed at his residence on the Champs-Élysées and from other properties he later acquired—an estate at Versailles, a hunting lodge in Scotland, a villa near Monte Carlo, and a yacht, *Namouna,* that in 1900 he replaced with the massive *Lysistrata,* a vessel featuring such cutting-edge amenities as electric fans and an onboard dairy farm to provide fresh milk to passengers. He kept homes in New York and Newport for visits back to the nation he'd scorned but always defended, his editorials knocking this or that American policy paling in venom to his attacks on foreigners who might express the very same criticism.

It was said that to work for the *Herald* was to endure a "pulping process" under Bennett's capricious fist. Yet men flocked there for the prestige it offered—and the high pay, which came in the form of eye-popping bonuses augmenting an already ample wage. Bennett liked to see men swoon when he took out the wad of bills. There was a dark side to this hands-on style: if an employee was to be fired, he preferred personally to break the news and observe the shocked reaction—just another sensation to savor.

In 1887 he started the Paris *Herald,* a breezy affiliate conceived as a village newspaper for rich Americans abroad. Full of gossip, scandal, cultural news, and sports coverage, it was a hit and a money loser. Its snappy layout and color graphics perfectly caught the wave of Europe's belle époque, when the continent exchanged the traumas of war for an end-of-century romp of irreverence, art, and joyful living. But the paper's popularity couldn't replenish the costs of making it so wittily written and visually stunning.

Two years later Bennett added a London edition, but folded it without hesitation when it too started losing money. The Paris *Herald* remained his pet, however. Every line reflected the madcap sensibility of its founding credo, "A dead dog in the Rue de Louvre is more interesting than a devastating flood in China"—a precursor of sorts to *The New York Times*'s "All the News That's Fit to Print." Born of whimsy (he ran the same item on its letters page, an inquiry from "An Old Philadelphia Lady" on how to convert centigrade to Fahrenheit, for almost twenty years), the Paris *Herald* would merge in 1924 with the remnants of the newspaper founded by Bennett Senior's lifelong foe, Horace Greeley, to form today's *International Herald Tribune.*

Immersed in pleasures and pastimes, Bennett lapsed in minding the finances of his New York flagship. A proliferation of papers with aggressive young owners began to cut into the *Herald*'s circulation. In the past, he'd deployed his editorial pages against two targets above all—Germany and Jay Gould. But toward the end of the century a new foe emerged, the San Francisco newspaper titan William Randolph Hearst. In a rare instance of Bennett taking a higher road, the *Herald* owner shunned the circulation war between Hearst's *Morning Journal* and Joseph Pulitzer's *New York World* that was fought via headlines of sensationalized, war-mongering "yellow journalism" that drove the nation's frivolous charge into the Spanish-American War.

Hearst tried to nullify the *Herald*'s attacks on him by denouncing Bennett for peddling smut in the paper's personal classifieds. Living in progressive Paris, Bennett didn't grasp that the charge could stick. When the U.S. government announced it would bring an obscenity lawsuit against the *Herald,* Hearst sent a taunting telegram asking if the paper might now be for sale. Bennett's reply was quick: "Three cents daily. Five cents Sunday." He retaliated by unleashing the *Herald* against Hearst's ultimately unsuccessful bids to become mayor of New York City and governor of New York. Hearst in turn kept up the morals attack. Hit with a federal indictment, Bennett wired Hearst, "I will never forgive you for this." To which Hearst replied, "I hope you never will." When the trial day came, Bennett walked into the courtroom, pleaded guilty, and paid the $31,000 fine in bills peeled from a roll in his pocket. He boarded a ship bound for Europe that night.

His squabbles with Hearst, Pulitzer, and other newspaper entrepreneurs whom he regarded as upstart punks forced him to refocus on the *Herald*'s New York operation. His first reflex was to reach into his wallet and steal talent from the competition. One of his gets was George Smalley of the *Tribune*. The venerable columnist, always looking to climb in social circles, had accepted an offer from the London *Times* in 1895 to write commentary from New York about Anglo-American relations. Bennett offered him a simultaneous position as associate editor for the *Herald*. The publisher gained a name pundit for his roster, and Smalley gained a hefty double paycheck.

Smalley missed London, however. When he decided to return a few years later, his wife announced she'd had enough and would live with him no longer; his shock multiplied when all his children sided with their mother. Rather than some single offense, the apparent cause was his infatuation with lordly English airs. He returned "home" to Hyde Park in 1903, seventy and alone.

Retired from newspaper work, he published books and articles about his career. The reception was lukewarm, and he became pinched for funds. His book production accelerated as if in anger, each successive tome more strident as he proclaimed the truths of journalism with himself as the shining example. "For the purposes of news-gathering," he told aspiring correspondents, "never go to see anyone." If that wasn't strange enough, "Never ask a question." At the Battle of Antietam, he'd carried military messages while under fire. All proper reporters must likewise dive into events rather than merely observe them, he wrote.

Smalley came to look down on reporting as "not professional. It is a trade." It was editors who raised journalism to its highest expression, editors like himself, that is, who used "the conservative instinct" to cull true news from sensational pulp. He defined that instinct in terms of comportment rather than politics, of standards of decorum that were, he said, "the means by which journalism may express the spirit of the best people." Nor did he doubt who the best people were. They were "the thoughtful minority," undazzled by fashion, celebrity, or crass wealth. Among journalists, that included men whose values resisted the bleating popular chorus and therefore put them on par with "Socrates, Christ and his apostles, the Protestants, the Puritans, the abolitionists." Lustrous company indeed.

Smalley died in 1916 an isolated man, dismayed that the international stature he'd once enjoyed was long gone. One of his last published statements about his profession carried beneath its calm appraisal a simmer of deep lament: "I do not know whether any work in journalism has elements of permanency. Probably not."

"Until my work is done I cannot die," began John Russell Young's favorite saying. "And then, I would not live." After leaving the *Herald* to write *Around the World with General Grant,* he went on to become ambassador to China, president of the Union League, Librarian of Congress, and a prolific contributor to literary magazines such as *McClure's, North American Review, Lippincott's,* and *Harper's,* which in those days were popular household staples and so enabled hardworking men of letters to earn a very comfortable living.

Depression clouded him. "Busy, tired, ill" is a common refrain in his diary. But his path to better spirits was invariably lighted by labor. Appropriately, he claimed "felicity" as one of his life goals. He treasured the English lexicon, and the word's two meanings captured his dual hope for joy and true expression.

Each December at the end of that year's diary, he recorded "friends gone." The lists feature dozens of names, many famous. Since he seems to have met all the notables of his age, obituaries became his specialty. They often turned into vehicles for what he called "self-communion," using each subject's individual biography as a window on the passing parade of Young's sense of American life. Grace and optimism—ironically, given his chronic moroseness—comprise the predominant mood of these pieces. For example, Charles Longfellow, the poet's son who'd been Bennett's sailing mate in the transatlantic race in 1866, was an inveterate sportsman and partygoer till burning out in his early forties—but Young spun the tale generously: "Free from the cares of life, he had an inherited income, was a bachelor, and spent his days in travel and in the sunny, sparkling coteries called 'society' in England and France." Lest readers think Longfellow frivolous, Young accorded him undying honor for taking a bullet as a Union volunteer in the Civil War and for being simply decent: "He was like all truly brave men, gentle, low-voiced, amiable, considerate, polite—with mild, winning eyes." Young's eulogies for Lincoln and Grant were scarcely more admiring.

He coedited a ten-volume collection, *The Literature of All Nations,* that offered translations of stories and poems from Hebrew, Arabic, Sanskrit, Persian, and Chinese. But American literature remained his passion, and Walt Whitman the author he championed. As a young man, he'd stumbled on Whitman's *Leaves of Grass* and made the mistake of quoting from it in respectable company. "Out of this book,"

John Russell Young, in his official portrait as Librarian of Congress in 1897, religiously kept a daily diary, "a kind of rosary on one's life, and I do not like to miss a bead." In times of personal tragedy, the pages went blank—but never his literary output to newspapers and magazines such as *Harper's* and *McClure's*.

he wrote, "I had dug something which seemed to beautify my composition. Whitman was the author of the lines, and my quoting them unspeakable. Yet somehow there were things that I found in no other book. The wanting in 'good morals' never occurred to me. He was an exemplification of nature."

Young visited his friend Whitman for the last time in Camden, New Jersey, in 1891. Books and papers were scattered "higgledy-piggledy" around the small apartment. Seventy-two, his white beard big as a spray of dried flowers, Whitman swayed in a rough-hewn rocking chair. Young asked him what he saw ahead for America.

The old poet pondered. "The greed for money is not pleasant. The hurry-scurry after the material, the deadening of finer thought, is distressing. We will come out of it, triumphant, fruitful—but I won't live to see it."

Contemplating the future seemed to light up Whitman's face, Young wrote—it likewise was much on Young's mind. "Conglomerate, composite America. Melted, fused. The glowing mass with its Magyar, Saxon, Hebrew, Slavic, and Asian ingredients embedded. What would it be? What would be the ideal America when the twenty-fifth century bloomed?" He believed the answer to that question was contained in Whitman's uplifting, embracing art—

Great are the plunges and throes and triumphs and falls of
   democracy,
Great the reformers with their lapses and screams,
Great the daring and venture of sailors on new explorations.
Great are yourself and myself,
We are just as good and bad as the oldest or youngest or any,
What the best and worst did we could do,
What they felt . . . do we not feel it in ourselves?
What they wished . . . do we not wish it ourselves?

Young was married for the third time by then. After losing his daughter and first wife to illness shortly after the Russo-Turkish War, he'd wed twenty-four-year old Julia Coleman, from a wealthy Connecticut family, and taken her to Paris. Almost simultaneously the news came that she was pregnant and that President Chester A. Arthur wanted Young, on the basis of his experience touring Asia with Grant, to be ambassador to China. In a replay of his experience with Rose, Young left Julia in the care of friends and his former employer, James Gordon Bennett, Jr., and went to China to begin his three-year tour. In August 1883, Bennett wired him the happy news that Julia had given birth to "a fine boy." Two months later the publisher sent another message: Julia had taken ill and died.

Bennett arranged with the Coleman family to ship her body to Hartford and deliver the child, named Russell, into their care. Young stayed in China. He calculated that he and Julia had been married 542 days, of which they'd spent seven months together. Insomnia plagued him in the aftermath. His diary notations are succinct: "Delirious all day. Bleak and exhausted." On December 31, 1881, he wrote, "So ends a very sad year. Amen! Amen! Amen!"

Returning from China to head Philadelphia's Union League, a philanthropic organization founded in 1862 to support and defend Abra-

Walt Whitman, "a wolf skin from the Mongolian plains over his shoulders," was months from death when his friend John Russell Young last visited him in 1891. Whitman spoke without rancor of his struggle for literary recognition. "Building cities and cutting away forests—America has no time for poems," he said.

ham Lincoln's Civil War policies, Young concluded that Russell would be happiest remaining in Connecticut with Julia's family. They spent little time together after that. "My dear son," he wrote in his diary on the boy's sixth birthday. "I wonder if he will know in the far away future how much I have loved him."

Young married again in 1890; "very ill and tired after the ceremony." Son Gordon was born the next year. In 1896 President William McKinley asked Young to become America's seventh Librarian of Congress. A Washington newspaper profiled the appointee as having risen from childhood poverty to accumulate "ample pecuniary resources." His present duties, the article said, included writing obituaries for the *Herald* along with an output of reviews and commentary whose volume was remarkable given his frequent bouts of ill health. Young's work with the library was full of innovation and lively industry, yet in private he struggled to stay positive. "The angel stands on the threshold," he wrote in his diary. "The name is called. We go. But is that all?"

Bright's disease, a kidney infection, killed him two years later. He was fifty-eight. While assembling his papers afterward, his wife found in his desk a handwritten snippet of *Leaves of Grass* sent by Walt Whitman many years earlier.

Wrath, argument, praise, comic leer, or prayer, or love's caress—
Within these pallid shivers, waiting.

"Personal. Don't print" was scribbled on the paper.

On the Ellipse, the circular park adjacent to the White House in Washington, D.C., there's a twelve-foot-high monument that was dedicated in 1914 to commemorate two friends, Francis Millet and Major Archibald Butt. Originally designed to double as an artistic fountain and a watering trough for horses, it has a central granite column with two bas-reliefs carved by Daniel Chester French, who sculpted the Lincoln Memorial's statue of the seated president. One side shows a helmeted soldier from ancient times, symbolizing Butt's military career. The other depicts a gauze-draped woman, a muse or minor goddess, holding a paintbrush and a painter's palette in delicate, fanlike fashion under her chin. She represents Millet's life in art.

French's incorporation of masculine and feminine imagery stemmed from the classic symbols associated with his subjects' professions. But because the sculptor knew both men well, it's been suggested that he intended the paired carvings to signal that Millet and Butt were lovers. Millet, thirty-three years married and a father of three, had a comfortable arrangement with his wife Lily wherein they lived mostly apart while he managed his art projects and his duties as a museum trustee and leader of several international arts societies. "Archie" Butt, nineteen years younger, was a lifelong bachelor whose marriage engagements never quite worked out; he lived with his mother in stylish quarters on G Street in Washington until her death in 1908, whereupon Millet, at Archie's invitation, stayed there whenever his work brought him to the capital, which was often.

Butt was one of the most charming and hardworking men in Wash-

Archibald Butt, 1910. When Frank Millet painted him the year before, every medal and braid on the major's dress blues was exquisitely rendered. Friends teased Archie, who loved to show off the portrait, that it was the best painting of a uniform they'd ever seen.

ington, managing the social schedules of presidents Theodore Roosevelt and William Taft in his position as White House protocol officer. He was also a proud dandy. In March 1912 *The New York Times* did a feature on his sartorial ensemble upon embarking from New York to vacation in Italy with Millet: "He wore a bright copper-colored Norfolk jacket fastened by big ball-shaped buttons of red porcelain, a lavender tie, tall baywing collar, trousers of the same material as the coat, a derby hat with broad, flat brim, and patent leather shoes with white tops. The major had a bunch of lilies in his buttonhole, and appeared to be delighted at the prospect of going away. He said that he had lost twenty pounds in weight."

Butt and Millet's vacation was cut short by a summons to the artist to attend to urgent business in America. On April 10 they took first-class cabins on separate decks aboard the White Star line's massive new ocean liner, *Titanic*. When the ship docked in Ireland prior to heading into the North Atlantic, Millet posted a letter to his friend, Alfred Parsons, praising the *Titanic's* sumptuous accommodations ("she has everything but taxicabs and theaters") though not the privileged clientele, who seemed insufferably self-satisfied for gracing the vessel's maiden voyage. "Looking over the list," he wrote, "I only find three or four people I know, but there are a good many of 'our people' I think and a number of obnoxious ostentatious American women, the scourge of any place they infest and worse on shipboard than anywhere. Many of them carry tiny dogs and lead husbands around like pet lambs. I tell you the American woman is a buster. She should be put in a harem and kept there."

Parsons was a painter and therefore, like Millet, operated at the edges of convention. That alone may have qualified him as "our people," though the designation could refer to any number of shared affinities, including politics, sexuality, or social sensibility. Millet's friend J. M. Barrie, the Scottish novelist and playwright, gave perhaps the best hint of what Millet meant by the phrase after he learned that Millet had died when the *Titanic* sank on April 15.

Survivor accounts of the vessel's last hours appeared in the press for days and weeks afterward. Millet and Butt had been seen assisting women and children into the lifeboats. Marie Young, a music teacher who got away in the last boat, said Major Butt tucked blankets around her "as courteously as though we were preparing for a motor ride." Then he stepped back and tipped his hat:

"Goodbye, Miss Young. Luck is with you. Kindly remember me to the folks back home."

Millet went to his cabin after the vessel hit the iceberg to change out of his dinner jacket into a blazer and topcoat. Back topside, he used his fluency in French and familiarity with other languages to explain to passengers rushing up from steerage the procedures for abandoning ship. A woman asked from her lifeboat if he had any message for home. He asked her to send his love to his wife.

Archibald Gracie, one of the few who survived the leap into the frigid water to be rescued later, recalled looking back into the *Titanic's* smoking room and seeing Millet and Butt sharing drinks and cigars. Butt's body was never found. Millet's was picked up by the rescue vessel *Mackay-Bennett* and cataloged as "NO. 249—MALE—ESTIMATED AGE, 65—HAIR, GREY." Later his ashes were divided between the

Daniel Chester French commemorated Frank Millet in feminine form, to signify Millet's career as a painter. Millet's brotherhood of war reporters would likely have approved. As Archibald Forbes wrote, "It may humbly be advanced that the true journalist must always be an artist, and make his artistic gift a handmaid to the loftier cult."

Millet family plot in Massachusetts and his home in the English Cotswolds.

"Brave and true and loyal," his friend Barrie wrote of him, adding, "he was a man one would choose to be on a liner with when it was going down." A curious compliment, it undoubtedly would have made sense to Millet, Butt, and to other of Millet's "people," including those now-distant companions from his days with the *Herald* and *The Daily News* more than thirty years earlier. A good man to die with, Barrie was saying. Or in the words of Barrie's famous creation, Peter Pan, a good man with whom to embark on "an awfully big adventure."

Epilogue

After taking the *Herald*'s Balkan beat as a twenty-three-year-old in 1889, Stephen Bonsal served there three years. Deluging the New York office with news cables, he was slow to realize that without a major war, reader interest was slight and his editors were printing few of the stories. Figuring he'd be better off covering domestic affairs, he got approval from James Gordon Bennett, Jr., the Commodore, to return to the States. He wrote a parting study of regional strife but feared the effort was wasted: "Americans will only become interested in the Balkans when happenings there affect Wall Street. And that will never be."

His trip home included a stopover in Britain, where, always looking to cultivate the old newsmen "in whose footsteps I hoped to follow," he called on Archibald Forbes. "He was happy in his marriage but not in other respects," Bonsal wrote. "He felt the weight of years, and his iron constitution was undermined by years of exposure." The Scotsman was working on a study of Julius Caesar's *Commentaries*. The Roman emperor's journal of fighting in Gaul in the first century B.C. had been a revelation to Forbes. "He was the greatest war correspondent who ever lived," he told Bonsal.

"Well, he wouldn't go far today. He'd be on the copy desk and told to reduce five columns to two and not leave out a single fact."

Forbes nodded. Everything in news was about speed and brevity now. "And it was one of your men who started us down the road to ruin."

"Who?"

"MacGahan."

"You didn't like him?"

"He was a wonderful, wonderful man. He had lightning flashes at his command. But oh Lord, how he jolted us!" Forbes was fifty-four. He could barely walk due to arthritis and would die eight years later, his last words a frantic raving: "The guns, man! Don't you hear the guns?"

In parting, Forbes took Bonsal's hand and spoke in the firm tone of an address to posterity: "Of all who have gained reputation as war correspondents, I regard MacGahan as the most brilliant." He added, "I do not believe that any two men loved each other more than Mac-Gahan did me and I did MacGahan."

A few evenings later Bonsal and some young colleagues, "after a gay dinner at the Café Royal," piled into a coach and headed for Victoria Street and the home of their profession's most esteemed member, William Howard Russell. "Today is his birthday," said one of the revelers. "No one has taken any notice of it. Let's drop in on the old man and let him see that he's not forgotten."

Russell would become *Sir* William Howard Russell when Queen Victoria knighted him in 1895. Seven years later her son, King Edward VII, would make him Commander of the Royal Victoria Order. Edward and Russell had caroused together at the Garrick Club when the king was still the feckless prince of Wales. So when he leaned to Russell's ear as the elderly correspondent strained to receive the award around his neck, Edward was speaking to an old chum. "Don't kneel, Billy," he whispered. "Stoop."

But on that rowdy night in 1892, the great reporter was merely "Bull Run" Russell to the young men pounding on his door, his lowest career moment defining how many of his journalistic children knew him: "'Bull Run' was awake when he greeted us, but it was quite evident that a few minutes before he'd been sound asleep."

When his visitors announced why they'd come, Russell laughed. "Everyone else has forgotten my birthday," he told them. "I'm trying to as well."

Bonsal recalled, "It was not difficult to see that the charming old boy was touched with our remembrance of him. He was quite alone now, and our tribute brought tears to his eyes."

Always up for a party, Russell got drinks for his guests. They had places to go, however, and after listening to some of his stories, they made polite goodbyes. "God bless you, and thank you," he said. Noting that Bonsal was an American, Russell drew him aside at the door. "I had a controversy with Burton Harrison I'd like to tell you about."

"Who?"

"Secretary to Jefferson Davis. Very talented man." Russell insisted that the little-known matter marked a crucial turn in Civil War history.

Bonsal wasn't interested in some forgotten item contained "in yellowing newspaper files." He shook hands with the doddering fellow, whose crypt at St. Paul's Cathedral would proclaim him "The First and Greatest of War Correspondents," and headed into the night with his pals.

In New York he reported to the *Herald*'s editor, Bennett's longtime cohort, Edward Flynn. He gave Flynn his Balkan piece, dramatically titled, "The European Powder Mine," and assured him its prediction of war was dead on. Flynn turned it down. Bonsal went on to place it with *Harper's*. This prompted a telegram from Bennett three weeks later: "Tell Bonsal he will write for the *Herald* again. When hell freezes over."

Flynn called the reporter into his office. "Well, young man," the editor snorted, "I'm indebted to you for the most complete dressing down I've ever received from that sonofabitch. I told him I'd refused your goddamn story but that there was no reason in hell why you shouldn't sell it to *Harper's*. Then I suggested he make you foreign editor."

Bonsal was stunned. "You did?"

"I'd welcome it. I'd tell you how many columns you'd be allotted each day and you could fill them with whatever rubbish you want. Bennett said no—you had too many ideas. But he does want you reinstated at full salary. Another thing," Flynn said. "He cabled the Senate Foreign Relations committee. You're to brief them on activities in the Balkans. Better your gibberish goes there than to the *Herald*."

At Bonsal's subsequent appearance before the Senate committee in Washington, Cushman Davis of Minnesota led the questioning: "Why don't these people in the Balkans leave off killing each other and burning down each other's houses? Why can't they just do what's right?"

"Because they're convinced that what they're doing *is* right," Bonsal explained. "If only they could be enlightened with the virus of modern skepticism, there might come about an era of peace. As justification for their merciless warfare, the Christians point to Joshua and the Muslims point to Mohammed. These wars are inspired by spiritual advisors, and the luckless contestants find full warrant for it in scripture which they accept as holy writ."

The reporter concluded his statements with a warning that "world conflagration is inevitable" unless tensions in the Balkans improved. He would recall this prediction when Austria's Archduke Franz Ferdinand was assassinated in Sarajevo in 1914, lighting the fuse of hostile alliances that ignited into World War I: "In this venture into prophecy, I had scored a bull's eye." At the time, however, the Senate committee barely reacted. "At least none of the senators went to sleep on you," someone told him as he left the committee chamber.

Bonsal served as a lieutenant colonel in the Great War. Afterward he was President Woodrow Wilson's translator at the peace conference in Paris in 1919 that led to the Treaty of Versailles. The treaty's arbitrarily redrawn borders and oppressive punishment of Germany by the European powers laid the ground for World War II less than thirty years later—a consequence foreshadowed in Bonsal's daily journal of his work with Wilson and the American delegation. Published under the title *Unfinished Business,* the book would win the Pulitzer Prize in 1945.

He always saw himself as a reporter above all. More exactly, he saw himself as that dashing globetrotter he'd set out to become as a young man—a foreign correspondent for *The New York Herald.* After testifying before the Senate in 1893, he'd hesitated to resume his international beat in Europe; he knew it meant he'd have to endure the volatile lash of the Commodore. But then he recalled advice given him by the correspondent who'd been Bennett's "greatest glory," as Bonsal put it— the inimitable Henry Stanley. "We must always give our vagrant chief a little leeway," the explorer said, when the young reporter had sought him out a few years earlier. "Because stop and think what a dull drab place our world would be without him."

Bonsal reminded him that Bennett had shown Stanley no respect

Stephen Bonsal, photographed here in Cuba in 1898, was inspired by Januarius MacGahan and Archibald Forbes to become a correspondent for *The New York Herald*. The future Pulitzer Prize winner even became fond of the newspaper's cantankerous publisher, James Gordon Bennett, Jr. "I liked him despite his faults," Bonsal said. "And because of them."

after his star-making discovery of Dr. Livingstone. Stanley smiled. "I advise you to grin and bear it, and to hang on. He never forgets a piece of good work or the man who did it—although he tries to."

"I thanked the great explorer," Bonsal wrote. "I would hang on."

Bennett died in 1918. He'd had premonitions that it would come at age seventy-seven. At least he lived long enough to see Germany, a nation he'd detested ever since Bismarck put France under his boot in the Franco-Prussian War, come to crashing defeat in World War I. ("How many Boche were killed today?" was his first question each morning in the *Herald*'s Paris newsroom.) The publisher had shocked everyone three years earlier by marrying the widowed daughter-in-law of the founder of the Reuters news agency. A baroness by title, she was the former Maud Potter of Philadelphia and had been friends with Bennett for years. Though brief, their union was calm and affectionate.

He spent a lot of time planning his funeral. He'd initially wanted to lie in New York City's Washington Heights, his sarcophagus suspended on chains inside a hollow stone owl 125 feet high. Ever since that midnight hoot he credited with saving his schooner from running aground in the Civil War, his faith in owls as protective charms had

Herald publisher James Gordon Bennett, Jr., regarded owls as good luck charms. Those lining the eaves of his Herald Square headquarters couldn't prevent his newspaper's demise after his death in 1918. Images of owls were carved on Bennett's Paris gravestone. He stipulated that the marker be otherwise blank.

been absolute. He went so far as to tell the sculptor the bird must glare "quite ferociously" toward Manhattan, but ultimately he scrapped the plan and was buried under a simple stone in the Passy section of Paris.

The *Herald* steadily lost money after the turn of the century. In addition to Bennett's yachts and mansions, his perennial sponsorship of international competitions in hot air ballooning, polo, and auto racing drained his bank account. In 1920, two years after their owner's death, the New York and Paris *Herald*s were sold at a fire-sale price of $4 million to retail magnate Frank A. Munsey, whom Bennett had once called "that grocer." It seemed to many veteran newsmen a sad fate for a once mighty institution founded twenty-five years before the Civil War by a cranky Scots visionary whose answer to society's complaints about his profits and prejudices was a taunting cackle, "I print my newspaper every day"—which more or less translates to *I do what I want—try and stop me.*

His son appears to have seen the end coming. After spending a fortune to construct a massive new *Herald* headquarters, completed in 1895, at the triangular intersection of Broadway, Sixth Avenue, and Thirty-fourth Street, Bennett had surveyed the building's two-block length and rooftop array of bronze owls with glowering electric eyes. "I fear my renaissance palace looks like an Italian fish market," he sighed.

His construction foreman assured him it was beautiful, though he did regret that it was built on a lot leased only for thirty years— a lot soon called Herald Square by every New Yorker, even after Frank Munsey tore the building down in 1921.

"Thirty years?" Bennett threw back his head and laughed. "Let's not worry about that. Thirty years from now the *Herald* will be in Harlem and I'll be in hell."

He was definitely wrong on one count.

Author's Note

Historians seem to conceive their subjects in one of two ways—as big or little, panorama or portrait. Then in the writing they add elements of individual experience or big-picture significance, depending on what's needed to balance the recipe. My last book fell into the former category. It began as a revision of Revolutionary War history, highlighting unsung maritime privateers who played a major role in America's War of Independence; the emergence of some compelling characters was an expected offshoot, and I found it most fulfilling to bring their stories to light. This book followed an opposite path. The people attracted me from the start. Their larger impact was icing on the cake.

I can imagine scholars aghast at my broad-brushing of the cultural and political complexities of Europe's upheaval in the late 1800s. So I'll lean on George Smalley's contention in 1866 that while that upheaval's roots meant "not much more to the masses of Americans than the Peloponnesian War," it didn't hinder their interest in the distant human drama described in their newspapers. I undertook this book expecting that its drama would come from reporters competing with one another for wartime scoops. But it turned out broader than that. *Tribune* and *Herald* became Greeley and Bennett; emancipation and slavery; letter and telegram; keel and centerboard; Harvard and Oxford; Dickens and Whitman; Stanley and Livingstone; *Daily News* and London *Times;* musket and machine gun; imperialism and republicanism; mercy and massacre; Christianity and Islam—all demanding historical context somehow not covered in my university studies of modern American literature.

Primary source material and Internet prospecting were great for turning up colorful nuggets, but a number of authors laid the path that got me through. MacGahan, Millet, Smalley, and Stanley have terrific biographers in Dale O. Walker, Peter A. Engstrom, Joseph J. Mathews, Martin Dugard, and Tim Jeal. Douglas Fermer can't be topped for his study of the *Herald*-Lincoln relationship. John Steele Gordon uses the story of Cyrus Field to open a window on American entrepreneurialism and the birth of global communication. Mountains of comment on the Paris Commune become a poignant tale in the hands of Alistair Horne. Dorothy Anderson finds in Emily Strangford and the Balkan volunteers paragons of selflessness who were also endearingly flawed. And while Geoffrey Wawro calls himself a beneficiary of a new style of military history that places strategy and tactics in larger contexts of society, politics, economics, and culture, he is, more than its beneficiary, a brilliant practitioner of that style, which in his case doesn't skimp on great storytelling either. His several volumes of nineteenth-century European history were invaluable to my understanding of the period. Needless to say, any errors in this telling are mine.

Readers may note that my correspondents use the terms "Islam" and "Muslim" when "Mohammadism" and "Musselman" (and variations thereof) were common at the time; I made the change for clarity's sake. And I gave myself leeway in taking legend as fact if it fit the characters and historical situations as I'd come to understand them. For example, in April 1879 *The New York Times* ran an item from the *Moscow Gazette* (of all places!) repeating an anecdote told by William Howard Russell about Emily Strangford claiming to have been spat on by Joseph Gourko. The story's multiple layers of hearsay didn't keep me from using the scene. Should some diligent scholar verify the scandal of my misrepresentation, I'll take heart in knowing that at least someone has been moved to care about two people, Strangford and Gourko, who were as extraordinary as they are unremembered.

Lastly, some personal thanks—to my editor, Victoria Wilson, and my agent, Harvey Klinger; to my family; and most of all to my wife, Vicki, with love.

Notes

INTRODUCTION

xv "**The miserable parent**": Knightley, *First Casualty,* 2.

xvi "**splendid little war**": Sweeney, *From the Front,* 73.

xvi "**Cavalry regiments**": "How I Became a War Correspondent," chap. 2 in Forbes, *Souvenirs,* 47–70.

PROLOGUE

3 "**I love America**": O'Connor, *Scandalous Mr. Bennett,* 185.

3 "**I'm surprised**": Bonsal, *Heyday,* 271.

4 "**You men have done wonders**" through "**Envelop your mission**": "The Story of a Great Beat," chap. 9, ibid., 144–75.

6 "**No one is indispensable**": O'Connor, *Scandalous Mr. Bennett,* 166.

6 "**Since my letter of yesterday**": MacGahan and Schuyler, *Turkish Atrocities,* 18.

6 "**It was pleasant to learn**" through "**Man is an incomprehensible animal**": "Court Life in Bulgaria," chap. 10 in Bonsal, *Heyday,* 261–94.

1. NOBODY'S CHILD, 1854–1866

11 "**the year of grace**": Chapman, *Russell,* 15.

11 "**big, bluff, genial Irishman**": Bullard, *War Correspondents,* 32.

12 "**a guinea a day**": Ibid.

12 "**You will be back**": Chapman, *Russell,* 16.

12 "**nobody's child**": Bullard, *War Correspondents,* 35.

12 "**an infinite adaptability**": Kipling, *Light That Failed,* 26.

13 "**but I suspect**": Bullard, *War Correspondents,* 37.

13 "**Are there no devoted women**": Ibid., 42.

13 "**nightmares for a lifetime**": Ibid., 41.

13 "**I shall proceed to describe**" through "**Went into action**": Carey, *Eyewitness,* 333–44.

15 "**Of course there would be a charge**": D'Este, *Warlord,* 91.

15 "**Not a very great general**": Hibbert, *Destruction,* 296.

15 "**bald as a round shot**": Bullard, *War Correspondents,* 38.

16 "**The Atlantic is dried up!**" through "**Please send something**": "Lightning Through Deep Waters," chap. 8 in Gordon, *Thread Across the Ocean,* 121–41.

18 "**For your kindness**": Field, *Atlantic Telegraph,* 210.

18 "**His gallery is filled**": Meredith, *Lincoln's Camera Man,* 54.

18 "**How many shares**": Field, *Atlantic Telegraph,* 215.

21 "**exhilarate the breakfast table**": Burrows and Wallace, *Gotham,* 526.

21 "**the nigger**": Fermer, *Bennett and the Herald,* 140.

21 **"oceans of blood"**: Ibid., 183.

21 **"He will receive such a greeting"** through **"the most sudden and total"**: "The Conversion: The *Herald* and the Outbreak of War, 1861," chap. 7, ibid., 187–98.

22 **"illiterate Western boor"**: Ibid., 131.

23 **"so sincere"**: Villard de Borchgrave and Cullen, *Villard,* 136.

23 **"a queer sort"**: Seitz, *James Gordon Bennetts,* 215.

23 **"Someone, possibly a servant"**: O'Connor, *Scandalous Mr. Bennett,* 37.

23 **"Intercourse with the old man"**: Carlson, *Man Who Made News,* 316.

23 **"The last wish"**: Ibid.

25 **tattooed on her knees**: O'Connor, *Scandalous Mr. Bennett,* 199.

25 **"a trifle presumptuous"**: Ibid., 40.

25 **"You'da thought he ordered"** through **"Send the bill to me"**: Seitz, *James Gordon Bennetts,* 234.

26 **"village idiot"**: Fermer, *Bennett and the Herald,* 132.

26 **"niggerism"**: Ibid., 249.

26 **"It is important to humor"**: Ibid., 209.

27 **"I felt like a man"**: Russell, *My Diary,* 86.

27 **"trifling"**: Ibid.

27 **"where great crimes"**: Chapman, *Russell,* 59.

27 **"A sickening anguish"**: David, *Indian Mutiny,* 256.

27 **"A glorious sight"**: Ibid., 327.

27 **"I believe we permit"**: Bullard, *War Correspondents,* 54.

28 **"put alive into boxes"**: Lal, "Crawling Lane," 38.

28 **"sewing Muslims in pigskins"**: Chapman, *Russell,* 78.

28 **"The impression of homeliness"**: Russell, *My Diary,* 55.

28 **"His game"**: Ibid., 29.

28 **"hunted down all his Indians"**: Harris, *Blue & Gray,* 35.

28 **"slave pens"**: Russell, *My Diary,* 36.

28 **"a cancer"**: Ibid., 7.

28 **"whippings and brandings"**: Ibid., 122.

29 **"take the field"**: Ibid., 251.

29 **"Brilliant Union Victory!"** Perry, *Bohemian Brigade,* 31.

29 **"We're whipped"**: Harris, *Blue & Gray,* 73.

29 **"but I might as well have talked"**: Russell, *My Diary,* 270.

30 **"the snob correspondent"**: Hohenberg, *Foreign Correspondence,* 66.

30 **"a startling pull"**: Russell, *My Diary,* 266.

30 **"the best abused man"**: Hohenberg, *Foreign Correspondence,* 66.

30 **"I failed to discover"**: Russell, *My Diary,* 265.

30 **"My unpopularity"**: Ibid., 311.

30 **"He hates our country"**: Ibid., 13.

30 **"thank Heaven, towards Europe"**: Ibid., 314.

31 **"bullet, ball, and grapeshot"**: Villard de Borchgrave and Cullen, *Villard,* 161.

31 **"A number of distinguished representatives"**: "The Battle of Bull Run," in Young, *Men and Memories,* 1:6–16.

31 **"humdrum laborer"**: Ibid., 207.

32 **"a lovable cuss"**: "Commentary," December 15, 1888, Whitman Archive.

32 **"You ran into him"**: "Walt Whitman," in Young, *Men and Memories,* 1:76–108.

32 **"He's a man with real guts"**: "Commentary," December 15, 1888, Whitman Archive.

32 **"slight and boyish"**: Young, *Men and Memories,* 1:110.

33 **"As lovely as a woman"**: Ibid., 1:ix.

33 **"There is nothing"**: Ibid., 1:162.

33 **"the advocate"**: Ibid., 1:163.

33 **"a vast, sinister shape"**: Ibid., 1:208.

33 **"beauty of being"**: Young, "Diaries," entry for June 21, 1872.

33 **"Forward to Richmond!"**: Maihafer, *General and Journalists,* 70.

33 **"brilliant, capable"**: Young, *Men and Memories,* 1:114.

33 **"the Union is irrevocably gone"**: Maihafer, *General and Journalists,* 71.

33 **"brain fever"**: Ibid., 70.

34 **"The *Herald* is constantly ahead"**: Fermer, *Bennett and the Herald,* 201.

34 **"our heavy battalions"**: Harris, *Blue & Gray,* 83.

34 **"The whole world"**: Fermer, *Bennett and the Herald,* 202

34 **"unorthodox remarks"**: Perry, *Bohemian Brigade,* 117.

34 **"That's good news!"**: Fermer, *Bennett and the Herald,* 205.

34 **"past facts"**: Carlson, *Man Who Made News,* 340.

34 **"I cannot remember"**: Lincoln to A. G. Hodges, April 4, 1864, Library of Congress, Washington, D.C.

34 **"If I could save the Union"**: Lincoln to Greeley, August 22, 1862, Abraham Lincoln Online, www.abrahamlincolnonline.org.

35 **"the only man"**: Fermer, *Bennett and the Herald,* 216.

35 **"God bless Abraham Lincoln!"**: Ibid., 222.

35 **"Unnecessary, unwise"**: Ibid., 277.

36 **"In broad daylight"**: Mathews, *Smalley,* 13.

36 **"a natural soldier"**: Ibid., 16.

36 **"the adventure"**: Ibid., 19.

36 **"I say this"**: Ibid., 181.

36 **"a sort of uniform"** through **"Don't let the next man"**: Smalley, *Anglo-American Memories,* 1:145–47.

37 **"more tranquil fortitude"**: Starr, *Bohemian Brigade,* 141.

37 **"Haven't you been in battle"**: Ibid., 143.

37 **"Fierce and desperate battle"**: "The Battle of Antietam," in Mathews, *Smalley,* 175–88.

38 **"They are just as good"**: Fermer, *Bennett and the Herald,* 235.

38 **"There being no slavery"**: Ibid., 251.

38 **"Apparently Greeley and Raymond"**: Ibid., 241.

39 **"incompetent driveller"**: Ibid., 258.

39 **"Honest Old Abe"**: Ibid., 250.

39 **"who knows how to tan leather"**: Ibid., 254.

39 **"Bennett has made"** through **"with sentiments of the highest respect"**: "The *Herald* for the Union and Bennett, 1864–5," chap. 13, ibid., 271–96.

39 "**He has proved himself**": Ibid., 282.

40 "**Should he accept**": Carlson, *Man Who Made News,* 371.

40 "**morally magnificent**": Fermer, *Bennett and the Herald,* 296.

40 "**to comprehend the genius**": Carlson, *Man Who Made News,* 372.

40 "**entire confidence**": Fermer, *Bennett and the Herald,* 311–13.

40 "**Should history condescend**": Carlson, *Man Who Made News,* 380.

41 "**overnight**": Ibid., 382.

41 "**I lingered to see the effect**": Villard de Borchgrave and Cullen, *Villard,* 189.

41 "**Decomposition had swelled**": Ibid., 203.

42 "**If I were a commanding general**": Ibid., 173.

42 "**With no more fighting**": Smalley, "Chapters in Journalism," 430.

42 "**We were still in that state**": Smalley, *Anglo-American Memories,* 1:164.

43 "**A journalist of genius**": Smalley, "Chapters in Journalism," 430–31.

43 "**I went to Europe**": Ibid.

43 "**to sink the Spanish Armada**": Field, *Atlantic Telegraph,* 254.

44 "**All well**": Gordon, *Thread Across the Ocean,* 202.

44 "**little more than wastepaper**": Mathews, *Smalley,* 29.

44 "**a glory to our age**": Ibid., 200.

44 "**Treaty of peace signed**": Field, *Atlantic Telegraph,* 339.

44 "**It would have made a difference**": Smalley, *Anglo-American Memories,* 1:165.

45 "**from the bankruptcies**": O'Connor, *Scandalous Mr. Bennett,* 173.

2. AMERICAN METHODS, 1865–1870

47 "**curiosities and monstrosities**": Carlson, *Man Who Made News,* 378.

47 "**Swedish Nightingale**": Seitz, *James Gordon Bennetts,* 142.

47 "**Fiji mermaids**": Carlson, *Man Who Made News,* 257.

48 "**I don't make child's bargains**" through "**Not yet**": Ibid., 150–52.

48 "**I want you fellows**": O'Connor, *Scandalous Mr. Bennett,* 77–79.

49 "**Bennetting**": Ibid., 51.

49 "**One rode better**": Ibid., 46.

49 "**merry despotism**": Fiske, *Off-Hand Portraits,* 199.

49 "**I want to be able to breathe**": O'Connor, *Scandalous Mr. Bennett,* 49.

49 "**It depends what you mean**": Ibid., 60.

49 "**Put it to the test**": Ibid., 53.

50 "**Only then can we count on wind enough**": Ibid., 54.

50 "**secret ocean path**": Maddocks, *Atlantic Crossing,* 101.

50 "**from a sense of filial duty**": Young, *Men and Memories,* 2:382.

50 "**The season selected**": "Yacht Race," *New York Times,* December 17, 1866.

51 "**a specially malignant billow**": "Ocean Yacht Races: The Present Contest and the Former One," *New York Times,* July 22, 1870.

51 "**of endurance rather than speed**": "Ocean Yacht Race: Full Account," *New York Times,* January 9, 1867.

51 "**who goes in his own boat**": Fiske, *Off-Hand Portraits,* 34.

52 "**HENRIETTA THE WINNER**": O'Connor, *Scandalous Mr. Bennett,* 59.

52 "**We hope the young gentlemen**": Ibid.

52 **"When he returned"**: Fiske, *Off-Hand Portraits*, 34.

52 **"a creature of unrestrained desires"**: Crockett, *Caliph of Baghdad*, 11.

53 **"kindly heart"**: Fermer, *Bennett and the Herald*, 314.

53 **"Though the announcement disappeared"**: Fiske, *Off-Hand Portraits*, 35.

53 **"In soul I long had worshipped"** through **"Shakespeare, with some threads"**: "Charles Dickens as I Knew Him," in Young, *Men and Memories*, 1:121–22.

55 **"we wasted no words"**: Smalley, *Anglo-American Memories*, 1:165.

55 **"they looked like"** through **"at the beginnings of what was foreordained"**: "How the Prussians After Sadowa Came Home to Berlin" and "A Talk with Count Bismarck in 1866," ibid., 1:170–93.

58 **"The proposal was far-reaching"** through **"a rival office to New York"**: "Some Account of a Revolution in International Journalism," ibid., 1:220–34.

58 **"hearty hate of all things English"**: Mathews, *Smalley*, 41.

59 **"In London"**: Smalley, "Notes on Journalism," 218.

59 **"paradise"**: Mathews, *Smalley*, 32.

60 **"We might question"** through **"He saw the material gain"**: "Horace Greeley," in Young, *Men and Memories*, 1:112–19.

60 **"instinctive dislike"**: Maihafer, *General and Journalists*, 236.

61 "Sneak News Thief": Ibid., 251.

61 **"A false treachery"**: Young, "Diaries," entry for April 21, 1869.

61 **"permeated with Democrats"**: "Horace Greeley," in Young, *Men and Memories*, 1:112–19.

61 **"Greeley surrendered me"**: Young, "Diaries," entry for November 5, 1869.

61 **"Everybody liked him"**: Fiske, *Off-Hand Portraits*, 267.

62 **"manly response"** through **"fare with muscle in it"**: Blaikie, "University Rowing Match," 49–67.

63 **"The usual amount of drunkenness"** through **"Our boys scattered their splendid qualities"**: Conway, "International Boat-Race," 912–15.

64 **"The victory"**: Mathews, "First Harvard-Oxford Boat Race," 74–82.

64 **"Such a defeat"**: Dickens, "Speech."

64 **"If I should ever send you"**: Matthews, *Smalley*, 55–56.

64 **"You may laugh at me"**: Ibid.

64 **"It does not matter"** through **"The year 1870"**: "Some Account of a Revolution in International Journalism," chap. 22 in Smalley, *Anglo-American Memories*, 1:220–34.

67 **"personals"**: O'Connor, *Scandalous Mr. Bennett*, 273.

67 **"We make bold to say"**: Mathews, *Smalley*, 33.

67 **"pleasure pilgrimage"**: Twain, *Innocents*, xxiv.

67 **"We always took care"**: Ibid.

68 **"these blazing farms"**: Jeal, *Impossible Life*, 67.

68 **"fierce-eyed and imperious"**: Ibid., 69.

69 **"superiority in writing style"**: Dugard, *Into Africa*, 60.

69 **"It widened my knowledge"**: Bonsal, *Heyday*, 411.

70 **"My name is Stanley"** through **"I mean that you should go"**: Dugard, *Into Africa*, 107.

71 **"He developed journalism"**: Fiske, *Off-Hand Portraits,* 36.

71 **"Everybody is going to Europe!"**: Twain, *Innocents,* 12.

71 **"mere existing"** through **"*Voilà la guerre!*"**: "Up From Pigeon Roost Ridge," chap. 1 in Walker, *Januarius MacGahan,* 3–16.

3. WILD WORK, 1870–1871

75 **"so free from clouds"**: Smalley, *Anglo-American Memories,* 1:230.

76 **"I will go to sleep"**: Wawro, *Franco-Prussian War,* 19.

77 **"I owe this mess"** through **"far less to deploy in great masses"**: "Causes of the Franco-Prussian War," chap. 1, ibid., 16–40.

79 **"one way is to send"**: *Anglo-American Memories,* 1:231–34.

80 **"not an important one"**: Ibid.

81 **"As a child might sigh"**: Forbes, *Souvenirs,* 53.

81 **"The battle was fought"** through **"every opportunity to admire"**: "Some Account of a Revolution in International Journalism," chap. 22 in Smalley, *Anglo-American Memories,* 1:220–34.

82 **"a very Napoleon of journalism"**: Hatton, *London,* 56.

82 **"We had ceased"**: Smalley, *Anglo-American Memories,* 1:226.

82 **"a modest mistrust"**: Forbes, *Souvenirs,* 85.

83 **"we shall be outstripped!"**: Chapman, *Russell,* 151.

83 **"These are terrible and painful sights"**: Atkins, *Russell,* 2:177.

83 **"I should not have thought"**: Forbes, *Memories,* 222.

84 **"Bismarck, with an elaborate assumption"**: Ibid., 7.

84 **"Where is all this to end?"**: Chapman, *Russell,* 140.

84 **"Who won?"**: Bullard, *War Correspondents,* 63.

84 **"a strange mental condition"**: Chapman, *Russell,* 138.

85 **"it is not the besieged army"**: Wawro, *Warfare and Society,* 115.

85 **"the prodigious force"**: Chapman, *Russell,* 143–44.

85 **"It is not a pleasant thing"**: Ibid.

86 **"had lost all their bloom"**: Atkins, *Russell,* 2:200.

86 **"Since I could not die"**: Chapman, *Russell,* 145–46.

86 **"wondering what I was to do"** through **"never thought it worthwhile"**: "Holt White's Story of Sedan and How It Reached the *New York Tribune,*" chap. 24 in Smalley, *Anglo-American Memories,* 1:235–42.

89 **"coil upon coil"** through **"Don't be a fool!"**: Bullard, *War Correspondents,* 70–72.

89 **"It is possible"**: Forbes, *Souvenirs,* 69.

90 **"It was cabled forthwith"** through **"The *Daily News* service"**: "Great Examples of War Correspondence," chap. 25 in Smalley, *Anglo-American Memories,* 1:243–50.

91 **"His one great aim"**: Villiers, *Peaceful Personalities,* 243.

91 **"the *Tribune* in the end profited"** through **"Holt White is entitled to be remembered"**: "Great Examples of War Correspondence," chap. 25 in Smalley, *Anglo-American Memories,* 1:243–50.

92 **"Every man is expected to write"**: Walker, *Januarius MacGahan,* 33.

92 **"How they manage to get on"**: Ibid.

93 "**no laziness in killing**": Wawro, *Franco-Prussian War,* 279–80.

94 "**This is the end**": Ibid., 283.

95 "**So moderate a victor**": Ibid., 305.

95 "**Prussian spy!**": Chapman, *Russell,* 159.

96 "**disturbant elements**": Forbes, *My Experiences,* 2:465–67.

97 "**wild work**": Ibid.

97 "**bourgeois battalions**": Horne, *Fall of Paris,* 253.

97 "**Vigilance Committee**" through "**All were shrieking**": Ibid., 270–72.

4. PARIS IS BURNING, 1871

99 "**People threw flowers**": Robb, *Victor Hugo,* 464.

99 "**The old story**" through "***Napoléon le Petit***": *New York Herald,* March 4, 1871.

101 "**I had supposed**": Walker, *Januarius MacGahan,* 33.

101 "**The mob is triumphant**": *New York Herald,* March 21, 1871.

102 "**principles of disorder**": *New York Herald,* March 30, 1871.

102 "**the watchword of the Commune**": *New York Herald,* March 21, 1871.

102 "**pitiful pygmy of insurrection**": *New York Herald,* March 30, 1871.

102 "**painful, but short**": Horne, *Fall of Paris,* 307.

102 "**The royalist conspirators**": Ibid., 308.

103 "**a horde of turbulent picnickers**": Ibid., 309.

103 "**The word *guillotine***": *New York Herald,* April 1, 1871.

104 "**Bergeret's Bosh**": *New York Herald,* May 26, 1871.

104 "**it is not for me to support**": Ibid.

104 "**Citizen Delescluze**": Ibid.

105 "**mutilated forms**": *New York Herald,* June 1, 1871.

105 "**they smoked, drank**": Ibid.

106 "**Will you come with me?**" through "**Dombrowski took off his hat**": Ibid.

108 "***Herald* Correspondent Wounded**" through "**The French Horror**": *New York Herald,* May 19, 1871.

108 "**His world was the world we live in**": Young, *Men and Memories,* 1:145–48.

109 "**What mere soldier**": "Grant: An Estimate," in Young, *Men and Memories,* 2:463–84.

109 "**a symbol of brute force**" through "**lacked buoyancy**": "John Russell Young on the Commune," in Young, *Men and Memories,* 1:166–95.

112 "**The Guards spat into its face**": *New York Herald,* June 1, 1871.

112 "**I visited every part**" through "**The destroying angel**": "John Russell Young on the Commune," in Young, *Men and Memories,* 1:166–95.

113 "***cocotte* train**" through "**he was last seen fighting**": Forbes, "What I Saw of the Paris Commune," 803–917.

116 "**menacing and discontented**": *New York Herald,* June 1, 1871.

116 "**In the extremity of panic**" through "**They were not clean**": Forbes, "What I Saw of the Paris Commune," 803–917.

118 "**The cause of justice**": Horne, *Fall of Paris,* 377.

118 "**They were demoralized**" through "**Where had people secreted the tricolor**": Forbes, "What I Saw of the Paris Commune," 803–917.

120 "**evidently with a Legion of Honor**": Young, *Men and Memories*, 1:176.

120 "**Ha! You're a plucky one!**": Carey, *Eyewitness*, 380.

120 "**We see the red, white, and blue**": Young, *Men and Memories*, 1:176.

120 "**a little grig of a fellow**" through "**Will they roast**": Forbes, *Memories and Studies*, 157–64.

122 "**If we are to fall**" through "**I can now understand**": "John Russell Young on the Commune" and "Commune of Paris," in Young, *Men and Memories*, 1:166–207.

124 "**The Hotbed of Communism**": *New York Herald,* May 26, 1871.

124 "**No mercy is to be shown**": *New York Herald,* May 29, 1871.

124 "**The last relics**": Horne, *Fall of Paris,* 387.

124 "**Government shells**": *New York Herald,* May 28, 1871.

124 "**dividing sense**" through "**They made him to kneel**": Ibid.

125 "**reception centers**": Carey, *Eyewitness,* 382–85.

125 "**You have five minutes**": Horne, *Fall of Paris,* 388.

125 "**But Monsieur Thiers declined**": Young, *Men and Memories,* 1:190.

126 "**What a war!**": Horne, *Fall of Paris,* 472.

126 "**after so many others**": Ibid., 477.

126 "**Bismarck wants his money**": Young, *Men and Memories,* 1:206.

126 "**Definitely one too many**": Horne, *Fall of Paris,* 487.

127 "**There they lay**" through "**Never again may the civilized world**": "The Crushing of the Commune," chap. 6 in Forbes, *Memories and Studies,* 188–251.

128 "**both the ladies and gentlemen**": Walker, *Januarius MacGahan,* 38.

128 "**The insurrection is writhing**": *New York Herald,* June 14, 1871.

128 "**The truth must be told**" through "**The bitterest letters**": Walker, *Januarius MacGahan,* 39–40.

129 "**The *Herald* Paris Correspondent**": *New York Herald,* May 25, 1871.

129 "**I changed my politics**": Walker, *Januarius MacGahan,* 39–40.

129 "**I have made up my mind**": Ibid.

129 "**holy work**": "John Russell Young on the Commune" and "Commune of Paris," in Young, *Men and Memories,* 1:166–207.

130 "**I am confident the time will come**": Ibid., 1:207.

130 "**a land of terror**": Ibid., 1:128.

130 "**France will rise again**": Ibid., 1:206.

130 "**innocent, believing days**": Ibid., 1:126.

130 "**my folly**": Young, "Diaries," entry for December 31, 1878.

130 "**I hang like Mohammed's coffin**": Ibid., entry for June 22, 1871.

130 "**fairness, breadth, feeling**": Young, *Men and Memories,* 1:165.

131 "**very old and feeble**": Ibid., 1:210.

5. PRIMITIVE PEOPLE, 1871–1873

133 "**cannibal country**": Jeal, *Impossible Life,* 287.

134 "**positive intelligence**": Dugard, *Into Africa,* 229.

134 "**experienced and well-qualified Europeans**" through "**everything that is noble and right**": "The Searchers," chap. 37, ibid., 269–84.

135 "**the great traveler**": Ibid., 286.

136 **"You are now as famous"**: Jeal, *Impossible Life*, 134.

136 **"Stop talking"**: O'Connor, *Scandalous Mr. Bennett*, 116.

136 **"intolerably dull"** through **"I used to have to do that myself"**: Ibid., 117–19.

138 **"wreathed in courtesy"** through **"The things we called men"**: "James Gordon Bennett," in Young, *Men and Memories*, 1:207–14.

138 **"My new arrangement"**: Ibid., 1:213.

139 **"He was aware"**: Carlson, *Man Who Made News*, 391–94.

139 **"utterly indifferent"**: Ibid.

139 **"astonished at his appreciation"**: Young, *Men and Memories*, 1:213.

139 **"begin in clouds"**: Young, "Diaries," entry for July 16, 1877.

140 **"not only news"**: Young, *Men and Memories*, 1:212.

141 **"chains"** through **"You know my friendly sentiments"**: "Varvara," chap. 4 in Walker, *Januarius MacGahan*, 41–60.

142 **"Being a man of peace"**: MacGahan, *Campaigning on the Oxus*, 30.

142 **"He was not such a man"**: Walker, *Januarius MacGahan*, 59.

143 **"to float in a shadowy way"**: MacGahan, *Campaigning on the Oxus*, 114.

143 **"I feel sometimes"**: Walker, *Januarius MacGahan*, 66.

143 **"I was not preparing joy"**: Ibid., 108.

143 **"Bennett never let him dwell"**: Ibid., 59.

143 **"a strong love of luxury"**: through **"the other side of his nature"**: Schuyler, *Selected Essays*, 43.

144 **"to leave them to anarchy"**: Schuyler, *Turkistan*, 2:388.

144 **"The harder you hit them"**: Hopkirk, *Great Game*, 4.

145 **"but simply impossible"** through **"brave fellow"**: MacGahan, *Campaigning on the Oxus*, 120–39.

151 **"MacGahan's ride across the desert"**: Schuyler, *Turkistan*, 1:65.

151 **"I was in every way good-natured"** through **"the Great White Czar"**: MacGahan, *Campaigning on the Oxus*, 128–270.

166 **"family never made men great"**: Novikova, *Skobeleff*, 3.

166 **"Forty brigands killed"**: Verestchagin, *Painter, Soldier*, 257.

166 **"Now his life"**: Nemirovitch-Dantchenko, *Personal Reminiscences*, 189.

166 **"Squalidness had changed"**: MacGahan, *Campaigning on the Oxus*, 430.

166 **"an eccentric country squire"**: Novikova, *Skobeleff*, 39.

167 **"Although he has not yet received"**: *Daily News*, 1:87.

6. PURE AND SAVAGE FREEDOM, 1872–1877

169 **"amorous escapades"**: O'Connor, *Scandalous Mr. Bennett*, 76.

169 **"The whole middle part"**: Seitz, *James Gordon Bennetts*, 212.

170 **"Bennett has led"**: Fiske, *Off-Hand Portraits*, 36.

171 **"the gold-gobbling gorilla"**: O'Connor, *Scandalous Mr. Bennett*, 95.

171 **"I have known you many years"**: Ibid., 176–77.

171 **"the progress of science"**: Maihafer, *General and Journalists*, 246.

172 **"I stand naked before my God"**: Ibid.

172 **"the field for advantages"**: Mathews, *Smalley*, 71.

172 **"other journals have since followed"**: Smalley, "Chapters in Journalism," 432.

173 "**aristocratic drawing rooms**": Mathews, *Smalley,* 90.

173 "**A great deal of my work**": Ibid., 100.

173 "**perennial favorites**": Ibid., 72.

174 "**he wanted to give himself**": Walker, *Januarius MacGahan,* 110.

174 "**AWFUL CALAMITY**" through "**to test the city's preparedness**": "The Wild Animal Hoax," chap. 13 in Seitz, *James Gordon Bennetts,* 304–39.

175 "**No such carefully prepared story**": O'Connor, *Scandalous Mr. Bennett,* 132.

175 "**the advertisements of abortionists!**": Ibid., 99.

176 "**My foreign policy**": Ibid., 286.

176 "**seduction under promise of marriage**": Ibid.

176 "**impartially annexed**": Seitz, *James Gordon Bennetts,* 217.

177 "**the Cossack Correspondent**": Heath, "Januarius MacGahan," 1.

178 "**I knew him fairly well**": Young, "Diaries," entry for December 31, 1878.

178 "**As fascinating as a novel**": "Editor's Literary Record," 137.

178 "**I would pawn the watch**": Walker, *Januarius MacGahan,* 113.

178 "**The Carlists**": Ibid., 123.

179 "**We think our correspondent**": Ibid., 124.

179 "**dullish, courteous**": Young, "Diaries," entry for October 14, 1875.

179 "**Young and brave**" through "**finally he would sit down**": "Riding with Don Carlos," chap. 8 in Walker, *Januarius MacGahan,* 113–36.

180 "**He put the question**": Ibid., 140.

180 "**A world of pure and savage freedom**": MacGahan, *Northern Lights,* 3.

180 "**I forgave all**": Walker, *Januarius MacGahan,* 140.

181 "**It now became necessary to decide**": Ibid., 303.

182 "**the pleasant side of Arctic life**" Ibid., vi.

182 "**They have the darkest, demurest eyes**": Ibid., 47–49.

182 "**Do not think I have exaggerated**": Ibid., 83.

182 "**when he becomes thoroughly civilized**": Ibid., 120.

182 "**We shall never see them again**": Ibid., 60.

183 "**There is something oppressive**": Ibid., 226.

183 "**He said he would not go**": Ibid., 158–59.

183 "**sixpence a head**": MacGahan, *Northern Lights,* 322.

184 "**In the volume**": Walker, *Januarius MacGahan,* 165.

184 "**The truth is**": Ibid.

184 "**Gird up your loins!**": Ibid., 164.

185 "**Dark rumors**": Ibid., 166.

185 "**the sick man of Europe**": Ibid., 183.

185 "**checkered, with opposites much mingled**": James, "Our Artists," 53.

186 "**Only in flight**": Sharpey-Schafer, "In Search of an Ancestor."

186 "**Went to draining wounds**": Millet, "Civil War Diary."

186 "**I stole from and abused**": Ibid.

187 "**worldliness and the devil**": Millet (grandson), "A Sketch," 4.

187 "**It seems to have required a degree of skill**": Adams, *Autobiography,* 189.

187 "**The mere utterance of those names**": Ibid., 151.

188 **"It was not heroic"**: Ibid., 154.

188 **"years of waste"**: Ibid., 197.

188 **"Looking back"**: Ibid., viii.

188 **"By severe lessons"**: Sharpey-Schafer, *Soldier of Fortune,* 15.

189 **"slender, boyish"**: Ibid., chap. 4, 1–6.

189 **"dangerous facility"**: Sharpey-Schafer, "In Search of an Ancestor," 6.

189 **"a rare flower"**: Sharpey-Schafer, *Soldier of Fortune,* 72.

189 **"I act as my nature prompts me"** through **"a thousand vulturous individuals"**: "Empty Chair, Empty Bed, Empty House," chap. 14, in Katz, *Love Stories,* 202–19.

190 **"the old Bohemian life"**: Ibid., 216.

190 **"a different set of friends"**: Sharpey-Schafer, "In Search of an Ancestor," 7.

190 **"talked art"**: Young, "Diaries," entry for August 10, 1873.

191 **"There is style and beauty here"**: Sharpey-Schafer, "In Search of an Ancestor," chap. 7, 5.

191 **"A fool's paradise"**: Ibid., chap. 8, 1.

7. RED HANDS, 1876–1877

193 **"reputation for sensational proclivities"**: Walker, *Januarius MacGahan,* 170.

194 **"generally terminate"**: Ibid., 314.

194 **"I came in a spirit of scientific inquiry"** through **"Mr. Disraeli was right"**: MacGahan and Schuyler, *Turkish Atrocities.*

200 **"I want the people of England"**: Walker, *Januarius MacGahan,* 181.

200 **"it is utterly impotent"**: MacGahan and Schuyler, *Turkish Atrocities,* 87.

200 **"that romantic school of journalism"**: Heath, "Januarius MacGahan," 201.

200 **"a damned Yankee newspaper fellow"**: Ibid., 188.

200 **"You must find another solution"**: Walker, *Januarius MacGahan,* 182.

200 **"Will Mr. Schuyler succeed"**: Ibid., 183.

201 **"In less than a year"**: Walker, *Januarius MacGahan,* 184.

201 **"cheap frippery"**: Anderson, *Balkan Volunteers,* 20.

202 **"We were three ladies"**: Strangford, *Eastern Shores,* 8.

202 **"The danger with us"**: Ibid., 365.

202 **"A child of light"**: Strangford, *Selection,* 297.

203 **"dazzling wit"**: Sydney-Smythe, *Pisani,* xxix.

203 **"illegitimate love"**: Millar, *Disraeli's Disciple,* 302.

203 **"Who is Lady Strangford?"**: Anderson, *Balkan Volunteers,* 18.

203 **"Englishmen are sometimes"**: Strangford, "Letter to *Diplomatic Review,*" 311.

203 **"She will appear in Bulgaria"**: Anderson, *Balkan Volunteers,* 17.

203 **"in this case"**: Ibid., 18.

203 **"dirty and so tired"** through **"A Heaven sent"**: "Balkan Diary," Viscountess Strangford Papers.

204 **"I never saw a fellow"**: Forbes, *Souvenirs,* 127.

204 **"Mr. MacGahan straightened things"** through **"He was so kind to me"**: "Balkan Diary," Viscountess Strangford Papers.

209   **"Is not humanity better"**: Anderson, *Balkan Volunteers,* 81.

209   **"Last year was the saddest"** through **"It distressed me so much"**: Young, "Diaries," entry for January 1, 1876–January 9, 1877.

211   **"with a cowhide whip"**: Seitz, *James Gordon Bennetts,* 268.

211   **"It kills or wounds"** through **"monstrously unfair"**: "Bennett and May's Duel," *New York Times,* May 19, 1878.

213   **"He hoped to get some good work"**: Young, "Diaries," entry for March 28, 1877.

213   **"Received a letter"**: Ibid., entry for July 6, 1877.

214   **"After a man is thirty-five"**: Ibid., entry for July 10, 1877.

214   **"The General has asked"**: Ibid., entry for June 2, 1877.

214   **"hero of ten thousand dinners"**: Ibid., entry for June 17, 1877.

215   **"a man's true and honorable career"** through **"This new adventure"**: Ibid., entry for October 1, 1877–December 4, 1877.

8. GREEN LEAVES IN A FURNACE FLAME, 1877

217   **"We still loved one another"**: Walker, *Januarius MacGahan,* 192.

217   **"You are too accustomed"**: Ibid., 292.

218   **"coffee-house babble"**: Heath, "Januarius MacGahan," 198.

218   **"men traveling in railway carriages"**: Forbes, *Souvenirs,* 123.

218   **"This thorough riddance"**: Gladstone, *Bulgarian Horrors,* 38.

218   **"Witness *Northern Lights*"**: Walker, *Januarius MacGahan,* 191.

218   **"They are looking to patch up"**: Ibid., 206.

219   **"the loathsome, vice-stricken leper"**: Ibid., 181.

219   **"I have fought several pitched battles"**: Ibid., 205.

219   **"a very polite telegram"**: Ibid., 206.

219   **"square shoulders, superb head"**: "Archibald Forbes," *New York Times,* December 17, 1899.

219   **"as prognosis or presentiment"** through **"a certain heroic young officer"**: "MacGahan, the American War Correspondent" and "Skobeleff" in Forbes, *Souvenirs.*

221   **"Needful severities"**: Ibid., 6.

221   **"two thousand turbans"**: *Daily News,* 1:86.

221   **"scented like a popinjay"**: "Skobeleff," in Forbes, *Souvenirs.*

222   **"millions of rubles"**: Ibid.

222   **"He had a habit"**: Forbes, *Czar and Sultan,* 31.

222   **"a genius for plundering"** through **"it seemed he had been everywhere"**: "Skobeleff," in Forbes, *Souvenirs.*

223   **"You have not seen him fight"**: *Daily News,* 1:87.

223   **"it will be seen"**: Ibid.

223   **"The risk of life"**: James, *Varieties,* 146.

223   **"Still mentally"**: Grondahl, *Like a Rocket,* 251.

224   **"To the remains of our friend"**: Samuel Clemens to Frank Millet, August 7, 1877, in Clemens, *Letters to Millet.*

224   **"dread information"**: Frank Millet to Samuel Clemens, June 9, 1877, in Millet, *Letters to Clemens.*

224 "**I write with the gravity**": Clemens to Millet, August 7, 1877.

224 "**strange and perhaps silly**" through "**do not stir us as much**": Millet to Clemens, June 9, 1877.

226 "**Reports are flying**": *Daily News,* 1:163–80.

226 "**It is impossible to say**": Ibid., 1:182.

226 "**in strained silence**": "Skobeleff," in Forbes, *Souvenirs.*

226 "**Get up, my brothers**": Ibid.

227 "**all the idiots in this army**": Millet to Clemens, October 18, 1877.

227 "**motley**" and "**sinister**": *Daily News,* 1:205.

227 "**quite medieval in appearance**": Ibid., 1:603.

228 "**all the men watched**" through "**It was a flagrant insult**": Forbes, *Souvenirs,* 19.

229 "**The Russian carried a weapon**": Millet, "From Plevna to Constantinople," 10.

230 "**Everything has been mismanaged**": Millet to Clemens, October 18, 1877.

230 "**It would be embarrassing**": *Daily News,* 1:298.

231 "**Fever, wounds, and various disabilities**": Millet, "From Plevna to Constantinople," 28.

231 "**broken carts, piles of bags**": Ibid., 23.

231 "**It was the most horrible experience**": Millet, "War Correspondence," 37.

232 "**The Turks so far have shown**": *Daily News,* 1:244.

232 "**The Turks rarely gave quarter**": Millet, "From Plevna to Constantinople," 9.

232 "**a forlorn wandering Jew**": Forbes, *Souvenirs,* 134.

232 "**fires yet burning**": *Daily News,* 1:258.

233 "**Indian fighting**": Ibid., 1:197.

233 "**like a promenade**": Walker, *Januarius MacGahan,* 235.

234 "**How miserably raw and chill**": *Daily News,* 1:322–23.

234 "**malarious fever**": Ibid.

234 "**killed as uselessly**": Ibid., 1:351.

234 "**indomitable resolution**": Walker, *Januarius MacGahan,* 220.

235 "**He composed easily**": Ibid., 226.

235 "**Notebooks, sketchbooks, writing materials**" through "**with patient pathos**": Millet, "Courier's Ride."

236 "**the fat salary**": Millet to Clemens, October 18, 1877.

236 "**his brawny chest half bare**" through "**My ambition for adventure**": Millet, "Courier's Ride."

238 "**I beg your pardon**" through "**a merry night**": Millet, "War Correspondence," 19.

238 "**and held it until further orders**" through "**like a bear with a sore head**": Forbes, *Czar and Sultan,* 85.

238 "**to feel the enemy**": *Daily News,* 1:368.

239 "**I suppose you want to go**": Millet, "War Correspondence," 20.

239 "**Go where you please**": Ibid.

239 "**Do any of you fellows**": Forbes, *Czar and Sultan,* 148.

239 "**I've a good mind to desert**": Ibid.

239 "**All those in high command**": *Daily News,* 1:520.

240 "**Our fellows have got**": Forbes, *Czar and Sultan,* 157.

240 "**making a splendid target**": Ibid.

240 "**The bullets must be falling like hail**": *Daily News*, 1:370.

240 "**The Russians hung somewhat around it**" through "**the hero of Loftcha!**": Forbes, *Czar and Sultan*, 162.

241 "**It is not given to many men**": Forbes, *Souvenirs*, 19.

241 "**Poor Papa!**": Forbes, *Czar and Sultan*, 158.

241 "**Skobelev himself owned**": Ibid., 180.

241 "**with complacent contentment**": Forbes, *Souvenirs*, 20–21.

242 "*Morituri te salutant*" through "**They would talk over Balzac's novels**": Forbes, *Czar and Sultan*, 167–81.

242 "**I hate deliberate swagger**": Millet to Clemens, June 1, 1878.

242 "**strangely jolly**": Millet, "War Correspondence," 24–25.

243 "**Not much to accomplish**" through "**I'm a humane man**": Forbes, *Czar and Sultan*, 155.

243 "**the Russians preface every act**": Millet, "Campaigning—Summer," 239.

243 "**they were shriveling up**": *Daily News*, 1:616.

243 "**When they begin to hang**" through "**God bless you**": Forbes, *Czar and Sultan*, 183–84.

244 "**Did but one bullet in ten**" through "**Having seen as much as I have seen**": *Daily News*, 1:477–80.

245 "**a stout officer**": Nemirovitch-Dantchenko, *Personal Reminiscences*, 395.

245 "**but was met by a stream**" through "**I did my best**": *Daily News*, 1:482–84.

246 "**To find a parallel**": Ibid., 1:354.

246 "**The generals complain**": Ibid., 1:401.

246 "**the argument of starvation**": Forbes, *Czar and Sultan*, 166.

247 "**It is a kind of monster picnic**": *Daily News*, 2:16.

247 "**The break in the monotony**": Ibid., 1:699.

247 "**Why didn't they send**" through "**I blame no one**": Ibid., 1:483.

248 "**My honor forbids it**": Millet, "From Plevna to Constantinople," 10-c.

248 "**They poured into the battery**" through "**And so ended this eventful day**": *Daily News*, 2:140–57.

252 "**Thin and tired**": Walker, *Januarius MacGahan*, 405.

252 "**Those who had the good fortune**": Ibid., 270.

252 "**I who have been lucky**": Ibid., 283.

252 "**Until then I was young**": Nemirovitch-Dantchenko, *Personal Reminiscences*, 99–100.

253 "**They came often**": Walker, *Januarius MacGahan*, 267.

253 "**I can't sleep**": Nemirovitch-Dantchenko, *Personal Reminiscences*, 141–42.

253 "**a monstrous spider**": *Daily News*, 1:698.

253 "**He was carried up to his room**": Ibid., 2:221.

253 "**We talked nonsense**": Walker, *Januarius MacGahan*, 267.

253 "**I have been pursued**": Ibid., 283.

254 "**Lightning never strikes twice**": "Millet Remembers MacGahan," *Brisbane Courier*, December 30, 1896.

254 "**Russians are very fond of sweets**": Millet, "From Plevna to Constantinople," 15.

254 "**the terrible impressions**": Nemirovitch-Dantchenko, *Personal Reminiscences*, 142.

254 **"I never saw water"** through **"At 11:30 I turned in"**: Young, "Diaries," entries for December 13, 1877–January 1, 1878.

9. THE PAUSE OF AN INSTANT, 1877–1890

255 **"so loyal"** through **"Between them"**: Millet, "Campaigning—Winter."

257 **"On a plain outside town"** through **"the final act from the drama"**: *Daily News,* 2, chap. 7.

259 **"I believe you are the correspondent"** through **"I've ordered correspondents away"**: Millet, "War Correspondence," 30.

259 **"are simply sublime"**: *Daily News,* 2:292.

260 **"These men have stood the long siege"**: Millet, "From Plevna to Constantinople," 12–13.

261 **"a veritable Capua"**: Millet, "War Correspondence," 34.

261 **"such as could walk"** through **"this leader of dogs"**: *Daily News,* 2:318–31.

262 **"They say I am mother"** through **"put cotton in my ears"**: "Lady Strangford's New Venture," chap. 13 in Anderson, *Balkan Volunteers.*

262 **"We are the greatest possible friends"** through **"I don't speak Russian"**: "Sifting a Story Down," *New York Times,* June 2, 1879.

263 **"There was some difficulty"**: *Daily News,* 2:320–21.

263 **"A more dramatic scene"** through **"They have no poets"**: Millet, "From Plevna to Constantinople"; Millet, "War Correspondence."

265 **"I laid my hand"**: *Daily News,* 2:401.

265 **"It will be many years"**: Ibid., 2:372.

265 **"No chloroform?"**: Barry, "Skobeleff," 381.

265 **"virtually over"**: *Daily News,* 2:381.

265 **"English friends of the Turk"** through **"In the case of declaration of war"**: Ibid., 2:381–495.

266 **"He wanted Russia to conquer"**: "Skobelev the Madcap," *Ellensburgh Capital,* February 15, 1914.

267 **"The following letter"** through **"So ends the war"**: *Daily News,* 2:578–83.

268 **"I look with trepidation"** through **"General Grant, with his dislike of grand reviews"**: Young, "Diaries," entries for January 6–March 1, 1878.

269 **"Grant is very strong"** through **"whisky toddy and cigars"**: Schuyler, *Selected Essays,* 122–25.

269 **"I must say that the peace"**: *Daily News,* 2:581.

269 **"Everywhere"**: Young, "Diaries," entry for March 30, 1878.

270 **"My little daughter is born!"**: Young, "Diaries," entries for March 8–28, 1878.

270 **"Some cities have the great misfortune"**: Young, *Around the World,* 1:348.

270 **"I was disgusted with the bluster"**: Millet to Clemens, June 1, 1878.

270 **"When I get to believing"**: Millet to Clemens, October 18, 1877.

271 **"malady"**: Sharpey-Schafer, "In Search of an Ancestor," chap. 10.

271 **"a first-rate young Greek"**: Engstrom, *Francis David Millet,* 98.

271 **"Keeping the market supplied"**: Millet (grandson), "Frank Millet: A Sketch," 10.

272 **"quietly raised their family"**: Ibid.

272 **"We shall have to do today"**: Engstrom, *Francis David Millet,* 322.

273 "**Gastric fever**": Walker, *Januarius MacGahan,* 297.

273 "**He ate quinine**": Villiers, "Story of a War Correspondent's Life."

273 "**He was the delight**": Pears, *Forty Years,* 24.

274 "**this crazy love**" through "**I asked him to lie down**": Walker, *Januarius MacGahan,* 292–300.

275 "**But you English**": Villiers, "Story of a War Correspondent's Life," 715.

276 "**They raised him**": "The Fourth Waits," in Millet, *Capillary Crime.*

276 "**You will be grieved to hear**": Millet, "War Correspondence," microfilm, frame 1136.

276 "**In my reverence for the memory of him**": Millet, "From Plevna to Constantinople," 20.

277 "**Dear brother**": "Skobeleff and MacGahan," *New Zealand Tablet,* May 15, 1882.

277 "**I lost my senses**": Walker, *Januarius MacGahan,* 304.

277 "**brother correspondents**": Villiers, "Story of a War Correspondent's Life," 715.

277 "**a wilderness of neglected graves**": Walker, *Januarius MacGahan,* 306.

277 "**with an inscription**": Forbes, *Souvenirs,* 139–40.

278 "**apparatus for artificial arms and legs**" through "**by friends and strangers**": "Lady Strangford's New Venture," chap. 13, and "Constantinople," chap. 16, both in Anderson, *Balkan Volunteers.*

278 "**impossible stories**": Ibid., 203.

279 "**singing the praises of the Turk**": Pears, *Forty Years,* 23.

279 "**the wilderness**": Walker, *Januarius MacGahan,* 293.

279 "**Dr. Stephenson accompanies me**": Anderson, *Balkan Volunteers,* 204.

279 "**Why am I so persistently ignored?**": "Salisbury Banquet," Viscountess Strangford Papers.

279 "**I wish you could go**": Gaulton, "Army Hospital Services," 123.

280 "**should I die**": "Last Will and Testament," Viscountess Strangford Papers.

280 "**miserable, wasted, futile**": "Skobelev the Madcap," *Ellensburgh Capital,* February 15, 1914.

280 "**old woman**": Barry, "Skobeleff," 381.

281 "**a riotous carnival**": Armstrong, "Blood and Iron," 12.

281 "**He did not commit suicide**": "Skobeleff," in Forbes, *Souvenirs.*

281 "**ten lives in ten years**": Ibid., 69.

281 "**The incomparable Archibald!**": Bullard, *War Correspondents,* 69.

282 "**How I wish all those hideous scenes**": Schuyler, *Selected Essays,* 72.

282 "**I feel desperately like writing novels**": Ibid., 202.

282 "**strong and positive**": Walker, *Januarius MacGahan,* 312.

10. OUR PEOPLE, 1884–1912

283 "**John**": Walker, *Januarius MacGahan,* 306.

283 "**This donkey**": O'Connor, *Scandalous Mr. Bennett,* 148.

283 "**He had not been tenderly reared**": Ibid., 160.

284 "**pulping process**": Ibid., 206.

284 "**A dead dog**": Ibid., 187.

284 "**An Old Philadelphia Lady**": Ibid., 200.

285 "**Three cents daily**": Ibid., 268–75.

286 "**For the purposes of news-gathering**" through "**I do not know whether any work**": Smalley, "Notes on Journalism."

286 "**Until my work is done**": Young, "Diaries," entry for December 31, 1889.

287 "**Busy, tired, ill**" through "**self-communion**": Ibid., entry for October 13, 1883.

287 "**Free from the cares of life**": "Charles Longfellow," in Young, *Men and Memories,* 1:2.

287 "**Out of this book**": "Walt Whitman," in Young, *Men and Memories,* 1:76–108.

288 "**Conglomerate, composite America**": Ibid.

289 "**Great are the plunges and throes**": Whitman, *Leaves of Grass.*

289 "**a fine boy**": Young, "Diaries," entry for August 15, 1883.

289 "**Delirious all day**": through "**ample pecuniary resources**": Ibid., entries for December 31, 1886–April 26, 1888.

290 "**The angel stands on the threshold**": Young, *Men and Memories,* 1:367.

291 "**Personal. Don't print**": Ibid., 1:107.

292 "**He wore a bright copper-colored Norfolk jacket**": "Major Butt's Suit a Wonder," *New York Times,* March 3, 1912.

292 "**she has everything but taxicabs**": Millet to Alfred Parsons, April 11, 1912, *Encyclopedia Titanica.*

293 "**as courteously**": "Butt a Courtier to Death, Says Woman," *Cleveland Plain Dealer,* April 20, 1912.

293 "**NO. 249**": "Mr. Francis Davis Millet," *Encyclopedia Titanica.*

294 "**Brave and true and loyal**": J. M. Barrie to Charles Turley Smith, April 1912, J. M. Barrie Online Database, http://www.jmbarrie.co.uk/view/3378/.

EPILOGUE

295 "**Americans will only become interested**": Bonsal, *Heyday,* 439.

295 "**in whose footsteps**" through "**in yellowing newspaper files**": Ibid., 413–15.

297 "**The First and Greatest of War Correspondents**": Bullard, *War Correspondents,* 68.

297 "**The European Powder Mine**" through "**At least none of the senators went to sleep**": "Home—Defeat and Victory," chap. 19 in Bonsal, *Heyday,* 416–40.

298 "**greatest glory**" through "**I thanked the great explorer**": Ibid., 410–11.

299 "**How many Boche**": O'Connor, *Scandalous Mr. Bennett,* 317.

300 "**that grocer**": Ibid., 320.

300 "**I print my newspaper**": "James Gordon Bennett, I Presume," New York Yacht Club.

301 "**I fear my renaissance palace**" through "**Thirty years?**": O'Connor, *Scandalous Mr. Bennett,* 223.

Bibliography

Adams, Charles Francis. *Charles Francis Adams 1835–1915: An Autobiography with a Memorial Address delivered November 17, 1915, by Henry Cabot Lodge.* Boston: Houghton Mifflin, 1916.

Anderson, Dorothy. *The Balkan Volunteers.* New York: Hutchinson, 1968.

"Archibald Forbes." *New York Times,* December 17, 1899.

Armstrong, Richard. "Blood and Iron." *Pacific Quarterly* 1, no. 1 (1890): 6–12.

Atkins, John Black. *The Life of Sir William Howard Russell.* 2 vols. London: John Murray, 1911.

"Atlantic Yacht Race." *New York Times,* November 29, 1866.

Austen, Roger. *Genteel Pagan: The Double Life of Charles Warren Stoddard.* Amherst: University of Massachusetts Press, 1991.

Barry, Richard. "Skobeleff, Russia's Chief War-Hero." *Century Magazine* 87, no. 1 (November 1913): 376–82.

Baxter, Sylvester, William A. Coffin, Edwin Howland Blashfield, Carroll Beckwith, and George W. Maynard. "Francis Davis Millet: An Appreciation." *Art and Progress* 3, no. 9 (July 1912): 635–57.

Beebe, Lucius. *The Big Spenders.* New York: Pocket Books, 1967.

"Bennett and May's Duel." *New York Times,* May 19, 1878.

Blaikie, William. "The University Rowing Match." *Harper's,* December 1869, 49–67.

Blakely, Walter J. "Januarius A. MacGahan." *Missouri Historical Society Collections* 4, no. 1 (1912): 1–8.

Blunt, Alison. "Embodying War: British Women and Domestic Defilement in the Indian 'Mutiny,' 1857–8." *Journal of Historical Geography* 26, no. 3 (2000): 403–28.

Bocca, Geoffrey. *The Adventurous Life of Winston Churchill.* New York: Julian Messner, 1958.

Bonsal, Stephen. *Heyday in a Vanished World.* New York: W. W. Norton, 1937.

Bullard, F. Lauriston. *Famous War Correspondents.* Boston: Little, Brown, 1914.

Burrows, Edwin G., and Mike Wallace. *Gotham: A History of New York City to 1898.* New York: Oxford University Press, 1999.

"Butt a Courtier to Death, Says Woman." *Cleveland Plain Dealer,* April 20, 1912.

Chapman, Caroline. *Russell of "The Times": War Despatches and Diaries.* London: Bell & Hyman, 1984.

Carey, John, ed. *Eyewitness to History.* New York: Avon, 1987.

Carlson, Oliver. *The Man Who Made News: James Gordon Bennett.* New York: Duell, Sloan & Pierce, 1942.

Carter, Samuel III. *Cyrus Field: Man of Two Worlds.* New York: G. P. Putnam's Sons, 1968.

Clemens, Samuel L. *Letters to Francis D. Millet.* Mark Twain Project Online. Berkeley, Los Angeles, and London: University of California Press, 2011.

Conway, Moncure Daniel. "The International Boat-Race." *Harper's,* November 1869, 912–15.

Crockett, Albert Stevens. *When James Gordon Bennett Was Caliph of Baghdad.* New York: Funk & Wagnalls, 1926.

Daily News. The War Correspondence of the "Daily News" 1877–78. 2 vols. London: Macmillan, 1878.

David, Saul. *The Indian Mutiny.* New York: Penguin, 2003.

D'Este, Carlo. *Warlord: A Life of Winston Churchill at War, 1874–1945.* New York: HarperCollins, 2008.

Dickens, Charles. "Speech: The Harvard and Oxford Boat Race. Sydenham, August 30, 1869." ClassicAuthors.net, http://bit.ly/16ld82h.

Dorsey, Hebe. *Age of Opulence: The Belle Epoque in the Paris Herald 1890–1914.* New York: Harry N. Abrams, 1986.

Drury, Ian, and Raffaele Ruggeri. *The Russo-Turkish War 1877.* London: Osprey, 1994.

Dugard, Martin. *Into Africa: The Epic Adventures of Stanley and Livingstone.* New York: Doubleday, 2003.

Durick, William G. "The Gentlemen's Race: An Examination of the 1869 Harvard-Oxford Boat Race." *Journal of Sport History* 15, no. 1 (Spring 1988): 41–63.

Dym, Jordana. "The Paris Commune." Skidmore College, http://bit.ly/18pK6S9.

"Editor's Literary Record." *Harper's,* December 1864, 137–38.

Engstrom, Peter A. *Francis Davis Millet: A Titanic Life.* East Bridgewater, Mass.: Millet Studio, 2010.

"European News: Henrietta Arrives." *New York Times,* December 30, 1866.

Faithfull, Emily. "Viscountess Strangford." *Victoria Magazine* 32 (November 1879): 389–91.

Fermer, Douglas. *James Gordon Bennett and "The New York Herald."* New York: St. Martin's, 1986.

Field, Henry M. *The Story of the Atlantic Telegraph.* New York: Charles Scribner's Sons, 1898.

Fiske, Stephen. *Off-Hand Portraits of Prominent New Yorkers.* New York: Geo. R. Lockwood & Son, 1884.

Forbes, Archibald. *Czar and Sultan: The Adventures of a British Lad in the Russo-Turkish War of 1877–78.* London: J. W. Arrowsmith, 1894.

———. *Memories and Studies of War and Peace.* New York: Charles Scribner's Sons, 1895.

———. *My Experiences of the War Between France and Germany.* 2 vols. London: Hurst & Blackett, 1871.

———. *Souvenirs of Some Continents.* London: Macmillan, 1885.

———. "War Correspondence as a Fine Art." *Century Magazine* 45, no. 23 (November 1892): 290–304.

———. "What I Saw of the Paris Commune." *Century Magazine* 44, no. 6 (October 1892): 803–17.

Gaulton, Douglas C. B. "Army Hospital Services." *Fortnightly Review* 34 (July 1–December 1, 1883). London: Chapman & Hall, 1883.

Gladstone, William E. *Bulgarian Horrors and the Question of the East.* New York: Lovell, Adam, Wesson & Co., 1876.

Goodwin, Doris Kearns. *Team of Rivals: The Political Genius of Abraham Lincoln.* New York: Simon & Schuster, 2005.

Gordon, John Steele. *A Thread Across the Ocean: The Heroic Story of the Transatlantic Cable.* New York: Perennial, 2003.

Greene, Francis V. *Sketches of Army Life in Russia.* New York: Charles Scribner's Sons, 1880.

Grondahl, Paul. *I Rose Like a Rocket: The Political Education of Theodore Roosevelt.* New York: Free Press, 2004.

Harris, Brayton. *Blue & Gray in Black & White.* Washington, D.C.: Brassey's, 2000.

"Harvard and Oxford Boat Race." *Nation,* June 30, 1869, 431–32.

Hastings, Max, ed. *The Oxford Book of Military Anecdotes.* New York: Oxford University Press, 1985.

Hatton, Joseph. *Journalistic London.* London: Sampson, Low, Marston, Searle & Rivington, 1882.

Heath, Roy E. "Januarius MacGahan and His Role in the Liberation of Bulgaria." *Southeastern Europe* 6, no. 2 (June 1979): 194–208.

Hibbert, Christopher. *The Destruction of Lord Raglan.* Boston: Little, Brown, 1961.

Hohenberg, John. *Foreign Correspondence: The Great Reporters and Their Times.* New York: Columbia University Press, 1964.

"Honors to MacGahan." *New York Times,* August 26, 1884.

Hopkirk, Peter. *The Great Game: The Struggle for Empire in Central Asia.* New York: Kodansha America, 1994.

Horne, Alistair. *The Fall of Paris: The Siege and the Commune 1870–71.* New York: Penguin, 1981.

James, Henry. "Our Artists in Europe." *Harper's,* June 1889, 50–55.

James, William. *The Varieties of Religious Experience.* 1901–2. Reprint, Stilwell, Kan.: Digireads, 2007.

"James Gordon Bennett, I Presume." New York Yacht Club, http://bit.ly/16eunt3.

Jamieson, Patrick C. "Foreign Criticisms of the 1871 Paris Commune: The Role of British and American Newspapers and Periodicals," *Intersections* 11, no. 1 (2010): 100–115.

Jeal, Tim. *Stanley: The Impossible Life of Africa's Greatest Explorer.* New Haven, Conn.: Yale University Press, 2007.

Katz, Jonathan Ned. *Love Stories: Sex Between Men Before Homosexuality.* Chicago: University of Chicago Press, 2001.

Kelley, J. D. Jerrold. *American Yachts: Their Clubs and Races.* New York: Charles Scribner's Sons, 1884.

Kipling, Rudyard. *The Light That Failed.* London: Macmillan, 1891.

Knightley, Phillip. *The First Casualty: From the Crimea to Vietnam: The War Correspondent as Hero, Propagandist, and Myth Maker.* New York: Harvest, 1976.

Lal, Vinay. "The Incident of the Crawling Lane: Women in the Punjab Disturbances of 1919." *Genders* 16 (Spring 1993): 35–60.

Laney, Al. *Paris Herald: The Incredible Newspaper.* New York: D. Appleton-Century, 1947.

Leslie, Anita. *The Remarkable Mr. Jerome.* New York: Henry Holt, 1954.

Levene, Mark, and Penny Roberts, eds. *The Massacre in History.* New York: Berghan Book, 1999.

MacGahan, J. A. *Campaigning on the Oxus and the Fall of Khiva.* New York: Harper & Brothers, 1874.

———. *Under the Northern Lights.* London: Sampson Low, Marston, Searle & Rivington, 1876.

MacGahan, J. A., and Eugene Schuyler. *The Turkish Atrocities in Bulgaria.* London: Bradbury, Agnew & Co., 1876.

"MacGahan Obituary." *Nation* 27, no. 25 (July 1–December 31, 1878).

MacPherson, R. B. *Under the Red Crescent; or, Ambulance Adventures in the Russo-Turkish War of 1877–78.* London: Hamilton, Adams, 1885.

Maddocks, Melvin. *The Atlantic Crossing.* Chicago: Time-Life Books, 1981.

Maihafer, Harry J. *The General and the Journalists: Ulysses S. Grant, Horace Greeley, and Charles Dana.* Washington, D.C.: Brassey's, 2001.

"Major Butt's Suit a Wonder." *New York Times,* March 3, 1912.

Mathews, Joseph J. "The First Harvard-Oxford Boat Race." *New England Quarterly* 33, no. 1 (March 1960): 74–82.

———. *George W. Smalley: Forty Years a Foreign Correspondent.* Chapel Hill: University of North Carolina Press, 1973.

———. *Reporting the Wars.* Minneapolis: University of Minnesota Press, 1957.

Meredith, Roy. *Mr. Lincoln's Camera Man: Mathew B. Brady.* New York: Dover, 1964.

Millar, Mary S. *Disraeli's Disciple: The Scandalous Life of George Smythe.* Toronto: University of Toronto Press, 2006.

Miller, Bill. "The Great International Boat Race." *Friends of Rowing History,* February 2006, http://www.rowinghistory.net/1869.htm.

Millet, Francis Davis. "A Balkan Bivouac." Smithsonian Archives of American Art, Washington, D.C., undated.

———. "Campaigning with the Cossacks I—A Summer Campaign." *Harper's,* January 1887, 235–50.

———. "Campaigning with the Cossacks II—A Winter Campaign." *Harper's,* February 1887, 397–411.

———. *A Capillary Crime and Other Stories.* New York: Harper & Brothers, 1892.

———. "Civil War Diary." Francis Davis Millet and Millet Family Papers, Smithsonian Archives of American Art, Washington, D.C. (hereafter Millet Papers), 1864–65.

———. "A Courier's Ride." *Harper's,* October 1891, 756–65.

———. "From Plevna to Constantinople." Millet Papers, undated.

———. "Letter to Alfred Parsons." April 11, 1912. *Encyclopedia Titanica,* http://bit.ly/sweY48.

———. *Letters to Charles Warren Stoddard, May 10, 1875—January 3, 1900.* Outhistory.org, 2011.

———. *Letters to Samuel L. Clemens.* Mark Twain Project Online. Berkeley, Los Angeles, and London: University of California Press, 2011.

————. "Millet Remembers MacGahan." *Brisbane Courier,* December 30, 1896. National Library of Australia, http://bit.ly/15cj3HO.

————. "War Correspondence." Speech to Buffalo Club, April 23, 1904. Millet Papers.

Millet, Francis Davis (grandson). "Frank Millet: A Sketch." Millet Papers.

Morris, Edmund. *The Rise of Theodore Roosevelt.* New York: Modern Library, 2001.

"Mr. Francis Davis Millet." *Encyclopedia Titanica,* http://bit.ly/HtU36s.

"Mr. Lincoln and New York." Lincoln Institute, http://bit.ly/14qDNya.

Myer, Karl E., and Shareen Blair Brysac. *Tournament of Shadows: The Great Game and the Search for Empire in Central Asia.* New York: Basic Books, 2006.

Nemirovitch-Dantchenko, V. I. *Personal Reminiscences of General Skobeleff.* London: W. H. Allen & Co., 1884.

Novikova, Olga Alekseevna. *Skobeleff and the Slavonic Cause.* London: Longmans, Green & Co., 1883.

"Ocean Yacht Race: Full Account." *New York Times,* January 9, 1867.

"Ocean Yacht Races: The Present Contest and the Former One." *New York Times,* July 22, 1870.

O'Connor, Richard. *The Scandalous Mr. Bennett.* New York: Doubleday, 1962.

Palgrave, Francis Turner. "Elegy in Memory of Percy, Eighth Viscount Strangford." *Lyrical Poems.* New York: MacMillan, 1871.

Pears, Edwin. *Forty Years in Constantinople: The Recollections of Sir Edwin Pears, 1873–1915.* New York: D. Appleton & Co., 1916.

Perry, James M. *A Bohemian Brigade: The Civil War Correspondents—Mostly Rough, Sometimes Ready.* New York: John Wiley & Sons, 2000.

Powers, Ron. *Mark Twain: A Life.* New York: Free Press, 2005.

"Powhatan in Port." *New York Times,* August 22, 1884.

Randall, David. *The Great Reporters.* London: Pluto Press, 2005.

Reid, James J. "Batak 1876: A Massacre and Its Significance." *Journal of Genocide Research* 2, no. 3 (2000): 375–409.

"Reminiscences of Skobeleff and MacGahan." *Review of Reviews* 6 (July–December 1892): 564.

Robb, Graham. *Victor Hugo: A Biography.* New York: W. W. Norton, 1997.

Roth, Mitchel P. *Historical Dictionary of War Journalism.* London: Greenwood Press, 1997.

Russell, William Howard. *My Diary North and South.* Edited by Eugene H. Berwanger. New York: Alfred A. Knopf, 1988.

Schudson, Michael. *Discovering the News: A Social History of America's Newspapers.* New York: Basic Books, 1978.

Schuyler, Eugene. *Selected Essays. With a Memoir by Evelyn Schuyler Schaeffer.* New York: Charles Scribner's Sons, 1901.

————. *Turkistan: Notes on a Journey in Russian Turkistan, Khokand, Bukhara, and Kuldja.* 2 vols. New York: Charles Scribner's Sons, 1885.

Seitz, Don C. *The James Gordon Bennetts.* Indianapolis: Bobbs-Merrill, 1928.

Sharpey-Schafer, Joyce A. "In Search of an Ancestor." Millet Papers.

————. *Soldier of Fortune: F. D. Millet 1846–1912.* Utica, N.Y.: Sharpey-Schafer, 1984.

"Sifting a Story Down." *New York Times,* June 2, 1879.

"Skobeleff and MacGahan." *New Zealand Tablet,* May 15, 1882, http://paperspast
.natlib.govt.nz.

"Skobelev the Madcap." *Ellensburgh Capital,* February 15, 1914.

Smalley, George W. *Anglo-American Memories.* New York: G. P. Putnam's Sons, 1911.

———. *Anglo-American Memories.* 2nd series. New York: G. P. Putnam's Sons, 1912.

———. "Chapters in Journalism." *Harper's,* August 1894, 426–35.

———. "English Men of Letters I." *McClure's,* November 1902, 53–66.

———. "English Men of Letters II." *McClure's,* January 1903, 296–306.

———. *London Letters.* 2 vols. New York: Harper & Brothers, 1891.

———. "Notes on Journalism." *Harper's,* July 1898, 213–23.

———. *Studies of Men.* New York: Harper & Brothers, 1895.

Spiring, Paul. "Sir John Richard Robinson (1828–1903)." BFRonline.BIZ, 2007.

Starr, Louis M. *Bohemian Brigade: Civil War Newsmen in Action.* Madison: University
of Wisconsin Press, 1987.

Stefanov, Archimandrite Pavel. "Crossing the Borders of Indifference: Lady Emily
Strangford and Her Charitable Work in Bulgaria." Shoumen University, Bulgaria.

Stone, Candace. *Dana and "The Sun."* New York: Dodd, Mead, 1938.

Strangford, Viscountess Emily Anne Beaufort Smythe. *The Eastern Shores of the Adriatic in 1863.* London: Richard Bentley, 1864.

———. "Letter to *The Diplomatic Review*." *Diplomatic Review,* book 6, *Vols. 22 to 25,
January 1874 to January 1877,* 310.

———. Papers of Viscountess Strangford, 1838–1888. In Francis Beaufort (Sir) Papers,
Huntington Library, San Marino, Calif.

Strangford, Viscountess Emily Anne Beaufort Smythe, ed. *Original Letters and Papers
of the Late Viscount Strangford.* London: Trubner, 1878.

———. *A Selection from the Writings of Viscount Strangford.* London: Richard Bentley,
1869.

Sweeney, Michael S. *From the Front: The Story of War.* Washington, D.C.: National
Geographic, 2002.

Sydney-Smythe, George. *Angela Pisani.* London: Richard Bentley, 1875.

Thompson, Luther. *Wiring a Continent: The History of the Telegraph Industry in the
United States, 1832–1866.* Princeton, N.J.: Princeton University Press, 1947.

"Titanic Survivor Arrives." *Toronto Daily Star,* April 25, 1912. *Encylopedia Titanica,*
http://bit.ly/vBQolx.

Twain, Mark. *The Autobiography of Mark Twain.* Edited by Harriet Elinor Smith. Los
Angeles: University of California Press, 2010.

———. *The Innocents Abroad.* 1869. Reprint, New York: Modern Library, 2003.

Verestchagin, Vassily. *Painter, Soldier, Traveler: Autobiographical Sketches.* New York:
American Art Association, 1888.

Villard, Oswald Garrison. *Some Newspapers and Newspapermen.* New York: Alfred A.
Knopf, 1923.

Villard de Borchgrave, Alexandra, and John Cullen. *Villard: The Life and Times of an
American Titan.* New York: Nan A. Talese, 2001.

Villiers, Frederic. *Peaceful Personalities and Warriors Bold.* New York: Harper & Brothers, 1907.

———. "The Story of a War Correspondent's life (Parts 1–3)." *Cosmopolitan* 10 (November 1890–April 1891).

Walker, Dale L. *Januarius MacGahan: The Life and Campaigns of an American War Correspondent.* Athens: Ohio University Press, 1988.

———. *The Search for Januarius MacGahan.* Carl Hertzog Lecture Series. El Paso: Texas Western Press, 1990.

Waller, Bruce, ed. *Themes in Modern European History 1830–1890.* London: Unwin Hyman, 1990.

Wawro, Geoffrey. *The Austro-Prussian War: Austria's War with Prussia and Italy in 1866.* Cambridge: Cambridge University Press, 1996.

———. *The Franco-Prussian War: The German Conquest of France in 1870–1871.* Cambridge: Cambridge University Press, 2003.

———. *Warfare and Society in Europe, 1792–1914.* London: Routledge, 2000.

Whitman, Walt. *Leaves of Grass.* New York: Walt Whitman (self-published), 1855.

———. Walt Whitman Archive, www.whitmanarchive.org.

"Yacht Race." *New York Times,* December 17, 1866.

"Yacht Race of 1866." *New York Times,* August 30, 1920.

Young, John Russell. *Around the World with General Grant 1877, 1878, 1879.* New York: American News Co., 1879.

———. "Diaries 1865–1898." Library of Congress, Washington, D.C.

———. *Men and Memories.* 2 vols. New York: F. Tennyson Neely, 1901.

Index

Page numbers in *italics* refer to illustrations.